COMPANION DOGS

COMPANION DOGS

How to Choose, Train, and Care for Them

Revised Edition

by

Arthur Liebers

South Brunswick and New York:
A. S. Barnes and Company
London: Thomas Yoseloff Ltd

A. S. Barnes and Co., Inc.
Cranbury, New Jersey 08512

Thomas Yoseloff Ltd
108 New Bond Street
London W1Y OQX, England

ISBN 0-498-01177-1
Printed in the United States of America

CONTENTS

PICTURE CREDITS

The author wishes to express thanks to the owners of so many of America's outstanding show dogs who have made available photographs of their dogs, exemplifying the standards of excellence of the most popular breeds and varieties of canine "companions." The photographs that have been chosen for inclusion represent a cross section of the work of many of the leading present-day dog-photographers. Mrs. Alice Wagner, editor of *Popular Dogs Magazine,* and Ab Sidewater of that publication were especially helpful in establishing contact with owners of "Champion" dogs throughout the country and in obtaining photographs of dogs whose show careers have been followed in the columns of that magazine.

The photographs illustrating steps in dog training were provided by the American Society for the Prevention of Cruelty to Animals.

ILLUSTRATIONS

COMPANION DOGS

1

CHOOSING A DOG

thirty-two million dogs and their owners came together by chance. All puppies are appealing, and it is all too easy to succumb to the wiles of the first puppy that snuggles up against you and licks your face with his pink tongue.

But for the best dog-human relationship, you should try to select a type of dog that will meet your needs and that will fit in with your way of life and living conditions. The various breeds of dogs differ as much in temperament and behavior as they do in appearance.

PUREBRED, MIXED BREED, OR MONGREL?

A recent survey shows that about 61 per cent of dog owners received their dogs from neighbors, relatives or friends; about 14 per cent bought theirs from dog breeders; about 8½ per cent bred the dogs themselves. The rest were obtained from pet shops, from a dog pound, or from a veterinarian.

If you receive a gift dog, you will find that, like all dogs, he is basically friendly, faithful and protective.

But the advantage in selecting the dog you want, and in selecting a purebred dog, is that you can be reasonably sure of what he will look like when he grows up. Also, the different breeds have been standardized for special abilities and characteristics.

If the dog you select or receive is the offspring of two different types of pure-bred dog, he is called a "mixed breed" or "crossbreed." He will probably have some of the characteristics of each parent, although it is almost impossible to foresee just how the mixture will turn out; and he will usually be intermediate in size.

13

The "mongrel" or "mutt" is the dog whose parentage is unknown, or who is a combination of various breeds over many generations. The problem with a mongrel, if you acquire him as a puppy, is that you are never sure how he will turn out as an adult. A tiny puppy can grow into a big dog, and the common idea that you can anticipate the size of the adult dog by the size of the puppy's feet and legs doesn't always work out. Taking the "runt" of a litter on the theory that he will be smaller at maturity is not a safe guide either.

THE VARIOUS TYPES OF DOGS

There is really little known about the origin of the dog, although one accepted theory is that all dogs came from a common ancestor millions of years ago. It is known that man and dog have been companions from the earliest times. Throughout the ages dogs have changed first into different types and then into different breeds to suit the different climates in which they lived and the occupations into which man placed them.

The collie and shepherd-type herd dogs were selected for their weather-resistant coats and their cleverness and endurance. The sled dogs of the frozen north developed heavy coats and hairy, curled tails to protect their noses while they slept in the snow. Their powerful muscles made them useful for sleigh and draft work.

The sporting dogs helped early man in his quest for food and retained their characteristics in hunting as a sport. Most dogs hunt by air-borne scent; some are sight hunters; and others retrieve game on land and from the water. The sporting hounds are of two types. Those that hunt by sight are tall, speedy dogs, whereas the scent hunters are usually smooth-coated, slower-moving dogs.

The terriers and dachshund were bred as vermin catchers and diggers, with strong shoulders and forelegs and powerful jaws. The guard dogs are descended from the mastiff types of ancient Greece and Rome and probably carry the blood of the breed which fought in the Roman arenas and served as war dogs.

The tiny "toy" breeds originated for the most part in countries that had reached the stage of luxury which could support dogs as pets for women.

LARGE OR SMALL DOG?

Inclination toward a large or small dog is a matter of individual preference.

Although many feel that their choice is limited to a small dog because they live in an apartment or small house, this is not necessarily so. Many of the larger, quiet breeds are better adapted to apartment living than the smaller, livelier breeds. However, for the person who lives in a city apartment or travels considerably, the tiny toy breeds are ideal. They adapt themselves easily to restricted quarters, can get almost all the exercise they need indoors, and can even be toilet-trained on paper or use a litter tray as cats do. Also, the toy dog can be put in a travelling case and carried around where larger dogs would be "verboten."

The sporting breeds—spaniels, setters, pointers, beagles and other dogs of the hound family are for the active, outdoors type of dog owner. With plenty of outdoor space and a liking for really big dogs, you have a choice among the great Dane, Irish wolfhound, great Pyrenees, Newfoundland, St. Bernard, and others. But keep in mind that the food bill for a 150-pound dog can mount up over the years.

MALE OR FEMALE?

Dog owners may be divided into two groups: One would not have a female dog as a gift; the other would not have a male dog in the house. Actually, there is very little difference between the male and female of any breed as pets or as working dogs. Generally, the female is somewhat less inclined to wander away from home than the male. With a female, you have the twice-yearly problem of her "season" when you may have to keep her confined or board her out, unless you want a litter of pups. Having the female spayed will cost $20 to $30, and will not affect the disposition or physical condition of the animal. However, spaying does slow down the rate of metabolism slightly so that you must watch the spayed female's diet to keep her from putting on too much weight. Also, some spayed bitches find it difficult to control their urination, but this can be remedied by inoculation or by feeding the hormone drug suggested by your veterinarian.

Among the larger, more powerful breeds, females are usually a bit smaller in size and structure than the males and may be easier to handle on lead. Some females are easier to train and housebreak than males. Also, walking a female dog is simpler than walking the male. The female gets her business over with quickly. The male likes to prolong his outings with numerous stops at trees, bushes, hydrants, and places that other dogs have visited.

MATCHING DOGS AND CHILDREN

One of the leading excuses for buying a dog is that it is good for the children in the family to have a pet. However, for best results, the dog and the child or children must be well matched and the parents must face the grim fact that children's promises to "take care of the dog and walk him" are hardly ever fulfilled.

The first concern in obtaining a dog for a child is to get one that will be a good playmate. Very young puppies want to eat and sleep and very young children tend to treat a puppy as a plaything. A large and energetic dog or older puppy may unintentionally knock a child down and destroy their relationship at the start. Some of the terrier breeds and other smaller dogs are inclined to be "snappy" and may bite back at the child in self-defense.

The puppy must be protected against very young children. A puppy is as fragile as an infant, and being dropped, poked, pulled and teased may wreak havoc with him physically and emotionally.

For younger children of about two to six years old, choose one of the larger herding breeds, such as the collie, old English sheepdog, or the less common Briard or Puli. And start off with an older puppy or a young adult dog. These breeds have an ingrained herding instinct which makes them good caretakers for young children. In addition, they are easygoing dogs and sturdy enough to take childish mauling without offense.

If you have active boys in your family, a boxer or Dalmatian or one of the larger terriers may be a good choice, or any of the sporting dogs.

If you do get a young puppy, teach the children how to support him with both hands when they hold him, so that his hindquarters are not dangling; to respect his privacy; and to give him time to grow up before they can expect him to be an active playmate.

WHAT TO PAY FOR YOUR DOG

In many ways, buying a dog is like buying a car. If you are a status seeker, and want a flashy, outstanding specimen of the currently popular breed, you can pay well into the hundreds of dollars for a puppy or older dog. If you are willing to settle for a sturdy, secondhand model, you can get a dog that will give you affection and companionship for the price of the license fee from the S.P.C.A. the local Humane Society or the nearest dog pound.

If you want a purebred dog, the price depends on a number of factors. Females of the same quality are usually a bit cheaper than males; on the other hand, in many areas the license fee for an unspayed female is three times as much as for a male. Breeders generally prefer to sell their puppies at about eight weeks old, as they are weaned at that time and have had their puppy shots. Keeping them long means additional veterinary expense and care and feeding so that the price for older puppies goes up. Also, in a better quality dog, bred for show prospects, the older the dog, the more evident are its characteristics as a potential champion, so that, too, increases the price.

If you have no intention of showing your dog in breed shows or in breeding the female and selling the litters, it is unnecessary to spend the top price for a dog with the best bloodlines and champions in its background. A puppy that is not close to the standard of perfection for its breed as its littermates will cost far less and be just as good as a pet and companion. Many breeders set aside such puppies and sell them without "papers" at bargain prices.

If you are interested in a high-quality dog of a specific breed, your best source is probably a breeding kennel, although here the price includes the kennel's overhead, advertising, and the cost of attending shows and exhibiting the dogs. You can probably get a good dog from a private breeder who will be able to provide a pedigree and registration papers. (See next chapter for details.) Watch the dog advertising section of your local newspapers, where breeders usually advertise, or write to the secretary of the breed club for a list of breeders.

Department stores and pet shops usually offer both purebred and mongrel dogs at fairly reasonable prices, and most of the larger mail-order houses have gone into the dog business in recent years and will deliver purebred, registered dogs by express.

One way to meet people who breed dogs is to attend a dog show and visit among the exhibitors' benches; also watch the advertisements in the dog magazines and sporting journals.

Currently, a fairly good purebred dog should be available for about $50 to $200, depending on the breed.

THE DOG'S LIFE SPAN

Perhaps the one disturbing feature of dog ownership is that the dog's life span is relatively short. A dog aged seventeen is considered the equivalent of a human centenarian. While statistics on the longevity of dogs are lacking (the one insurance company that issues life insurance policies on purebred, registered dogs has not been operating long enough to have accurate actuarial information), it is known that some types of dogs generally live longer than others.

Studies in England have shown that, as in man, mortality among dogs favors the female. And the dog's life span is almost in inverse proportion to his size. In simpler words, the smaller the dog, the longer his anticipated life. Many of the toy dogs are exceptionally long-lived. It has been found that the larger breeds are more subject to cancer and skin tumors than the smaller breeds. This is a leading cause of death among the larger dogs, but is a strikingly minor cause of death among Pekingese and other small breeds.

Generally, the small and medium-sized breeds seem to have the best prospects for longer life. In a survey taken by the Gaines Dog Research Center a few years ago, it was found that fox terriers, cocker spaniels, dachshunds, Pekingese and Pomeranians, spitzes and Boston terriers were most often the longest-lived breeds and that crosses among these breeds also tend to live longer. A number of dogs were found who were eighteen, nineteen and twenty-one years old, and the oldest verified was twenty-six years old.

On the other hand, a study in England among Irish wolfhounds showed that the mean age at death of these large dogs was slightly under five years for males; a little over six and half years for bitches; and that few were found older than ten years.

THE BUSINESS OF PEDIGREE

You have to watch your language when you are in the company of "dog" people. If you refer to a blue-blooded canine as a "thoroughbred" or a "pedigreed" dog, that marks you as an outsider. The term thoroughbred is applied to horses or cattle, never to dogs. The pedigree is a chart showing the family tree of a particular dog or litter of pups.

The aristocrats of the dog world are always described as "purebred." By definition, a purebred dog is one belonging to a breed with recognized characteristics that have been maintained through many generations of unmixed descent. In actual practice, purebred dogs are those that are recognized by one or more of the established kennel clubs. The American Kennel Club now recognizes 116 different purebred dogs. Still other kinds of dogs are accepted by the United Kennel Club. To complicate the matter a bit, the *Field Dog Stud Book* maintains a registry of hunting (sporting) dogs of breeds which are also recognized by the A.K.C. Also, some breeds of dogs that are not considered purebred in America are registered by the kennel clubs of other countries.

The basic test of a purebred dog is that it must breed true to type. In other words, if you mate two specimens of any "pure" breed, the offspring will possess the characteristics of the parents and of the breed.

The dogs that have won recognition as purebred have gone through a lengthy process before becoming eligible for "registration" in the stud book of the A.K.C. Before any breed has been recognized, its sponsors have had to form a "specialty" club. The club's constitution, by-laws and membership lists have been submitted to the A.K.C. for approval, together with an acceptable "description and standard" which describes the traits of the breed in detail, and considerable supporting evidence that the dog in question is of a purebred type which reproduces its kind.

WHEN BUYING A DOG OR PUPPY

In making an investment in a purebred dog, you should be certain that you receive the dog's "papers." In the case of an older dog, he will probably have been registered with the appropriate kennel club and the owner provides you with the registration certificate. You sign it on the back, have the seller sign, and you send it to the kennel club with the required fee to record the change of ownership. This is necessary in the event that you plan to show the dog or to breed it and register the puppies.

If you are buying the dog from a kennel owner or breeder, he should be able to provide you with a copy of the pedigree which records the ancestors of the dog you are buying and also the designation "Ch." before the names of any champions in his ancestry. Where the dog is represented as a purebred, but no papers are available, the cost of the dog should be much less than for one that is documented.

The pedigree is not necessary for registration; it is merely for your information and to show the worth of the dog in terms of bloodlines. If you want an official pedigree of your dog, you can obtain it from the kennel club records by sending in an application form. The fee depends on how many generations back you want his ancestry traced.

When you buy a purebred puppy, he will probably not have been registered, though the litter is. The litter must be registered before any individual puppy can be. As the stud book maintains records from generation to generation, no dog may be registered unless both his parents are.

The seller of the puppy will give you an application for registration form. On this appear the names and stud book numbers of the dog's parents and the name of breeder who signs the form. You in turn must fill in the data which establish you as the new owner of the dog (a co-owner may be included) and the name you select for the dog. The name is limited to twenty-five letters. It must not be the name of a living person without that person's written permission, and must not duplicate the name used by another dog of the same breed. A space is provided for an alternate name in case your first choice is not allowed.

If your registration is with the American Kennel Club, send the completed application form to the A.K.C. at 51 Madison Avenue, New York, N. Y. 10010, with the registration fee of $2.00 ($4.00 if the dog is over eighteen months old). In a few weeks, if the papers are in order, you will receive a certificate of registration from the A.K.C. showing that your dog has been entered in the stud book of his breed. (The Kennel Club in England is located at 84 Piccadilly, London, W. 1. English readers may write to the Secretary for application forms.)

If your dog is one of the hunting breeds and you prefer to enter him in the

Sample pedigree certificate

Sample registration certificate

Field Dog Stud Book, you must obtain the following forms from the seller:

1. Certificate from owner of bitch which the breeder must fill out completely.

2. Certificate from owner of stud dog—if the litter has not already been registered with the *Field Dog Stud Book.*

3. Application for registration, which you, as the purchaser, fill out. Send the required certificates and the registration fee of $3.00 to the American Field Publishing Company, 222 West Adams Street, Chicago, Ill. 60606.

The *Field Dog Stud Book* registration is necessary if you plan to train your dog to work in the field and to run him in field trials.

The United Kennel Club, located at 321 West Cedar Street, Kalamazoo, Michigan, maintains a stud book for nineteen breeds which are not recognized by the American Kennel Club. Their registration procedure is similar to that of the other stud books, and similar forms are used. However, the $2.00 registration fee charged by the U.K.C. includes the preparation of a three-generation certified pedigree which is sent out with the registration certificate.

CERTIFICATE FOR OWNER OF BITCH

I HEREBY CERTIFY

That my bitch (Name)...*No.*...........
STUD BOOK NUMBER

Was bred to .... *on* ....
NAME OF STUD DOG   DATE OF SERVICE

Breed..*Color*....................................
OF BITCH   OF BITCH

Date of birth of Bitch ....

Number and sex in litter....................*Date puppies were whelped*...........................
DOGS   BITCHES

Dated at ....   *(Signed)* ....
OWNER OF BITCH AT TIME OF SERVICE

For the **FIELD DOG STUD BOOK**   Published by **AMERICAN FIELD PUBLISHING CO.**, Chicago (6)

CERTIFICATE FOR OWNER OF STUD DOG

I HEREBY CERTIFY

That my dog (Name)...*No.*...........
STUD BOOK NUMBER

Was bred to .... *on* ....
NAME OF BITCH   DATE OF SERVICE

Breed..*Color*....................................
OF STUD DOG   OF STUD DOG

Date of birth of Stud Dog...

Dated at ....   *(Signed)* ....
OWNER OF STUD DOG AT TIME OF SERVICE

For the **FIELD DOG STUD BOOK**   Published by **AMERICAN FIELD PUBLISHING CO.**, Chicago (6)

Sample stud dog and bitch certificates

Field Dog Stud Book Application for Registration—Fee $3.00

Published by the AMERICAN FIELD PUBLISHING CO., 222 West Adams Street, Chicago, Illinois 60606

Certificate of Registration Issued 30 Days After Receipt of Application

---

Application forms become a part of the files and records of the F. D. S. B. and will not be returned.

PUBLISHER FIELD DOG STUD BOOK:

I offer for registration the dog described below. Fee, THREE DOLLARS.

> Obtain a Certified Pedigree of the dog covered by this application at following rates:
> 3 generations, $ 3.00; with wins, $ 5.00   4 generations, $ 6.00; with wins, $ 9.00
> 5 generations, $12.00; with wins, $18.00
> **THE COST OF PEDIGREES IS IN ADDITION TO THE REGISTRATION FEE**

Owner_____
(Print or Typewrite to Avoid Errors)

Street_____

City_____ State_____ Zip Code_____

Name Claimed   Fill in three choices. Maximum, three words for each name or 20 letters. _____
(First Choice)

_____   _____
(Second Choice)   (Third Choice)

Breed_____ Sex_____

Color_____ Date Whelped_____
(Give predominating color first)

Indicate principal markings for identification

SIRE_____   { Sire's Sire_____
*(Certificate of Sire required unless litter is enrolled)
Registration No.   { Sire's Dam_____

DAM_____   { Dam's Sire_____
*(Certificate of owner of Dam at time of service must be furnished)
Registration No.   { Dam's Dam_____

Owner (or Lessee) of Sire_____ Address_____
(At time of service)

Owner (or Lessee) of Dam_____ Address_____
(At time of service)

If dog offered for registration is registered in any other stud book, give number_____

---

*If certificates from owners of sire and dam cannot be obtained, owner must execute following affidavit and attach statement explaining why certificates are not procurable.

State of_____ }
                   } ss
County_____ }

_____,
being first duly sworn, on oath says that he is the owner of the dog described, and that he knows the sire and dam to be as stated above; and the deponent further says that all information given is correct, to the best of his knowledge and belief.

Subscribed and sworn to before me this

_____day of_____, 19_____

Owner's Signature

_____
Notary Public   (OVER)

Registration forms of the Field Dog Stud Book. Similar forms are used by the American Kennel Club and the United Kennel Club.

THE FACTS ABOUT DOG BITES

A dog is after all an animal, and under some provocation, any dog may bite a person. One of the hazards of dog ownership is the possibility of the family pet inflicting injury on a person. Although the laws regarding the responsibility of the dog's owner for damages the animal may inflict vary slightly according to locality, the owner is generally liable for medical expenses and for compensation for permanent disability or disfigurement.

Most houseowners are protected against damages their dog may inflict by the public liability policy on their property, which includes a clause covering a dog bite that may occur on the premises. However, any dog owner may obtain a fairly inexpensive personal liability policy to protect him against such claims up to the face amount of the policy.

Until very recently, little was known about the incidence of dog bites, but a study made by several veterinary colleges and medical schools indicates that dog bites are a real hazard. Each year, six hundred thousand to a million persons are bitten by dogs in the United States.

Study of the victims of dog bites shows that the great majority of them are preschool and school children, with boys and girls between five and nine years old having the highest bite rate, and boys between ten and nineteen next highest. The greatest number of the bites reported were suffered by children and youths less than twenty years of age. It is this group which is most intimately associated with dogs as pets; they are often abusive to pets, and in many instances they do not know how to care for pets properly. Also, persons under twenty years of age are more likely to be engaged in activities which excite dogs, such as playing ball, running, riding bicycles, and delivering newspapers.

Who Gets Bitten

Definite categories of persons run a high risk of being bitten by dogs. School children and preschool children are the most frequent victims, especially if they own a dog or live within three houses of a dog owner's home. Persons coming to the dog owner's home in the line of work are also frequent victims, as are also veterinarians and their assistants.

An unfortunate aspect of the dog-bite situation is that a high percentage of the bites (about 16 per cent) occur on the victim's head, face and neck. In about 10 per cent of all dog bites, there are injuries which physicians classify as "moderately severe" and "severe."

Why Dogs Bite

A study of the causes of dog bites indicates fairly clearly that, while some dog bites are unprovoked, the human factor plays a big part, and the activity of the person involved led to the biting in about 50 per cent of the cases studied.

On the basis of the studies of dog biting, a number of recommendations for the reduction of dog bites can be made:

Do not give a dog to children under six years of age. About 18 per cent of the bites may thus be eliminated.

Teach children how to care for their pets and not to tease or abuse dogs.

Discourage playing ball with a dog, riding bicycles and vehicles in the vicinity of excited dogs, and running while playing with a dog if it excites him. These suggestions might eliminate another 10 per cent of the bites.

Exercise caution while assisting injured and sick animals, avoid abruptly arousing sleeping dogs, and be careful in picking up pups so as not to offend the mother dog. These measures might prevent another 3 per cent of all bites.

Do not pet, startle, or take food away from a dog while feeding him and do not intercede in dog fights. These suggestions might eliminate another 10 per cent of the bites.

Avoid holding your face next to a dog's; thus you will avoid disfiguring facial injuries.

Admittedly, this is confining for dog owners, but the rules are suggested as preventive measures. If these could be followed, 40 to 50 per cent of dog bites might be avoided.

Characteristics of Biting Dogs

A study of the types of dogs which are most prone to bite people produced some surprising results. Contrary to general belief, it was found that female dogs are almost twice as likely to bite a person as male dogs. Also contrary to popular notions, the sex difference in bite rates was not related to the females caring for newborn pups, as only a small percentage of the bites occurred while the victim was playing with a pup.

Another striking finding is that younger dogs are more likely to bite people than older dogs. This was most true for dogs between six and eleven months of age, while dogs over five years of age bite far less often than would be expected. Young dogs in intimate association with young people seem to invite frequent dog-bite incidents.

As to the breeds most guilty of inflicting bites, it was found that the working-dog group is much more likely to inflict bites than any other. This group includes the following breeds: boxers, collies, Eskimo dogs, German shepherds, great Danes, Saint Bernards and Doberman pinschers. This group inflicted almost twice as many bites as was expected statistically.

The sporting dogs, including the various breeds of pointers, setters, retrievers and spaniels, also inflicted more bites than had been expected.

Hounds, on the other hand, bite fewer people than would be expected, indicating that they are relatively safe dogs to own.

No significant differences in the frequency of bites could be found for mixed breeds, terriers, toys, nonsporting dogs and unrecognized breeds, and it was not possible to single out any individual breed as being particularly vicious.

As had been expected, it was found that certain individual dogs are chronic biters. However, it was observed that dogs which are pugnacious toward other dogs do not carry this tendency over to people, and there was no relationship between dogs fighting among themselves and biting persons.

On the basis of the study of biting dogs, it is suggested that dog owners should:

Try to avoid the association of young dogs (less than a year old) with young children (less than five years old).

When obtaining pets for children, consider the fact that female dogs inflict more bites than males.

Restrain or dispose of dogs that are frequent biters.

Immunize dogs against rabies; consult a veterinarian for the proper schedule.

Attach an identification tag to each animal's collar listing the dog's name and the owner's name and address.

Don't permit dogs to roam at large in a well-populated area.

BREEDS REGISTERED BY THE AMERICAN KENNEL CLUB

GROUP I—SPORTING DOGS

POINTERS	SETTERS (GORDON)
POINTERS (GERMAN SHORTHAIRED)	SETTERS (IRISH)
POINTERS (GERMAN WIREHAIRED)	SPANIELS (AMERICAN WATER)
RETRIEVERS (CHESAPEAKE BAY)	SPANIELS (BRITTANY)
RETRIEVERS (CURLY-COATED)	SPANIELS (CLUMBER)
RETRIEVERS (FLAT-COATED)	SPANIELS (COCKER)
RETRIEVERS (GOLDEN)	SPANIELS (ENGLISH COCKER)
RETRIEVERS (LABRADOR)	SPANIELS (ENGLISH SPRINGER)
SETTERS (ENGLISH)	SPANIELS (FIELD)

SPANIELS (IRISH WATER)   VIZSLAS
SPANIELS (SUSSEX)   WEIMARANERS
SPANIELS (WELSH SPRINGER)   WIREHAIRED POINTING GRIFFONS

GROUP II—HOUNDS

AFGHAN HOUNDS   GREYHOUNDS
BASENJIS   HARRIERS
BASSET HOUNDS   IRISH WOLFHOUNDS
BEAGLES   NORWEGIAN ELKHOUNDS
BLACK AND TAN COONHOUNDS   OTTER HOUNDS
BLOODHOUNDS   RHODESIAN RIDGEBACKS
BORZOIS   SALUKIS
DACHSHUNDS   SCOTTISH DEERHOUNDS
FOXHOUNDS (AMERICAN)   WHIPPETS
FOXHOUNDS (ENGLISH)

GROUP III—WORKING DOGS

ALASKAN MALAMUTES   KOMONDOROK
BELGIAN MALINOIS   KUVASZOK
BELGIAN SHEEPDOGS   MASTIFFS
BELGIAN TERVUREN   NEWFOUNDLANDS
BERNESE MOUNTAIN DOGS   OLD ENGLISH SHEEPDOGS
BOUVIERS DES FLANDRES   PULIK
BOXERS   ROTTWEILERS
BRIARDS   ST. BERNARDS
BULLMASTIFFS   SAMOYEDS
COLLIES   SHETLAND SHEEPDOGS
DOBERMAN PINSCHERS   SIBERIAN HUSKIES
GERMAN SHEPHERD DOGS   STANDARD SCHNAUZERS
GIANT SCHNAUZERS   WELSH CORGIS (CARDIGAN)
GREAT DANES   WELSH CORGIS (PEMBROKE)
GREAT PYRENEES

GROUP IV—TERRIERS

AIREDALE TERRIERS   BEDLINGTON TERRIERS
AMERICAN STAFFORDSHIRE TERRIERS   BORDER TERRIERS
AUSTRALIAN TERRIERS   BULL TERRIERS

CAIRN TERRIERS

DANDIE DINMONT TERRIERS

FOX TERRIERS

IRISH TERRIERS

KERRY BLUE TERRIERS

LAKELAND TERRIERS

MANCHESTER TERRIERS

MINIATURE SCHNAUZERS

NORWICH TERRIERS

SCOTTISH TERRIERS

SEALYHAM TERRIERS

SKYE TERRIERS

WELSH TERRIERS

WEST HIGHLAND WHITE TERRIERS

GROUP V—TOYS

AFFENPINSCHERS

BRUSSELS GRIFFONS

CHIHUAHUAS

ENGLISH TOY SPANIELS

ITALIAN GREYHOUNDS

JAPANESE SPANIELS

MALTESE

MINIATURE PINSCHERS

PAPILLONS

PEKINGESE

POMERANIANS

PUGS

SHIH TZU

SILKY TERRIERS

YORKSHIRE TERRIERS

GROUP VI—NONSPORTING DOGS

BOSTON TERRIERS

BULLDOGS

CHOW CHOWS

DALMATIANS

FRENCH BULLDOGS

KEESHONDEN

LHASA APSOS

POODLES

SCHIPPERKES

BREEDS REGISTERED BY THE UNITED KENNEL CLUB

American (pit) bull terrier

Toy fox terrier

American toy terrier

American black-and-tan coonhound

Bluetick coonhound

English coonhound

Plott hound

Redbone coonhound

Walker (treeing) coonhound

English bloodhound

English beagle

Miniature boxer

American Eskimo

Arctic huskie

Alaskan Malemute

American water spaniel

English shepherd

Columbian collie

Scotch collie

BREEDS REGISTERED BY THE ENGLISH KENNEL CLUB
SPORTING DOGS

Afghan
Basenji
Basset hound
Beagle
Bloodhound
Borzoi
Long-haired dachshund
Miniature dachshund
Short-haired dachshund
Wire-haired dachshund
Deerhound

Elkhound
Finnish spitz
Foxhound
Greyhound
Harrier
Irish wolfhound
Otter hound
Rhodesian ridgeback
Saluki
Whippet

Gun Dogs

English setter
Gordon setter
Red Irish setter
Setter (Crossbreed)
Pointer
German short-haired pointer
Curly-coated retriever
Flat-coated retriever
Golden retriever
Labrador retriever
Retriever (Interbred)

Retriever (Crossbreed)
Clumber spaniel
Cocker spaniel
English springer spaniel
Welsh springer spaniel
Field spaniel
Irish water spaniel
Sussex spaniel
Spaniel (Interbred)
Spaniel (Crossbreed)
Weimaraner

Terriers

Airedale terrier
Australian terrier
Bedlington terrier
Border terrier
Bull terrier
Miniature bull terrier
Cairn terrier
Dandie Dinmont terrier
Fox terrier (Smooth)
Fox terrier (Wire)
Irish terrier

Kerry blue terrier
Lakeland terrier
Manchester terrier
Norwich terrier
Scottish terrier
Sealyham terrier
Skye terrier
Staffordshire terrier
Welsh terrier
West Highland white terrier

NONSPORTING DOGS

Alsatian (German shepherd dog)
Bearded collie
Boston terrier
Boxer
Bulldog
Bull mastiff
Chowchow
Collie (Rough)
Collie (Smooth)
Dalmatian
Dobermann
French bulldog
Great Dane
Keeshond
Mastiff
Newfoundland

Old English sheepdog
Poodle
Miniature poodle
Toy poodle
Pyrenean mountain dog
Saint Bernard
Samoyed
Schipperke
Schnauzer
Miniature schnauzer
Shetland sheepdog
Shih Tzu
Tibetan terrier
Cardigan Welsh corgi
Pembroke Welsh corgi

TOYS

Miniature black-and-tan terrier
Chihuahua
Griffon Bruxelloix
Italian greyhound
Japanese spaniel
King Charles spaniel
Cavalier King Charles spaniel

Maltese
Miniature pinscher
Papillon
Pekingese
Pomeranian
Pug
Yorkshire terrier

OTHER ENGLISH BREEDS

Among breeds known in England which are not found in the current registry of the English Kennel Club:

Hounds
  Evissenc
  Lurcher

Mastiff-type Breeds
  Appenzell mountain dog
  Bernese mountain dog
  Rottweiler

Spitz-type Breeds
  Akita

Sheep dogs
  Armant
  Kelpie
  Kuvasz
  Maremma sheepdog

Spaniels
   Old English spaniel
Terriers
   Glen of Imaal terrier

Welsh sheepdog
Lhasa Apso
Parson Jack Russell terrier
Soft-coated Wheaten terrier

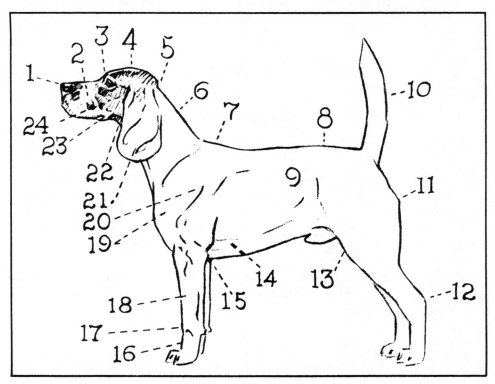

PARTS OF THE DOG

1. Nose.
2. Muzzle.
3. Stop.
4. Skull.
5. Occiput.
6. Arch or Crest.
7. Withers or Top of Shoulders.
8. Hip.
9. Loin.
10. Brush or Flag.
11. Point of Rump.
12. Hock.
13. Stifle.
14. Chest.
15. Elbow.
16. Pastern.
17. Knee.
18. Forearm.
19. Point of Shoulder.
20. Shoulder.
21. Ear or Leather.
22. Dewlap.
23. Lips or Flews.
24. Cheek.

Courtesy of Harry Miller, director Gaines Dog Research Center, New York, N.Y.

2

THE MOST POPULAR DOGS

SPORTING DOGS

FOR HUNDREDS of thousands of people the happiest day of the year is the one when the sign "CLOSED—GONE HUNTING" is hung up and the man and dog go off after birds or upland game. Since prehistoric times man and dog have hunted together, and whether the man's weapon was a stone ax, a crude net or a shotgun, the sporting dog has used his keener senses to find the game and wait for his reward when the man brings it down.

The "togetherness" inherent in the make-up of the sporting breeds extends to living with man as well as hunting with him, and the sporting dogs make ideal companions in the home.

BRITTANY SPANIEL

A product of France, this spaniel is unusual in that he works as a pointer in the field. In the United States only since 1931, the breed has become increasingly popular. Average weight 35 pounds, height 19 inches. Flat, wavy coat, white with orange or liver markings.

Developed in France, the Brittany spaniel probably has in his veins setter, pointer and spaniel blood, but enough spaniel characteristics to be kept within that group. He is the only spaniel that points game (other spaniels flush their prey); he is often born tailless or with a stub of a tail; and he resembles a setter in conformation.

This long-limbed spaniel is inclined to be a one-man dog. He is often rather sensitive and must be trained with kindness and mild correction when he errs.

In the few decades that he has been known to American hunters, the Brittany spaniel has shown himself to be an excellent companion to the man

32

Brittany Spaniel
Dual Ch. Helgramite Howie D'Acajou
Owner: W. E. Stevenson. Stamford, Connecticut

who hunts on foot. He ranges wider than the other spaniels—although he keeps closer to the hunter than the average pointer or setter, and he is particularly adept at working in brush and heavy cover. Despite the lack of a tail—which helps the hunter follow his dog's progress—the Brittany is the favorite of many hunters in Canada and New England.

In addition to his pointing instinct, the Brittany is good at retrieving game and he has the usual spaniel characteristics that make him an excellent house pet and family dog as well as a hunter. Not a kennel dog, he enjoys the comforts of the fireside as well as the work in the field.

Standard of the Breed

General Description: A compact, closely knit dog of medium size, a leggy spaniel with the appearance and agility of a great ground coverer. Strong, vigorous, energetic and quick of movement. Not too light in bone, yet never heavy-boned and cumbersome. Ruggedness without clumsiness is a characteristic of the breed. So leggy is he that his height at the withers is the same as the length of his body. He has no tail, or, at most, not more than four inches.

Weight: Should weigh between 30 and 40 pounds.

Height: 17½ to 20½ inches—measured from the ground to the highest point of the back—the withers.

Disqualification: Any Brittany spaniel measuring under 17½ inches or over 20½ inches is disqualified from bench show competition. Any black in the coat or a nose so dark in color as to appear black, disqualifies him. A tail substantially more than four inches is a disqualification.

Coat: Hair dense, flat or wavy, never curly. Not as fine as other spaniel breeds, and never silky. Furnishings not profuse. The ears should carry little fringe. Neither the front nor the hind legs should carry heavy featherings. *Note:* Long, curly or silky hair is a fault. Any tendency toward excessive feathering should be severely penalized as undesirable in a sporting dog which must encounter burrs and heavy cover.

Skin: Fine and fairly loose. (A loose skin rolls with briars and sticks, thus diminishing punctures or tearing. But a skin so loose as to form pouches is undesirable.)

Color: Dark orange and white or liver and white. Some ticking is desirable, but not so much as to produce belton patterns. Roan patterns or factors of orange or liver shade are permissible. The orange and liver are found in standard parti-color or piebald patterns. Washed-out or faded colors are not desirable. Black is a disqualification.

Skull: Medium length (approximately 4¾ inches). Rounded, very slightly wedge-shaped, but evenly made. Width, not quite as wide as the length (about 4⅜ inches) and never so broad as to appear coarse or so narrow as to appear racy. Well-defined but gently sloping stop effect. Median line rather indistinct. The occipital crest apparent only to the touch. Lateral walls well rounded. The Brittany spaniel should never be "apple-headed" and he should never have an indented stop. (All measurements of the skull are for a 19½-inch dog.)

Muzzle: Medium length, about two-thirds the length of the skull, measuring the muzzle from the tip to the stop, and the skull from the occipital crest to the stop between the eyes. Muzzle should taper gradually in both horizontal and vertical dimensions as it approaches the nostrils. Neither a Roman nose nor a concave (dish face) is desirable. Never broad, heavy or snipy.

Nose: Nostrils well open to permit deep breathing of air and adequate scenting while at top speed. Tight nostrils should be penalized. Never shiny. *Color:* fawn, tan, light shades of brown or deep pink. A black nose is a disqualification. A two-tone or butterfly nose should be severely penalized.

Ears: Set high, above the level of the eyes. Short and leafy, rather than pendulous, reaching about half the length of the muzzle. Should lie flat and close to the head, with the tip rounded very slightly. Ears well covered with dense but relatively short hair, and with little fringe.

Lips: Tight to the muzzle, with the upper lip overlapping the lower jaw only sufficiently to cover under lip. Lips dry so that feathers do not stick. Drooling receives a heavy penalty. Flews (chaps) are penalized.

Teeth: Well-joined incisors. Posterior edge of upper incisors in contact with anterior edge of lower incisors, thus giving a true scissors bite. Overshot or undershot jaw is penalized heavily.

Neck: Medium length. Not quite permitting the dog to place his nose on the ground without bending his legs. Free from throatiness, though not a serious fault unless accompanied by dewlaps. Strong, without giving the impression of being overmuscled. Well set into sloping shoulders. Never concave or ewe-necked.

Body Length: Approximately the same as the height when measured at the withers. Body length is measured from the point of the forechest to the rear of the haunches. A long body should be heavily penalized.

Withers: Shoulder blades should not protrude much. Not too widely set apart, with perhaps two thumbs' width or less between the blades. At the withers, the Brittany spaniel is slightly higher than at the rump.

Shoulders: Sloping and muscular. Blade and upper arm should form nearly a 90-degree angle when measured from the posterior point of the blade at the withers to the junction of the blade and the upper arm, and thence to the point of the elbow nearest the ribs. Straight shoulders do not permit sufficient reach.

Back: Short and straight. Slight slope from the highest point of withers to the root of the tail. Never hollow-, saddle-, sway- or roach-backed. Slight drop from hips to root of tail. Distance from last rib to upper thigh short, about three to four finger widths.

Chest: Deep, reaching the level of the elbow. Neither so wide nor so rounded as to disturb the placement of the shoulder bones and elbows, which causes a paddling movement, and often causes soreness from elbow striking ribs. Ribs well sprung, but adequate heart room provided by depth as well as width. Narrow or slab-sided chest is a fault.

Flanks: Rounded. Fairly full. Not extremely tucked up, nor yet flabby and falling. Loins short and strong. Narrow and weak loins are a fault. In motion the loin should not sway sideward, giving a zigzag motion to the back and wasting energy.

Hindquarters: Broad, strong and muscular, with powerful thighs and well-bent stifles, giving a hip well set into the loin and the marked angulation necessary for a powerful drive when in motion. Fat and falling hindquarters are a fault.

Tail: Naturally tailless, or not over four inches long. Natural or docked. Set on high, actually an extension of the spine at about the same level.

Front Legs: Viewed from the front, perpendicular, but not set too wide as in the case of a dog loaded in shoulder. Elbows and feet turning neither in nor out. Viewed from the side, practically perpendicular to the pastern. Pastern slightly bent to give cushion to stride. Not so straight as in terriers. Falling pasterns, however, are a serious fault. Leg bones clean, graceful, but not too fine. Extremely heavy legs are as much a fault as spindly legs. One must look for substance and suppleness. Height to the elbows should approximately equal the distance from elbow to withers.

Hind Legs: Stifles well bent. The stifle generally is the term used for knee joint. If the angle made by the upper and lower leg bones is too straight, the dog quite generally lacks drive, since his hind legs cannot drive as far forward at each stride as is desirable. However, the stifle should not be bent as to throw the hock joint far out behind the dog. Since factors not easily seen by the eye may give the dog his proper drive, a Brittany spaniel should not be condemned for straight stifles until the judge has checked the dog in motion from the side. When at the trot, a Brittany's hind foot should step into or beyond the print made by the front foot.

The stifle joint should not turn out, making a cow hock. (The cow hock moves the foot out to the side, thus driving out of line and losing reach at each stride.) Thighs well feathered, but not profusely, halfway to the hock. Hocks—that is, the back pasterns—should be moderately short, pointing neither in nor out; perpendicular when viewed from the side. They should be firm when shaken by the judge.

Feet: Should be strong, proportionately smaller than in other spaniels, with close-fitting, well-arched toes and thick pads. The Brittany is not "up on his toes." Toes not heavily feathered. Flat feet, splayed feet, paper feet, and the like, are heavily penalized. An ideal foot is halfway between the hare and cat foot.

SCALE OF POINTS. The points below indicate only relative values. To be taken into consideration are type, gait, soundness, spirit, optimum height, body length, and general proportions.

SCALE OF POINTS

Head	*25*
Body	*35*
Running gear	*40*
	100

CHESAPEAKE BAY RETRIEVER

A native American dog, its ancestry is traced to two dogs rescued from a wrecked brig off Maryland in 1807. An outstanding duck hunter. Average weight 70 pounds; height 24 inches. Dense brown or tan coat.

No attempts have been made by fanciers to beautify the Chesapeake Bay retriever. Descended from old ships' dogs that could carry a line ashore in

Chesapeake Retriever
Rigsbys Rosemont Dancer
Owner: Clyde D. Rigsby. Cedar Rapids, Iowa

heavy seas, the Chesapeake is endowed by nature with an oily coat that is fully waterproof and protects him from the coldest waters. He is one of the few dogs that will plunge fully under water on a retrieve, and his webbed feet aid him in swimming.

Although the Chesapeakes are traced back to the two shipwrecked animals, it is believed that there is much Newfoundland in their descent and that they share a common ancestry with the Labrador retriever.

Strictly a one-purpose dog, the Chesapeake plunges headlong into the iciest water after a duck, and many seem to enjoy swimming in frigid waters for the sheer sport of it.

Never popular as a show breed, the Chesapeake is not a particularly friendly dog and his propensity for getting into fights has made him an unpopular kennel mate. However, some owners have reported that these dogs, when raised in the home, show a high instinct for protecting children.

Originally known only on the Atlantic coast, the dog has also become fairly popular with duck hunters in the Midwestern swamps and marshes, and in Canada and England. He has also been used to some extent in retrieving upland game.

While even his staunchest admirers admit that he is a homely dog, they say that no other breed even approaches him in water retrieving. One of his assets is a phenomenal memory for downed birds. Hunters have said that Chesapeakes have noted as many as six fallen ducks and have retrieved them in turn, even getting those that had been swept a distance away by the currents.

Standard of the Breed

Height: 23–26 inches for males; 21–24 inches for females.

Weight: 65–75 pounds for males; 55–65 pounds for females.

Body Length: Medium.

Teeth: Not undershot or overshot.

Skull: Broad, round.

Eyes: Wide apart, medium in size, yellowish in color.

Ears: Small, set high, hanging loose; leather medium thick.

Neck: Medium length, strong muscular, tapering.

Stop: Medium.

Lips: Thin, not pendulous.

Muzzle: Medium short, not sharp.

Shoulders: Sloping.

Chest: Strong, deep, wide; barrel-round.

Back: short, well-coupled, sloping.

Hindquarters: Trifle higher than shoulders, extremely powerful.

Tail: Medium length, heavy at base, moderate feathering permissible.

Flanks: Well tucked up.

Hock to Heel: Not too long or too short.

Feet: Harelike, webbed toes well rounded.

Pasterns: Close, slightly bent, medium length.

Legs: Medium length, straight good bone, muscular, very powerful, no dewclaws.

Coat: Thick, short, not over 1¼ inches long; oily; undercoat dense, fine woolly; hair on legs short and straight; curly coat not desirable; outer coat harsh; coat water-resistant; feathering not over 1¾ inches.

Color: Dark brown to dead grass.

COCKER SPANIEL

One of the most popular dogs in England and America and in European countries. A distinctive American type has been developed. Average weight 25 pounds, height 14 inches. Wavy coat in three varieties: black; any solid color (including black and tan); parti-color.

Pet-shop owners have found that placing a merry, effervescent cocker spaniel puppy in a store window is a certain way to ensure a fast sale. But the purchaser of a cocker should be a bit wary. Many of the present-day strains have a tendency to shyness, some to hysteria, and about the only way to tell how any one cocker will turn out is to live with him. However, as with other breeds, the puppy usually inherits the characteristics of his immediate parents, and the offspring of two "good" cockers should be a satisfactory pet.

Basically, the cocker is a hunting dog and although extremely few of the modern cockers ever get into the field, the dog should have some interest in life that will keep his active character occupied. Many cockers have done remarkably well in obedience trials. Some owners have found that keeping a pair of cockers works out better than having one, as they keep each other occupied and alert.

Cockers differ considerably in behavior. Some will love swimming, others will refuse to enter the water; some will be natural retrievers, others will refuse to retrieve and must be taught; some will show complete attention and train readily; others may be stubborn and resist training.

The owner of a cocker should pay special attention to his dog's ears. Because of their long, floppy ears and long hair, cockers are particularly prone to ear cankers (sores in the ears) which become extremely painful when the dog's

ASCOB Cocker Spaniel
Int. Ch. Pinefair Pirate
Owner: Mrs. H. Terrell Van Inger. Greenwich, Connecticut

Parti-color Spaniel
Ch. Dau-Han's Dan Morgan
Owner: Mrs. Muriel R. Laubach. Norfolk, Virginia

Black Cocker Spaniel
Ch. Holly High Night
Owner: Mrs. William H. Edwards. Meriden, Connecticut

ears are touched, and for this reason many adult cockers become fretful "biters" of persons who attempt to pet them.

Standard of the Breed

Skull: Well-developed and rounded with no tendency toward flatness or pronounced roundness of the crown (dome). The forehead smooth, the eyebrows and stop clearly defined, the median line distinctly marked and gradually disappearing until lost rather more than halfway up to the crown. The bony structure surrounding the socket of the eye should be well chiseled; there should be no suggestion of fullness under the eye, nor prominence in the cheeks which, like the sides of the muzzle, should present a smooth, clean-cut appearance.

Muzzle and Teeth: To attain a well-proportioned head, which above all should be in balance with the rest of the dog, the distance from the tip of the nose to the stop, at a point on a line drawn across the top of the muzzle between the front corners of the eyes, should approximate half the distance from the stop at this point up over the crown to the base of the skull. The muzzle should be broad and deep, with square, even jaws. The upper lip should be of sufficient depth to cover the lower jaw, presenting a square appearance. The teeth should be sound and regular and set at right angles to the jaw. The relation of the upper teeth to the lower should be that of scissors, with the inner surface of the upper in contact with the outer surface of the lower when the jaws are closed. The nose of sufficient size to balance the muzzle and foreface, with well-developed nostrils, and black in color in the blacks and black-and-tans; in the reds, buffs, livers and parti-colors, and in the roans it may be black or brown, the darker color being preferable.

Eyes: The eyeballs should be round and full and set in the surrounding tissue to look directly forward and give the eye a slightly almond-shaped appearance. The eye should be neither weak nor goggled. The expression should be alert, intelligent, soft and appealing. The color of the iris should be dark brown to black in the blacks, black-and-tans, buffs and creams, and in the darker shades of the parti-colors and roans. In the reds, dark hazel; in the livers, parti-colors and roans of the lighter shades, not lighter than hazel, the darker the better.

Ears: Lobular, set on a line no higher than the lower part of the eye, the leather fine and extending to the nostrils; well clothed with long, silky, straight or wavy hair.

Neck and Shoulders: The neck sufficiently long to allow the nose to reach the ground easily, muscular and free from pendulous "throatiness." It should rise strongly from the shoulders and arch slightly as it tapers to join the head. The shoulders, deep, clean cut and sloping without protrusion and so set that the upper points of the withers are at an angle which permits a wide spring of rib.

Body: Its height at the withers should approximate the length from the withers to the set-on of tail. The chest deep, its lowest point no higher than the elbows, its front sufficiently wide for adequate heart and lung space, yet not so wide as to interefere with the straightforward movement of the forelegs. Ribs deep and well sprung throughout. Body short in the couplings and flank, with its depth at the flank somewhat less than at the last rib. Back strong and sloping evenly and slightly downward from the withers to set-on of tail. Hips wide, with quarters well rounded and muscular. The body should appear short, compact and firmly knit, giving the impression of strength.

Legs and Feet: Forelegs straight, strong-boned and muscular and set close to the body well under the scapulae. The elbows well let down and turning neither in nor out. The pasterns short and strong. The hind legs strongly boned and muscled, with well-turned stifles and powerful, clearly defined thighs. The hocks strong, well let down and parallel when in motion and at rest. Feet compact, not spreading, round and firm, with deep, strong horny pads and hair between the toes; they should turn neither in nor out.

Tail: Set on and carried on a line with the top line of the back, and when the dog is at work its action should be incessant.

Coat: Flat or slightly waved, soft and dense; the ears, chest, abdomen and legs well feathered.

Color and Markings: Blacks should be jet black, those showing shading of brown or liver in the sheen of the coat or feathering are penalized though not disqualified. Solid colors other than black should be of sound shade, but lighter-colored feathering, while not favored, does not disqualify. A small amount of white on chest and throat of solid colors should be penalized, but does not disqualify. White in any other location on solid colors does disqualify.

In parti-colors at least two definite colors appearing in clearly defined markings distinctly distributed over the body are essential. Dogs (excepting black-and-tans) which are in the opinion of the judge 90 per cent or more one solid color and possess limited markings of another color on the skull, neck, toes or other locations are to be disqualified as they are neither solids nor parti-colors. Roans may follow any typical roaning shade or pattern, and are classed as parti-colors.

Black-and-tans are shown under the variety classification of "solid color other than black." The marking of the black-and-tans should be definite. The black should be jet and the tan rich in shade. Tan pigmentation solely under the stern and on the underside of the ears does disqualify. The same penalties apply to white markings on black-and-tans as apply to solid colors.

Weight: Not under 22 or over 28 pounds. Weights under or in excess of these limits shall be severely penalized. Puppies are exempt from the minimum limitation.

General Description: Embodying the foregoing we have a serviceable-looking dog with a refinedly chiseled head; standing on straight legs and well up at the shoulders; of compact body and wide, muscular quarters. The cocker spaniel's sturdy body, powerful quarters and strong, well-boned legs show him to be a dog capable of considerable speed combined with great endurance. Above all, he must be free and merry, sound, well-balanced throughout, and in action show a keen inclination to work; equable in temperament with no suggestion of timidity.

SCALE OF POINTS

Skull	*8*
Muzzle	*10*
Teeth	*4*
Eyes	*6*
Ears	*3*
Neck and shoulders	*15*
Body	*15*
Legs	*9*
Feet	*6*
Stern	*3*
Coat	*6*
Color and markings	*3*
Action	*12*
Total	*100*

ENGLISH COCKER SPANIEL

Closely related to the American cocker, the English dog has a longer head and is "leggier." The two breeds were separated by the kennel clubs in 1935. Average weight 32 pounds; height 16 inches. Coat medium length, black, red, roan or parti-color.

The English cocker spaniel has much the same temperament and characteristics as the American cocker. In England, the English cocker is widely used in the field where his longer legs and longer muzzle—with a better grip for retrieving—give him a definite edge as a sporting dog. In an effort to keep the breed from deteriorating to a mere pet rather than remaining a true sporting breed, the British require that their cockers must display their skill in a field trial before being eligible to qualify as a bench (or breed) champion.

Although the American cocker is widely lauded as a perfect "apartment-size" dog, the English cocker is equally adaptable to city life and is fully as affectionate and intelligent. On the debit side, he may be high-strung and his protective instincts may lead him to snap at household visitors on slight provocation. His shorter coat may require somewhat less care than the American cocker's, but his long floppy ears make him equally prone to annoying ear cankers.

The family with small children may find that the stronger English cocker is better able to stand up to handling by a child than the American type.

Standard of the Breed

General Appearance: The English cocker spaniel is an attractive, active, merry sporting dog with short body and strong limbs, standing well up at the withers. His movements are alive with energy; his gait powerful and frictionless. He is alert at all times, and the carriage of head and incessant action of his tail while at work gives the impression that here is a dog that is not only bred for hunting but really enjoys it. He is well balanced, strongly built, full of quality, and is capable of top speed combined with great stamina. His head imparts an individual stamp peculiar to him alone and has that brainy appearance expressive of the highest intelligence, and is in perfect proportion to his body. His muzzle is a most distinctive feature, being of correct conformation and in proportion to his skull.

English Cocker Spaniel
Ch. Surrey On Time Morse Code
Owners: Mr. and Mrs. Seymour F. Praeger. Middle Valley, New Jersey

Character: The character of the English cocker is of extreme importance. His love for and faithfulness to his master and household, his alertness and courage are characteristic. He is noted for his intelligence and merry disposition; not quarrelsome; and is a responsive and willing worker both in the field and as a companion.

Head: The skull and forehead should be well developed with no suggestion of coarseness, arched and slightly flattened on top when viewed both from the stop to the end of the skull as well as from ear to ear, and cleanly chiseled under the eyes. The proportion of the desirable head is approximately one-half for the muzzle and one-half for the skull. The muzzle should be square with a definite stop where it blends into the skull, and in proportion with the width of the skull. As the English cocker is primarily a sporting dog, the muzzle and jaws must be of sufficient strength and size to carry game; and the length of the muzzle should provide room for the development of the olfactory sense to ensure good scenting qualities, which require that the nose be wide and well developed. Nostrils black in color except in reds, livers and parti-colors, and roans of the lighter shades, where brown is permissible, but black preferred. Lips should be square, full and free from flews. Teeth should be even and set squarely. *Faults:* Muzzle too short or snipy. Jaw overshot or undershot. Lips snipy or pendulous. Skull too flat or too rounded, cheeky or coarse. Stop insufficient or exaggerated.

Eyes: The eyes should be of medium size, full and slightly oval-shaped; set squarely in skull and wide apart. Eyes must be dark brown except in livers and light parti-colors where hazel is permissible, but the darker the better. The general expression should be intelligent, alert, bright and merry. *Faults:* Light, round, or protruding eyes. Conspicuous haws.

Ears: Lobular; set low and close to the head; leather fine and extending at least to the nose, well covered with long, silky, straight or slightly wavy hair. *Faults:* Set or carried too high; too wide at the top; insufficient feathering; positive curls or ringlets.

Neck: Long, clean and muscular; arched toward the head; set cleanly into sloping shoulders. *Faults:* Short; thick; with dewlaps or excessive throatiness.

Body: Close-coupled, compact and firmly knit, giving the impression of great strength without heaviness. Depth of brisket should reach to the elbow, sloping gradually upward to the loin. Ribs should spring gradually to middle of body, tapering to back ribs which should be of good depth and extend well back. *Faults:* Too long and lacking depth; insufficient spring of rib; barrel rib.

Shoulders and Chest: Shoulders sloping and fine; chest deep and well developed, but not too wide and round to interfere with the free action of the forelegs. *Faults:* Straight or loaded shoulders.

Back and Loin: Back short and strong. Length of back from withers to tail-set should approximate height from ground to withers. Height of the dog at the withers should be greater than at the hip joint, providing a gradual slope between these points. Loin short and powerful, slightly arched. *Faults:* Too low at withers; long, sway-back or roach back; flat or narrow loin; exaggerated tuck-up.

Forelegs: Straight and strong with bone nearly equal in size from elbow to heel; elbows set close to body with free action from shoulders; pasterns short, straight and strong. *Faults:* Shoulders loose; elbows turned in or out; legs bowed or set too close or too wide apart; knees knuckled over; light bone.

Feet: Size in proportion to the legs; firm, round and catlike with thick pads and strong toes. *Faults:* Too large, too small, spreading or splayed.

Hindquarters: The hips should be rounded; thighs broad; well developed and muscular, giving abundance of propelling power. Stifles strong and well bent. Hock to pad moderately short, strong and well let down. *Faults:* Excessive angulation; lightness of bone; stifle joints too short; hocks too long or turned in or out.

Tail: Set on to conform with the top line of the back. Merry in action. *Faults:* Set too low; habitually carried too high; too short or too long.

Color: Various. In self-colors a white shirt frill is undesirable. In parti-colors, the coloring must be broken on the body and be evenly distributed. No large portion of any one color should exist. White should be shown on the saddle. A dog of any solid color with white feet and chest is not a parti-color. In roans it is desirable that the white hair should be distributed over the body, the more evenly the better. Roans come in various colors: blue, liver, red, orange and lemon. In black-and-tans the coat should be black; tan spots over the eyes, tan on the sides of the muzzle, on the throat and chest, on forelegs from the knees to the toes and on the hind legs inside, also on the stifle and extending from the hock to the toes. *Faults:* White feet are undesirable in any specimen of self-color.

Coat: On head short and fine; on body flat or slightly wavy and silky in texture. Should be of medium length with enough undercoating to give protection. The English cocker should be well feathered but not so profusely as to hide the true lines or interfere with his field work. *Faults:* Lack of coat; too soft, curly or wiry. Excessive trimming to change the natural appearance and coat should be discouraged.

Height: Ideal height at withers, males 16 to 17 inches; females, 15 to 16 inches. Deviations are severely penalized but not disqualified.

Weight: The most desirable weights, males 28 to 34 pounds, females, 26 to

32 pounds. Proper physical conformation and balance should be considered more important than weight alone.

ENGLISH SETTER

These dogs have been used in England for game birds for at least 400 years, and in America since 1874. Average weight 65 pounds; height 25 inches. Long coat, white with black, lemon, orange, blue.

His coat, feathering, shape of head and intelligent eyes give the English setter an appearance that many fanciers claim is the most beautiful of purebred dogs.

Basically a hunting dog, the setter has been bred and trained for countless generations to approach quietly and "set"—sit or crouch, while the hunter bags the game he has scented.

This breed has a character all its own. The English setter responds only to unhurried and unforced training. Once he learns a lesson—whether in hunting or in obedience—he is unlikely to forget it. And the setter is strictly a one-man dog, with few exceptions.

In the field, English setters work a bit more slowly than the pointers, but they work the ground most thoroughly.

In choosing a setter for field work the coloring is important, as a dog with more body white will be more visible in the field than a darker specimen. In field trials, the setters are often surpassed by their flashier-working pointer rivals, but fanciers of the setters claim that in actual gunning the setters are unexcelled.

As the pet, the setter responds to kindly treatment and is highly affectionate and loyal to his master. However, the dog that is not used for hunting should get enough exercise to keep him hard-muscled and his diet should be watched to avoid overweight.

Standard of the Breed

Head: Long and lean with a well-defined stop. The skull oval from ear to ear, of medium width, giving brain room but with no suggestion of coarseness; with little difference between the width at base of skull and at brows and with a moderately defined occipital protuberance. Brows should be at a sharp angle from the muzzle. Muzzle should be long and square, of width in harmony with the skull, without any fullness under the eyes and straight from eyes to tip of nose. A dish face or Roman nose is objectionable. The lips square and fairly pendent. Nose should be black or dark liver in color, except in white, lemon

English Setter
Ch. Scyld's The Black Widow
Owner: E. S. Howell. Darien, Connecticut

and white, orange and white, or liver and white dogs, when it may be of lighter color. Nostrils should be wide apart and large in the openings. Jaws should be of equal length. Overshot or undershot jaw objectionable. Ears should be carried close to head, well set back, and set low, of moderate length, slightly rounded at the ends, and covered with silky hair. Eyes should be bright, mild, intelligent, and dark brown in color.

Neck: The neck should be long and lean, arched at the crest, and not too throaty.

Shoulders: Shoulders should be formed to permit perfect freedom of action to forelegs. Shoulderblades should be long, wide, sloping moderately well back and standing fairly close together at the top.

Chest: Chest between shoulderblades should be of good depth but not of excessive width.

Ribs: Ribs, back of the shoulders, should spring gradually to the middle of the body and then taper to the back ribs, which should be of good depth.

Back: Back should be strong at its junction with the loin and should be straight or sloping upward very slightly to the top of the shoulder, the whole forming a graceful outline of medium length, without sway or drop. Loins should be strong, moderate in length, slightly arched, but not to the extent of being roached or wheel-backed. Hipbones should be wide apart without too sudden drop to the root of the tail.

Forelegs: The arms should be flat and muscular, with bone fully developed and muscles hard and devoid of flabbiness; of good length from the point of shoulder to the elbow, and set at such an angle as will bring the legs under the dog. Elbows should not tend to turn in or out. The pastern should be short, strong and nearly round, with the slope from the pastern joint to the foot deviating very slightly forward from the perpendicular.

Hind legs: The hind legs should have wide, muscular thighs with well-developed lower thighs. Stifles should be well bent and strong. Hocks should be wide and flat. The pastern should be short, strong and nearly round, with the slope from the pastern joint to the foot deviating very slightly forward from the perpendicular.

Feet: Feet should be closely set and strong, with pads well developed and tough; toes well arched and protected with short thick hair.

Tail: Tail should be straight and taper to a fine point, with only sufficient length to reach the hocks or shorter. The feathering must be straight and silky, falling loosely in a fringe and tapering to a point when the tail is raised. There must be no bushiness. The tail should not curl sideways or above the level of the back.

Coat: The coat should be flat and of good length, without curl; not soft or woolly. The feathering on legs should be moderately thin and regular.

Height: Males about 25 inches; bitches about 24 inches.

Colors: Black, white and tan; black and white; blue belton; lemon and white; lemon belton; orange and white; orange belton; liver and white; liver belton; and solid white.

Markings: Dogs without heavy patches of color on the body, but flecked all over preferred.

Symmetry: The harmony of all parts to be considered. Symmetrical dogs will have level backs or be very slightly higher at the shoulders than at the hips. Balance, harmony of proportion, and an appearance of breeding and quality to be looked for and coarseness avoided.

Movement and Carriage: An easy, free and graceful movement, suggesting rapidity and endurance. A lively tail and a high carriage of head. Stiltiness, clumsiness, and a lumbering gait are objectionable.

SCALE OF POINTS

Head		20
Skull	5	
Ears	5	
Eyes	5	
Muzzle	5	
Body		27
Neck	5	
Chest and shoulders	12	
Back, loins and ribs	10	
Running gear		23
Forelegs	5	
Hips, thighs and hind legs	12	
Feet	6	
Coat		8
Length and texture	5	
Color and markings	3	
Tail		5
Length and carriage	5	
General appearance and action		17
Symmetry, style and movement	12	
Size	5	
Totals	100	100

ENGLISH SPRINGER SPANIEL

This breed's name comes from their manner of "springing" game from cover. Good retrievers, they are popular for pheasant hunting. Average weight 45 pounds; height 18 inches. Medium coat, white with liver or black.

The English springer spaniel is an enthusiastic aid to the hunter. Unlike the pointer or setter that freezes when he scents the game, the springer dashes right into the cover and flushes the fowl, then if the hunter brings it down, retrieves it.

The springer is favored by pheasant hunters, working closely with the gunner and pursuing the pheasant in its erratic course after it is flushed. Provided with a waterproof and briarproof coat and slightly webbed feet (like the water spaniel), the springer works equally well in the field or in swamps or tidal flats.

Although it has been recognized as a distinct breed only since the early

English Springer Spaniel
Ch. Melilotus Royal Oak
Owner: Mrs. R. Gilman Smith. Bethel, Connecticut

1900's, the English springer spaniel's ancestry can be traced back over six hundred years to the days when hunters using nets followed their hunting spaniels and netted the birds they flushed.

Close behind the Labrador retriever in popularity, this dog owes his following to the ease with which he can be trained and the fact that his field work follows his natural bent—chasing birds. In addition to flushing pheasants, he can also work on grouse and woodcock, and with a little training can adapt to rabbiting.

As a house pet, this spaniel is a warm companion, especially gentle with children, has a sturdy build and the stamina to cope with a houseful of children.

Standard of the Breed

General Appearance and Type: A hunting dog of all work. His qualities stated in this standard will give him speed, agility and endurance to cope with the most difficult field trial and hunting conditions. He is a medium variety of spaniel, active, symmetrical, upstanding, strong, built for endurance, but not in any way coarse or ponderous. A well-balanced sporting dog of distinct spaniel character, combining beauty and utility. Excessive lowness or length should be penalized as interfering with the dog's activity.

Foreface: Nostrils well developed, soft, liver color or black, according to color of coat. Muzzle deep, with plenty of upper lip and flew. Jaws good length, straight, fairly square, neither undershot nor overshot. Nicely chiseled below eyes.

Skull: Should rise from foreface without a pronounced stop. Skull of medium length and fairly broad. From the stop the median line or groove, continues backward to the front of the sagittal crest (forehead) forming two slightly rounded halves above the eyes. Eyebrows and temples well developed, not thick in cheeks. Top of skull flat from forehead to occiput and slightly rounded on sides and back; occiput not domed; the top of occiput bone should be rounded, not pointed or angular in contour.

The resulting appearance is a head of medium length, fairly broad and slightly rounded, with a well-defined stop effect—well chiseled under the eyes and free of cheekiness—with a strong, lean, fairly square jaw and well muzzled with plenty of lip, but not so thick or pendulous as in the hound; even-set teeth and well-developed nostrils—an impressive head without being heavy. A ponderous head is objectionable. *Faults:* Oval skull; cheekiness; too much stop which gives the clumber expression; head appears too heavy.

Eyes: Neither too full nor too small—medium size—not prominent or sunken, but well set in, not showing haws; of an alert and kindly expression. In color dark hazel, brown or nearly black, harmonizing with the coat. *Note:* Seldom darker than dark hazel in the liver and white. *Faults:* Light-yellow eyes, or eyes showing haws too prominently.

Ears: Lobular, long and wide, set on not higher than in line with level of eye, flaps hanging close to cheeks; well covered both inside and outside with fine feather, which should not be curly. The leather should not be longer than reaching the tip of the nose. *Faults:* Ears off line of level of eyes, or set too far back on head.

Neck: Moderately long, strong and muscular, coming out of the shoulders rather full and tapering to the head, slightly arched and free from throatiness. *Faults:* Too short or ewelike, set into head too heavily, causing throatiness.

Brisket: Not so wide as to interfere with the free action of the forelegs, but well developed and nicely rounded.

Shoulders: The blades wide, strong and sloping, well set back, forming a strong and powerful upper arm, muscular without being mutton-shouldered. *Faults:* Straight shoulders or mutton shoulders, which cause the dog to be paddle-gaited.

Body: The chest deep and well developed, with plenty of heart and lung room, but not too round or wide. Walls of chest deep, with well-sprung ribs. Back from withers to root of tail should equal height at shoulder. Back should be strong, straight, never sway-back. Strong loins, with hips nicely rounded; slight arch over loin and hip joints; thighs broad, well developed and muscular, the hindquarters giving the appearance of great driving power. Rump slightly sloping to base of tail, belly nicely curved from chest to flank, but not in any way "tucked up." *Faults:* Sway-back; ribs too round, too flat, or too hollow; body too long or loosely coupled; rump too high.

Legs: Forelegs—elbows well let down, setting close to body, with free action from the shoulder. Forearm straight, with the same degree of size to toes, with slightly flattened bone and muscle. Wrist, sometimes called the "knee," straight and almost flat. Pasterns short and strong. Feet strong and compact, with good strong round pads, well feathered between toes. Wavy feathering of moderate heaviness down to pastern. *Note:* When viewed from front the springer spaniel should be straight from shoulder to foot, elbow close to body and knee bending neither in or out. *Faults:* crooked legs; bones too light; splay or hare feet.

Hind Legs: From hip to hock, long and sinewy; hock to heel, short and strong. Stifles and hock moderately bent and not inclining in or out. Firm on feet; feet round and not too small, with strong, thick, close pads. Well feathered between toes, moderately feathered down to hock. Profuse feathering objectionable.

Stern: Set on low, well fringed with wavy feather. Preferably never carried above the level of the back. Of lively motion when dog is excited.

Coat: On head, front of forelegs and below hock on front of hind legs, flat or wavy (never curly), of medium length, but of sufficient texture to be waterproof, weatherproof and thornproof, glossy and refined in texture. A nice fringe of wavy hair on throat, brisket, chest and belly.

Weight: Males about 45 pounds, should not exceed 50 pounds; bitches about 42 pounds, should not exceed 47 pounds.

Color: Liver and white; black and white; liver and tan; black and tan; tan and white; black, white and tan; liver; black roan; anything except red and white and lemon and white, which should be penalized.

Gait: The springer gait is strictly his own. His forelegs should swing straight forward from the shoulder, throwing the foot well forward in an easy and free manner, not a paddle, nor with a choppy or terrier stride. In the rear his hocks must drive well under his body following on a line with the forelegs.

Note: At slow movement many springers have a pacing stride which is also acceptable for springer gait.

SCALE OF POINTS. The following table of positive and negative points is appended simply as a guide to the relative importance of perfect or defective features. The question of "type" and "balance," however, takes precedence over any scoring table which may be drawn up.

Positive Points

Head and Jaw	15
Eyes	5
Ears	5
Neck	5
Body	10
Forelegs	10
Hind legs	10
Feet	10
Stern	5
Coat and feather	10
General appearance	15
Total	100

Negative Points

Light eyes	5
Light nose	10
Poor ears	5
Bad neck	5
Curly coat	10
Weak or uneven jaw	15
Bad carriage of tail	5
Crooked legs	15
Poor gait	15
Excessive lowness or length	15
Total	100

GERMAN SHORT-HAIRED POINTER

The breed originated in Germany in the seventeenth century and was first brought to the United States in the 1920's. Average weight 65 pounds, height 23 inches. Coat short, liver-colored or ticked.

The German short-haired pointer is another example of the German thoroughness in creating a breed of dog almost to specifications. Their goal was to

German Short-haired Pointer
Dual Ch. Jones Hill Friedrich
Owner: Dr. Eugene McNinch. Dover, Delaware

develop a hunting dog that would work slowly and carefully both on waterfowl and on upland game. This breed will point game and retrieve from land and water. Its ancestry includes the old Spanish pointer, bloodhound, foxhound, and English pointer—and then generations of the most careful selective breeding.

The German short-haired pointer has been popular with hunters wherever there is a variety of game; the versatility of the breed makes him the hunter's valued aid. However, in many places where the hunters vie in open field trials against other breeds, the dog's somewhat bulky build and slowness in the field has worked against him in competition with the flashier pointers and setters.

As a house pet, the German short-haired pointer has an affectionate and mild disposition and is particularly good with small children. The dog is one of the more intelligent breeds, does well in obedience training and generally outperforms many other breeds in tracking tests.

The water-repellent coat makes him an all-climate animal and his webbed feet aid him in retrieving downed waterfowl. Some have been used in recent years as guide dogs for the blind with highly satisfactory results.

Standard of the Breed

General Appearance: The over-all picture created in the observer's eye should be that of an aristocratic, well-balanced, symmetrical animal with conformation indicating power, endurance and agility, and a look of intelligence and animation. The dog should be neither unduly small nor conspicuously large. He should rather give the impression of medium size but be like the proper hunter, "with a short back, but standing over plenty of ground." Tall, leggy individuals seldom possess endurance or sound movement.

Dogs which are ponderous or unbalanced because of excess substance should be definitely rejected. The first impression should be that of a keenness which denotes full enthusiasm for work without indication of nervous or flighty character. Movement should be alertly coordinated without waste motion.

Desired qualities are: grace of outline, clean-cut head, sloping shoulders, deep breast, powerful back, strong quarters, good bone structure, adequate muscle, well-carried tail and taut coat, all of which should combine to produce a look of nobility and an indication of anatomical structure essential to correct gait, showing a heritage of purposeful breeding.

Head: Clean cut, neither too light nor too heavy, in proper proportion to the body. Skull should be reasonably broad, arched on the side and slightly round on top. Scissura (median line between the eyes at the forehead) not too deep, occipital bone not as conspicuous as in the pointer.

The foreface should rise gradually from nose to forehead—not resembling the Roman nose. This is more strongly pronounced in the male, as befitting his sex, than in the bitch. The chops should fall away from the somewhat projecting nose. Lips should be full and deep, never flewy. The chops should not fall over too much, but form a proper fold in the angle. The jaw should be powerful and the muscles well developed.

The line to the forehead should rise gradually and should never possess a definite stop, but rather a stop-effect when viewed from the side, due to the position of the eyebrows.

The muzzle should be sufficiently long to enable the dog to seize properly and to facilitate his carrying game a long time. A pointed muzzle is not desirable. The entire head should not give the impression of tapering to a point. The depth should be the right proportion to the length, both in the muzzle and in the skull proper.

Ears: Ears should be broad and set fairly high, lie flat and not hang away from the head. Placement should be above eye level. The ears when laid in front without being pulled should meet the lip angle. In heavier dogs, they should be correspondingly longer.

Eyes: The eyes should be of medium size, intelligent and expressive, good-humored, and yet radiating energy, neither protruding nor sunken. The eyelids should close well. The best color is a dark shade of brown. Light yellow, china or owl (bird of prey) eyes are not desirable.

Nose: Brown, the larger the better; nostrils well opened and broad. Flesh-colored and spotted noses are not desirable.

Teeth: The teeth should be strong and healthy. The molars should inter-mesh properly. Incisors should fit close in a true scissors bite. Jaws should be neither overshot nor undershot.

Neck: Of adequate length to permit the jaws reaching game to be retrieved, sloping downward on beautifully curving lines. The nape should be rather muscular, becoming gradually larger towards the shoulder. Moderate hound-like throatiness permitted.

Breast and Thorax: The breast in general should give the impression of depth rather than breadth; for all that, it should be in correct proportion to other parts of the body, with fair depth of chest. The ribs forming the thorax should be well curved and not flat; they should not be absolutely round or barrel-shaped. Ribs that are entirely round prevent the necessary expansion of the chest when taking breath. The back ribs reach well down. The circumference of the breast immediately behind the elbows should be smaller than that of the breast about a hand's-breadth behind the elbows so that the upper arm has room for movement.

Back and Loins: The back should be short, strong and straight, with slight rise from root of tail to withers. Excessively long or hog-back should be penalized. Loins strong, of moderate length, and slightly arched. Tuck-up should be apparent.

Assembly of Back Members: The hips should be broad with hip sockets wide apart and fall slightly toward the tail in a graceful curve. Thighs strong and well muscled. Stifles well bent. Hock joints should be well angulated with strong, straight bone structure from hock to pad. Angulation of both stifle and hock joints should be such as to form maximum combination of both drive and traction. Hocks should turn neither in nor out.

Assembly of Front Members: The shoulders should be sloping, movable, well covered with muscle. The shoulder blades should lie flat. The upper arm (also called the "cross bar"—the bones between the shoulder and elbow joints) should be as long as possible, standing away somewhat from the trunk so that the straight and closely muscled legs, when viewed from the front should appear to be parallel. Elbows which stand away from the body or are pressed right into same indicate toes turning inward or outward, which should be regarded as faults. Pasterns should be strong, short and nearly vertical.

Feet: Should be compact, close-knit and round to spoon-shaped; the toes sufficiently arched and heavily nailed. The pads should be strong and hard.

Coat and Skin: The skin should look close and tight. The hair should be short and thick and feel tough and hard to the hand. It is somewhat longer on the underside of the tail and the back edge of the haunches. It is softer, thinner and shorter on the ears and the head.

Tail: Is set high and firm, and must be docked, leaving approximately two-fifths of length. The tail hangs down when the dog is still, is held horizontal when he is walking, never turned over the back or considerably bent but violently wagged when he is on the search.

Bones: Thin and fine bones are not desirable in a dog which should be able to work over any type of ground and should possess strength. The main importance is laid not so much on the size as being in proper proportion to the body. Dogs with coarse bones are handicapped in agility of movement and speed.

Weight and Height: Males, 55 to 70 pounds, 23 to 25 inches; bitches, 45 to 60 pounds, 21 to 23 inches.

Color: Solid liver, liver and white spotted and ticked, liver-and-white ticked, liver roan. Any colors other than liver and white (gray white) are not permitted.

SPECIAL POINTS. Symmetry and field quality are most essential. A dog well balanced in all points is preferable to one with outstanding good qualities and defects. A smooth, lithe gait is most desirable.

Faults: Bone structure too clumsy or too light, head too large, too many wrinkles in forehead, dish-faced, snipy muzzle, ears too long, pointed or fleshy, flesh-colored nose, eyes too light, too round or too closely set together, excessive throatiness, cow-hocked, feet or elbows turned inward or outward, down on pasterns, loose shoulders, sway-back, black coat or tricolored, any colors except liver or some combination of liver and white.

GOLDEN RETRIEVER

Descended from Russian sheepdogs, this breed was developed in England as a sporting dog. Has been increasingly popular since the early 1930's. Average weight 65 pounds; height 23 inches. Long, dense coat in golden-brown color.

An unusual history lies behind the development of the golden retriever—although, as with so many other breeds, many doubt this story of the golden's background. The generally accepted breed history started when an Englishman, Lord Tweethmouth, in the 1860's saw a troupe of performing Russian dogs and so admired them that he bought the entire troupe of eight dogs. Then

Golden Retriever
Ch. Pele of Flarewin
Owner: Jack Martin. Arcata, California

he interbred them with a bloodhound to reduce the size and enhance the sense of smell.

While the original dogs were used as sheepdogs in the Caucasus, the modern golden retriever has won high honors in field trials and in hunting. His water-resistant coat makes him a good retriever from water and he is equally adept at retrieving on land.

A flashier worker than the Labrador, with whom he competes in field trials, the golden retriever has made a strong place for himself as a house pet, and has adapted to life in the country or city with ease.

Highly intelligent, the golden retriever has also found a firm niche for himself in the obedience trial ring. He learns quickly, seems to remember everything he has learned and goes through the obedience routine with verve and seeming enjoyment.

Still more common as a sporting dog, this breed is seen more and more at shows and obedience trials and in the company of owners and families who have discovered his merits as a cooperative companion.

Standard of the Breed

General Appearance: A symmetrical, powerful, active dog, sound and well put together, not clumsy nor long in the leg, displaying a kindly expression and possessing a personality that is eager, alert and self-confident. Primarily a hunting dog, he should be shown in *hard working condition.* Over-all appearance, gait and purpose to be given more emphasis than any of his component parts.

Size: Males 23 to 24 inches in height at withers; females $21\frac{1}{2}$ to $22\frac{1}{2}$. Length from breastbone to buttocks slightly greater than height at withers in ratio of 12 to 11. Weight for dogs 65 to 75 pounds; bitches 60 to 70 pounds.

Head: Broad in skull, slightly arched laterally and longitudinally without prominence of frontal or occipital bones. Good stop. Foreface deep and wide, nearly as long as skull. Muzzle, when viewed in profile, slightly deeper at stop than at tip; when viewed from above, slightly wider at stop than at tip. No heaviness in flews. Removal of whiskers for show purposes optional.

Eyes: Friendly and intelligent, medium large with dark rims, set well apart and reasonably deep in sockets. Color preferably dark brown, never lighter than color of coat. No white or haws visible when looking straight ahead.

Teeth: Scissors bite with lower incisors touching inside of upper incisors.

Nose: Black or dark brown, though lighter shade in cold weather not serious. Dudley nose (pink without pigmentation) to be faulted.

Ears: Rather short, hanging flat against head with rounded tips slightly below jaw. Forward edge attached well behind and just above eye with rear edge slightly below eye. Low, houndlike ears to be faulted.

Neck: Medium long, sloping well back into shoulders, giving sturdy, muscular appearance with untrimmed, natural ruff. No throatiness.

Body: Well balanced, short-coupled, deep through the heart. Chest at least as wide as a man's hand including the thumb. Brisket extends to elbows. Ribs long and well sprung, but not barrel-shaped, extending well to rear of body. Loin short, muscular, wide and deep, with very little tuck-up. Top line level from withers to croup, whether standing or moving. Croup slopes gently. Slab-sidedness, narrow chest, lack of depth in brisket, excessive tuck-up roach- or sway-back to be faulted.

Forequarters: Forequarters well coordinated with hindquarters and capable of free movement. Shoulder blades wide, long and muscular, showing angulation with upper arm of approximately 90 degrees. Legs straight, with good bone. Pastern short and strong, sloping slightly forward with no suggestion of weakness.

Hindquarters: Well-bent stifles (angulation between femur and pelvis approximately 90 degrees) with hocks let down. Legs straight when viewed from rear. Cow hocks and sickle hocks to be faulted.

Feet: Medium size, round and compact, with thick pads. Excess hair may be trimmed to show natural size and contour. Open or splayed feet to be faulted.

Tail: Well set on, neither too high nor too low, following natural line of croup. Length extends to hock. Carried with merry action with some upward curve but never curled over back nor between legs.

Coat and Color: Dense and water-repellent, with good undercoat. Texture not as hard as that of a short-haired dog nor as silky as that of a setter. Lies flat against body and may be straight or wavy. Moderate feathering on back of forelegs and heavier feathering on front of neck, back of thighs and underside of tail. Feathering may be lighter than rest of coat. Color lustrous golden of various shades. A few white hairs on chest permissible, but not desirable. Further white markings to be faulted.

Gait: When trotting, gait is free, smooth, powerful and well coordinated. Viewed from front or rear, legs turn neither in nor out, nor do feet cross nor interefere with each other. Increased speed causes tendency of feet to converge toward center line of gravity.

DISQUALIFICATIONS

1. Deviation in height of more than one inch from standard either way.

2. Undershot or overshot jaws. This condition not to be confused with misalignment of teeth.

3. Trichiasis (abnormal position or direction of the eyelashes).

IRISH SETTER

One of the most majestic dogs in appearance, this breed came from Ireland in the early 1870's. Average weight 60 pounds; height 25 inches. Long, straight coat with fringes, deep, rich mahogany, chestnut or red.

His outstanding beauty has made the Irish setter more of a show dog than a field dog. The rich and shining coat, the aristocratic way in which he carries his head and his spirited stride assure him of acclaim from the ringsiders at any show.

Temperamentally, the breed is usually high-strung and requires more patient handling than most other breeds. Most Irish setters mature slowly, and while the average dog can begin serious training at the age of six months, many

Irish Setter
Ch. Flagstones Flame C.D.
Owner: Mrs. William Bolton Cook. Port Chester, New York

of this breed must wait until they are well over a year old before they respond to training. Any harsh treatment in training, whether for field work or obedience, may break the dog's spirit and make it almost impossible to teach him.

Among the sporting dogs, the Irish setter is the most likely to become a firm one-man dog and he remains more interested in having human companionship than in finding birds. In the field, he works slowly and fairly close to the gunner. While this breed shows "style" in the show ring, they work in the field their tails held low, and lack the "happy" tail of the golden retriever and some other sporting breeds, and this lack of field style has also worked against their wider use by hunters.

As a house pet, the Irish setter is affectionate and friendly, and seldom shows any vicious traits.

Standard of the Breed

Head: Should be long and lean. The skull oval (from ear to ear) having plenty of brain room and with well-defined occipital protuberance. Brows raised, showing stop. The muzzle moderately deep and fairly square at end. From stop to the point of the nose should be long, the nostrils wide and the jaws of nearly equal length, flews not to be pendulous. The color of the nose mahogany or dark chocolate and that of the eyes (which ought not to be too large) rich hazel or brown. The ears to be of moderate size, fine in texture, set on low, well back, and hanging in a neat fold close to the head.

Neck: Should be moderately long, very muscular but not too thick, slightly arched, free from all tendency to throatiness.

Body: Should be proportionately long, shoulders fine at the points, deep and sloping well back. The chest deep, rather narrow in front. The ribs well sprung, leaving plenty of lung room. The loins muscular and slightly arched. The hindquarters wide and powerful.

Legs and feet: The hind legs from hip to hock should be long and muscular, from hock to heel short and strong. The stifle and hock joints well bent, and not inclined either in or out. The forelegs should be strong and sinewy, having plenty of bone, with elbows free, well let down and, like the hock, not inclined either out or in. The feet rather small, very firm, toes strong, close together and arched.

Tail: Should be of moderate length, set on rather low, strong at root and tapering to a fine point; to be carried in a slight scimitar-like curve or nearly straight, nearly level with the back.

Coat: On the head, front legs and tips of ears should be short and fine, but on all other parts of body it should be of moderate length, flat and as free as possible from curve or wave.

Feathering: The feather on the upper portion of the ears should be long and silky, on the back of the fore- and hind legs long and fine, a fair amount of hair on belly, forming a nice fringe which may extend on chest and throat. Feet to be well feathered between the toes. Tail to have a nice fringe of moderately long hair, decreasing in length as it approaches the point. All feathering to be as straight and as flat as possible.

Color and Markings: The color should be a rich golden chestnut or mahogany red, with no trace whatever of black; white on chest, throat, or toes, or a small star on the forehead, or a narrow streak, or blaze on the nose or face not to disqualify.

SCALE OF POINTS

Head	*10*
Eyes	*5*

Ears	*5*
Neck	*5*
Body	*15*
Shoulders, forelegs and feet	*12*
Hind legs	*10*
Tail	*8*
Coat and feather	*8*
Color	*8*
Size, style and general appearance	*14*
Total	*100*

LABRADOR RETRIEVER

A native of Newfoundland, this breed first appeared in the United States in the 1920's and has become one of the most popular bird dogs. Average weight 70 pounds; height 23 inches. Coat short and dense, solid black or yellow.

Many of the old-time Labrador fanciers are worried that the increasing popularity of this dog as a pet may lead to a deterioration of the breed. In the field, the average Labrador trains easily and becomes a steady worker. As a pet, he is one of the best-natured dogs, almost invariably friendly, gets along well with children and adults and other dogs. Many Labradors have won their obedience degrees and they are much in demand as guide dogs for the blind. The thick coat of the Labrador enables him to withstand climatic changes and he gets along well in any part of the country.

Although he has risen to a place among the top dozen breeds in registration, the Labrador stock is still in good condition and the novice dog buyer can purchase a purebred Labrador with good assurance that he will conform to the favorable characteristics of his breed.

On the debit side however, most Labradors have one outstanding fault as a dog for the country or suburbs. They are natural roamers, and even the females often show an uncanny skill at getting out of a yard and taking off for a long jaunt on their own. The roaming Labrador is inclined to be highly sociable and will join any person in what seems to be an interesting activity. Though not destructive, the Labrador likes to swim, and a neighbor's lily pond or pool may attract him, to the detriment of neighborhood relations.

In the city, the Labrador needs plenty of on-leash walking to keep him in good physical condition. If he is to be kept in a suburban back yard, he should be provided with a tightly fenced-in run or an overhead suspended leash to give him room for exercise.

Labrador Retriever (Black)
Ch. Lockerbie Blackfella
Owner: Mrs. James Warwick. Little Silver, New Jersey

Labrador Retriever (Yellow)
Ch. Ballyduff Candy
Owner: Mrs. James Warwick. Little Silver, New Jersey

Standard of the Breed

General Appearance: The general appearance of the breed should be that of a strongly built, short coupled, very active dog. He should be fairly wide over the loins, and strong and muscular in the hindquarters. The coat should be dense, close, short and free from feather.

Head: The head should be wide, giving brain room; there should be a slight stop—the brow should be slightly pronounced, so that the skull is not absolutely in a straight line with the nose. The head should be clean cut and free from fleshy cheeks. The jaws should be long and powerful and free from snipiness; the nose should be wide and the nostrils well developed. Teeth should be strong and regular, with a level mouth.

Ears: The ears should hang moderately close to the head, rather far back, should be set somewhat low and not be large and heavy. The eyes should be of a medium size, expressing great intelligence and good temper, and can be brown, yellow or black, but brown or black is preferred.

Neck and Chest: The neck should be medium length, powerful and not throaty. The shoulders should be long and sloping.

The chest must be of good width and depth, the ribs well sprung and the loins wide and strong, stifles well turned, and the hindquarters well developed and of great power.

Legs and Feet: The legs must be straight from the shoulder to ground, and the feet compact with toes well arched, and pads well developed; the hocks should be well bent and the dog must neither be cow-hocked nor be too wide behind; in fact, he must stand and move true all around on legs and feet. Legs should be of medium length, showing good bone and muscle, but not so short as to be out of balance with rest of body. In fact, a dog well balanced in all points is preferable to one with outstanding good qualities and defects.

Tail: The tail is a distinctive feature of the breed; it should be very thick toward the base, gradually tapering toward the tip, of medium length, should be free from any feathering, and should be clothed thickly all around with the Labrador's short, thick, dense coat, thus giving that peculiar rounded appearance which is described as the "otter" tail. The tail may be carried gaily but should not curl over the back.

Coat: The coat is another very distinctive feature; it should be short, very dense and without wave, and should give a fairly hard feeling to the hand.

Color: The color is generally black, free from any rustiness and any white marking except possibly a small spot on the chest. Other whole colors are permissible.

Movement: Movement or action is the crucial test of conformation. The

Labrador's legs should be carried straight forward while traveling, the forelegs hanging perpendicular and swinging parallel with the sides, like the pendulum of a clock. The principal propulsive power is furnished by the hind legs, perfection of action being found in Labradors' possessing long thighs and muscular second thighs well bent at the stifles, which admit of a strong forward thrust or "snatch" of the hocks. When approaching, the forelegs should form a continuation of the straight line of the front, the feet being the same distance apart as the elbows. When the Labrador is standing still, it is often difficult to determine whether he is slightly out at the shoulder, but directly he moves, the defect—if it exists—becomes more apparent, the forelegs having a tendency to cross or "weave." When, on the contrary, the dog is tied at the shoulder, the tendency of the feet is to move wider apart with a sort of paddling action. When the hocks are turned in (cow hocks) the stifles and feet are turned outward, resulting in a serious loss of propulsive power. When the hocks are turned outward, the tendency of the hind feet is to cross, resulting in an ungainly waddle.

Weight and Height: Males, 60 to 75 pounds, 22½ to 24½ inches; bitches, 55 to 70 pounds, 21½ to 23½ inches.

WEIMARANER

The breed known as the "gray ghosts" of dogdom was developed at the Court of Weimar in Germany in the 1800's as big-game hunters. First brought to the United States in 1929. Average weight 75 pounds, height 25 inches. Smooth solid gray coat.

For the first hundred years of their existence, ownership of a Weimaraner was truly a sign of distinction. The breed was developed by the German nobility of Weimar as an all-around hunter and house dog and their ownership was rigidly restricted. The dog was developed to do everything in the field; point, trail and retrieve under any conditions and in any terrain.

Breeding was carried on under careful scrutiny of the Weimaraner club and only the finest specimens were bred. At no time were there more than about 1,500 of these dogs in Germany. Prospective owners could be "blackballed" and traveling club wardens passed on the merits of new litters; any puppies not coming up to standard were destroyed. In addition, there was a firm rule against allowing any outside of Germany.

It was not until 1929 that the first Weimaraners appeared in the United States when a pair were imported and later several others were brought in as a foundation stock. The Weimaraner Club of America has made a strong attempt to keep the standards of the breed high and to avoid exploitation despite the

Weimaraner
Ch. Gourmet's Garden
Owner: Erma E. Muster. Bensenville, Illinois

fanfare of publicity which the dog received in newspapers and dog magazines.

The breed received increased notice when President Eisenhower's bitch Heidi was noticed on the White House lawn and widely photographed and written up. In recent years, the Weimaraner has been up among the dozen most popular breeds in American Kennel Club registrations.

The Weimaraner has lived up to its advance publicity by obedience trial performance, especially when one dog won its obedience degree at the age of six months. However, like other dogs the Weimaraner must be trained, and while it is a fast learner and highly responsive and intelligent it is still a dog.

In field work, the Weimaraner has shown itself to be a thorough, though not especially flashy worker. One unusual feature of the Weimaraner is that he matures earlier than most other breeds and training can usually start several months earlier than with other breeds.

Some caution should be observed when buying a Weimaraner puppy—or older dog—as its popularity has led to some overbreeding and some strains exhibit physical faults and undesirable temperament.

Standard of the Breed

General Appearance: A medium-sized gray dog with light eyes. He should present a picture of great driving power, stamina, alertness and balance, Above all, the dog should indicate ability to work hard in the field.

Height: Height at withers: males 25 to 27 inches; bitches, 23 to 25 inches.

Head: Moderately long and aristocratic, with moderate stop and slight median line extending back over the forehead. Rather prominent occipital bones and trumpets set well back, beginning at the back of eye sockets. Measurement from tip of nose to stop equals that from stop to occipital bone. The flews should be moderately deep, enclosing a powerful jaw. Foreface perfectly straight, delicate at the nostrils. Skin tightly drawn. Neck clean cut and moderately long. Expression kind, keen, intelligent.

Ears: Long and lobular, slightly folded and set high. The ear when drawn snugly alongside the jaw should end approximately two inches from the point of the nose.

Eyes: In shades of light amber, gray or blue-gray, set well enough apart to indicate good disposition and intelligence. When dilated under excitement, the eyes may appear almost black.

Teeth: Well set, strong and even; well developed and proportionate to jaw with correct scissors bite, the upper teeth protruding slightly over the lower teeth, but not more than one-sixteenth of an inch. Complete dentition is greatly to be desired.

Nose: Gray.

Lips and Gums: Pinkish flesh shades.

Body: The back should be moderate in length, set in straight line, strong, and slope slightly from the withers. The chest should be well developed and deep, shoulder well laid on and snug. Ribs well sprung and long. Abdomen firmly held; moderately tucked-up flank. The brisket should drop to the elbow.

Coat: Short, smooth and sleek in shades of mouse-gray to silver gray, usually blending to a lighter shade on the head and ears. Small white mark allowable on the chest, but not on any other part of the body. White spots that have resulted from injuries not to be penalized.

Legs; Forelegs: Straight and strong, with the measurement from the elbow to the ground approximately the same as from the elbow to the top of the withers.

Hindquarters: Well-angulated stifles and straight hocks. Musculature well developed.

Feet: Firm and compact, webbed toes well arched, pads closed and thick, nails short and gray or amber in color.

Dewclaws: Allowable only on forelegs, there optional.

Tail: Docked. At maturity it should measure approximately six inches with a tendency to be light rather than heavy and should be carried in a manner expressing confidence and sound temperament.

Gait: The walk is rather awkward. The trot should be effortless, ground covering and should indicate smooth coordination. When seen from the rear, the hind feet should parallel the front feet. When viewed from the side, the top line should remain strong and level.

Temperament: The dog should display a temperament that is keen, fearless, friendly, protective and obedient.

Very Serious Faults: Any long-haired coat or coat darker than mouse-gray to silver-gray is considered a most undesirable recessive trait. White, other than a spot on chest. Eyes and color other than gray, blue-gray or light amber. Black, mottled mouth. Tail not docked. Dog exhibiting strong fear. Viciousness.

Serious Faults: Poor gait. Very poor feet. Faulty backs, either roached or sway. Badly overshot or undershot jaw. Snipy muzzle. Short ears. Yellow in white marking. Undersize.

Faults: Doggy bitches. Bitchy dogs. Improper muscular condition. Bad teeth. More than four missing teeth. Back too long or too short. Faulty coat. Low tail set. Elbows in or out; feet east and west.

Minor Faults: Tail too short or too long. Pink nose. Oversize not to be considered a serious fault, providing correct structure and working ability are in evidence.

HOUNDS

The sweetest music to the hunter's ear is the baying of a pack of hounds on the trail of game and their excited calls when the prey is treed or grounded. Ranging from the regal Afghan to the low-slung dachshund, these breeds offer a wide variety of choices to the person seeking a pet that will enjoy living-room comfort as much as the thrill of the chase.

AFGHAN HOUND

Rock carvings in Afghanistan dating back some 4,000 years show dogs which are identical with the modern Afghan. One of the fastest running dogs, he has been

used to hunt gazelles. He is a fairly recent import, known in England about 1907
and in the United States in the 1920's. Average weight 60 pounds, average height
27 inches. Long coat, flat on back, in tan; black; fawn; cream; blue.

Recent victories of the Afghan in Westminster shows have spurred the popularity of this large breed. While the Afghan does not shed—a point to be considered by the fastidious housewife—his coat requires regular grooming to prevent matting and a shaggy appearance.

One of the healthier, large breeds, the Afghan thrives on a regulated diet, but should be restricted to eating only at mealtimes.

In disposition, the Afghan is one of the most independent breeds and may be somewhat difficult to train. Faster than the racing hounds, the Afghan must be kept on leash where there is any traffic as his love of running may exceed his traffic sense, and he cannot outrun an automobile. Despite his large size, the Afghan is a good apartment dog. He is naturally quiet, and has considerable patience with children. On the other hand, he can be happy in surroundings where he has enough room to really run free.

The Afghan is basically a one-man dog, and in public his reaction to strangers may be timidity. He is seldom vicious. His size, dramatic coat, curled tail and general appearance make him a spectacular dog to be walked by his owner.

Standard of the Breed

General Appearance: The Afghan hound is an aristocrat, his whole appearance one of dignity and aloofness with no trace of plainness or coarseness. He has a straight front, proudly carried head, eyes gazing into the distance as if in memories of ages past. The striking characteristics of the breed, its exotic or "Eastern" expression, long silky topknot, peculiar coat pattern, very prominent hip bones, large feet, and the impression of a somewhat exaggerated bend in the stifle due to profuse trouserings stand out clearly, giving the Afghan hound the appearance of what he is, a king of dogs, that has held true to tradition throughout the ages.

Head: The head is of good length, showing much refinement, the skull evenly balanced with the foreface. There is a slight prominence of the nasal bone structure causing a slightly Roman appearance, the center line running up over the foreface with little or no stop, falling away in front of the eyes so that there is an absolutely clear outlook with no interference; the underjaw showing great strength, the jaws long and punishing; the mouth level, meaning that the teeth match evenly, neither overshot nor undershot. This is a difficult mouth to breed. A scissors bite is even more punishing and can be

Afghan Hound
Ch. Ben Ghazi's Kaman
Owner: Gran Ellen Kennels. Athens, Georgia

more eaily bred into a dog than a level mouth; a dog having a scissors bite, where the lower teeth slip inside and rest against the teeth of the upper jaw, should not be penalized. The occipital bone is very prominent. The head is surmounted by a topknot of long silky hair.

Ears: The ears are long, set approximately on level with the outer corners of the eyes, the leather of the ear reaching nearly to the end of the dog's nose, and covered with long silky hair.

Eyes: The eyes are almond-shaped (almost triangular), never full or bulgy and are dark in color.

Nose: Nose is of good size, black in color.

Faults: Coarseness, snipiness; overshot or undershot jaw; eyes round or bulgy or light in color; exaggerated Roman nose; head not surmounted with topknot.

Neck: The neck is of good length, strong and arched, running in a curve to the shoulders which are long and sloping and well laid back. *Faults:* Too short or thick in neck; a ewe neck; a goose neck; a neck lacking in substance.

Body: The back line appears practically level from the shoulders to the loin. Strong and powerful loin and slightly arched, falling away toward the stern, with the hipbones very pronounced; well ribbed and tucked up in flanks. The height at the shoulders equals the distance from the chest to the buttocks; the brisket well let down and of medium width. *Faults:* Roach-back, sway-back; goose rump; slack loin; lack of prominence of hip bone; too much width of brisket causing interference with elbows.

Tail: Tail set not too high on body, having a ring or curve on the end; should never be curled over or rest on the back, nor be carried sideways; and should never be bushy.

Legs: Forelegs are straight and strong with great length between elbow and pastern; elbows well held in; forefeet large in both length and width; toes well arched; feet covered with long thick hair; fine in texture; pasterns long and straight; pads of feet unusually large and well down on the ground. Shoulders have plenty of angulation so that the legs are well set underneath. Too much straightness of shoulder causes the dog to break down in the pasterns, and this is a serious fault.

All four feet of the Afghan are in line with the body, turning neither in nor out. The hind feet are broad and of good length; the toes arched, and covered with long thick hair; hindquarters powerful and well muscled, with great length between hips and hocks; hocks are well let down good angulation of both stifle and hock; slightly bowed from hock to crotch. *Faults:* Front or back feet thrown outward or inward; pads of feet not thick enough; or feet too small; or any evidence of weakness in feet, weak or broken-down pasterns; too straight in stifle; too long in hock.

Coat: Hindquarters, flanks, ribs, forequarters and legs well covered with thick, silky hair, very fine in texture; ears and all four feet well feathered. From in front of the shoulders and also backward from the shoulders along the saddle from the flanks and ribs upward, the hair is short and close, forming a smooth back in mature dogs—this is a traditional characteristic of the Afghan hound.

The Afghan is shown in his natural state; the coat is not clipped or trimmed; the head is surmounted (in the full sense of the word) with a topknot of long, silky hair—this is also an outstanding characteristic of the Afghan hound. Showing of short hair on cuffs on either front or back legs is permissible. *Fault:* Lack of short-haired saddle in mature dog.

Height: Males, 27 inches plus or minus one inch; bitches 25 inches, plus or minus one inch.

Weight: Males about 60 pounds; bitches about 50 pounds.

Color: All colors are permissible, but color or color combinations should be pleasing. White markings, especially on the head, are undesirable.

Gait: When running free, the Afghan hound moves at a gallop, showing great elasticity and spring in his smooth, powerful stride. When on a loose lead, the Afghan hound can trot at a fast pace. Stepping along, he has the appearance of placing the hind feet directly in the footprints of the front feet, both thrown straight ahead. Moving with head and and tail high, the Afghan's whole appearance is one of great style and beauty.

Temperament: Aloof and dignified, yet gay. *Faults:* Sharpness or shyness.

BASENJI

The only "barkless" dog, the Basenji was a hunter in its native African Congo. Was first brought to the United States in 1937. Average weight 20 pounds, height 16 inches. Coat short and silky, light brown or black with white markings.

Fanciers of the Basenji are certain that this small dog will rise to popularity when more people get to know him. He has some unique undoglike traits that make him an ideal house pet.

For one thing, he does not bark! However, he is not mute but snarls, growls and makes a sound somewhat like a soft yodel. When it comes to personal cleanliness, the Basenji is almost catlike, devoting much of his leisure time to keeping his coat clean and glossy by licking it; and he has no "doggy" odor.

The Basenji generally has a delightful personality. He wears a perpetually puzzled look, and when he wants attention he will rub his paw briskly over his muzzle. He always seems happy and is especially tolerant of children.

Although a native of the tropics, he seems to have adjusted to the American range of climates, and his coat becomes a bit coarser in colder regions.

The Basenji is rather fast for a small dog and should be kept on leash in the city, else his curiosity may send him dashing off after some interesting sight or scent.

Some of the earlier imports of Basenjis were lost to distemper, and owners should be careful to keep Basenji puppies off the streets until they have been immunized by injection against infectious canine diseases. Although they are probably not related, the Basenji has the same deerlike look as the miniature pinscher.

Basenji
Ch. Bettina's Oribi
Owner: Mrs. Bettina Belmont Ward. Middlesburg, Virginia

Standard of the Breed

Characteristics: The Basenji should not bark, but is not mute. The wrinkled forehead and the swift, tireless running gait (resembling a racehorse trotting full out) are typical of the breed.

General Appearance: The Basenji is a small, lightly built, short-backed dog, giving the impression of being high on the leg compared to its length. The wrinkled head must be proudly carried, and the whole demeanor should be one of poise and alertness.

Head and Skull: The skull is flat, well chiseled and of medium width, tapering toward the eyes. The foreface should taper from eye to muzzle and should be shorter than the skull. Muzzle, neither coarse nor snipy, but with rounded cushions. Wrinkles should appear on the forehead and be fine and profuse. Side wrinkles are desirable, but should never be exaggerated into dewlaps.

Nose: Black greatly desired. A pinkish tinge should not penalize an otherwise first-class specimen, but it should be discouraged in breeding.

Eyes: Dark hazel, almond-shaped, obliquely set and far-seeing.

Ears: Small, pointed and erect, of fine texture, set well forward on top of head.

Mouth: Teeth must be level, with scissors bite.

Neck: Of good length, well crested and slightly full at base of throat.

Forequarters: The chest should be deep and of medium width. The legs straight with clean fine bone, long forearm and well-defined sinews. Pasterns should be of good length, straight and flexible.

Body: The body should be short and the black level. The ribs well sprung with plenty of heart room, deep brisket, short-coupled, and ending in a definite waist.

Hindquarters: Should be strong and muscular, with hocks well let down, turned neither in nor out, with long second thighs.

Feet: Small, narrow and compact, with well-arched toes.

Tail: Should be set on top and curled tightly over to either side.

Coat: Short and silky. Skin very pliant.

Color: Chestnut red (the deeper the better) or pure black, or black-and-tan, all with white feet, chest and tail tip. White legs, white blaze and white collar optional.

Weight: Bitches about 22 pounds; males about 24 pounds.

Size: Bitches 16 inches and males 17 inches from the ground to the top of the shoulder. Bitches 16 inches and males 17 inches from the front of the chest to the farthest point of the hindquarters.

Faults: Coarse skull or muzzle. Domed or peaked skull. Dewlaps. Round eyes. Low-set ears. Overshot or undershot mouth. Wide chest. Wide behind. Heavy bones. Creams, shaded or off colors, other than those defined above, should be heavily penalized

BASSET HOUND

The basset hound is believed to be descended from an ancient line of French slow-trailing hounds. Average weight 45 pounds (although some reach 60 pounds), height 14 inches. Short coat, black, tan and white.

Thanks to the magic of the television screen and a mournful-looking canine actress named Cleo, the basset hound has begun to regain his popularity in recent years. Though he is not considered one of beauties of dogdom, with his bloodhound-like head on a low-slung body with crooked legs, he has many good qualities.

When it comes to scenting, the basset is second only to the bloodhound, and as a hunter he has worked well on pheasants. In the home, the basset is slow-

Basset Hound
Hartshead Red Dust
Owner: Hartshead Kennels. Muskegon, Michigan

moving, somewhat aloof and inclined to be a one-man dog. However, in the field he is far more agile than his appearance would indicate, and he has been used to hunt rabbits and foxes, and many have been taught to retrieve. In the field, the basset's voice has a deep and resonant bell-like timbre. If the dog is to be kept as a house pet, he should be restrained from using his voice too often as even a basset puppy's howls can carry for a considerable distance.

Most bassets get along well with children and it is almost impossible to make them lose their temper. Some owners report that their bassets get along well with their pet cats, birds, and even rabbits.

In training a basset, considerable patience is required, as the dog works slowly and responds at his own well-regulated pace. As a rule the breed is healthy and a less finicky eater than other of the small hounds. However, his diet should be watched to prevent overfeeding and a resultant excess of fat. To keep him in good condition, the basset needs many long, slow walks if he spends much of his time indoors.

Standard of the Breed

Head: The head should be large, the skull narrow and of good length, the peak being very fully developed, a characteristic point of the head, which should be free from any appearance of, or inclination to, cheek bumps. It is most perfect when it closest resembles the head of a bloodhound, with heavy flews and forehead wrinkled up to the eyes. The expression when sitting or when still should be very sad, full of reposeful dignity. The whole of the head should be covered with loose skin, so loose, in fact, that when the hound brings its nose to the ground the skin over the head and jaws should fall forward and wrinkle perceptibly.

Jaws: The nose itself should be strong and free from snipiness, while the teeth of the upper and lower jaws should meet. A pig-jawed hound or one whose jaw is underhung is distinctly objectionable.

Ears: The ears are very long and when drawn forward fold well over the nose. They are set on the head as low as possible and hang loose in folds, like drapery, the ends curling inward, in texture thin and velvety.

Eyes: The eyes should be deeply sunken, showing prominent haws, and in color they should be a deep brown.

Neck and Shoulders: The neck should be powerful, with heavy dewlaps set on sloping shoulders.

Forelegs: The forelegs should be short, very powerful, very heavy in bone, close-fitting to the chest, with a crooked knee and wrinkled ankle, ending in a massive paw. A basset hound must not be out at elbows, which is a bad fault.

Feet: He must stand perfectly sound and true on his feet, which should be thick and massive, and the weight of the forepart of the body should be borne equally by each toe of the forefeet so far as it is compatible with the crook of the legs. Unsoundness in feet or legs should absolutely disqualify a basset from taking a prize at a show.

Chest and Body: The chest should be deep and full. The body should be long and low and well ribbed. Slackness of loin, flat-sidedness and a roach- or razor-back are all bad faults.

Hocks: A basset hound should not be straight on his hocks, nor should he measure more over his quarters than he does at his shoulder. Cow hocks, straight hocks, or weak hocks are all bad faults.

Quarters: The quarters should be full of muscle which stands out so that when one looks at the dog from behind, he gives a round, barrel-like effect, with quarters round as an apple. He should be what is known as a good dog to follow, and when trotting away from you, his hocks should bend well and he should move true all around.

Stern: The stern is coarse underneath and carried "gaily," in hound fashion.

Coat: The coat should be like that of the foxhound, not too fine and not too coarse, but yet of sufficient strength to be of use in bad weather. The skin is loose and elastic.

Color: No hound color is a bad color, so that any recognized foxhound color should be acceptable to the judge, and only in the very closest competition should the color of a hound have any weight in a judge's decision.

SCALE OF POINTS

Head, skull, eyes, muzzle, flews	*14*
Ears	*10*
Neck, dewlap, chest and shoulders	*18*
Forelegs and feet	*18*
Back, loins, hocks and hindquarters	*18*
Stern	*5*
Coat and skin	*5*
Color and markings	*5*
Basset hound character and symmetry	*7*
Total	*100*

BEAGLE

Originally an English hunting dog, used for rabbits and hares, the beagle has been for some years one of the most popular breeds. Comes in two sizes: under 13 inches, weight 18 pounds; 13 to 15 inches, about 30 pounds. Short coat, white with black-and-tan saddle markings.

In 1953 the beagle pushed the cocker spaniel out of first place in American Kennel Club registrations and since then he has been at or near first place in canine popularity. It is easy to account for the beagle's success. He's small, quiet around the house, always cheerful, carrying his tail high, and very friendly. His short coat needs little care and he is a sturdy, long-lived dog.

As a hunter, the beagle seems born with the ability to hunt rabbits and other game, and with a little "showing" he can do fairly well on pheasants. He is less temperamental than some of the other hounds and adaptable to life in a small apartment or on a farm.

While a grown beagle can put up with a young child, or children, it is not a good idea to get a beagle puppy for a family with human toddlers, as the small dog needs a quieter atmosphere and gentle handling during his early growth.

The adult beagle needs exercise and may run to fat unless he get enough outdoor running or frequent long hikes with his master. His preferred exercise is following the trail of a cottontail, and many beagle owners have found

Beagle
Ch. Forest Festivity
Owner: Edward Jenner. Libertyville, Illinois

themselves becoming rabbit hunters after a beagle joined their family circle.

Standard of the Breed

Head: The skull should be fairly long, slightly domed at the occiput, with cranium broad and full.

Ears: Ears set on moderately low, long, reaching when drawn out nearly, if not quite to, the end of nose; fine in texture, fairly broad, and with almost entire absence of erectile power—setting close to the head, with the forward edge slightly in-turning to the cheek—rounded at tip.

Eyes: Large, set well apart, soft and houndlike, of a brown or hazel color, expression gentle and pleading.

Muzzle: Of medium length; straight and square cut; the stop moderately defined.

Jaws: Level. Lips free from flews; nostrils large and open.

Defects: A very flat skull, narrow across the top; excess of dome; eyes small, sharp and terrier-like, or prominent and protruding; muzzle long, snipy or cut away below the eyes, or very short. Roman or upturned nose, giving a dish-faced expression. Ears short, set high or with a tendency to rise above the point of origin.

Neck and Throat: Neck rising free and light from the shoulders, strong in substance, yet not loaded, of medium length. The throat clean and free from folds of skin; a slight wrinkle below the angle of the jaw, however, may be allowable. *Defects:* A thick, short, cloddy neck carried on a line with the top of the shoulders. Throat showing dewlaps and folds of skin to a degree termed "throatiness."

Shoulders and Chest: Shoulders sloping, clean, muscular, not heavy or loaded —conveying the idea of freedom of action with activity and strength. Chest deep and broad, but not broad enough to interfere with the free play of the shoulders. *Defects:* Straight, upright shoulders. Chest too wide or with lack of depth.

Back, Loin and Ribs: Back short, muscular and strong. Loin broad and slightly arched. Ribs well sprung, giving abundance of lung room. *Defects:* Very long or swayed or roach-back. Flat, narrow, thin loin. Flat ribs.

Forelegs and Feet: Forelegs straight, with plenty of bone in proportion to size of dog. Pasterns short and straight. Feet, close, round and firm. Pads full and hard. *Defects:* Out at elbows. Knees knuckled over forward or bent backward. Forelegs crooked or dachshund-like. Feet long, open or spreading.

Hips, Thighs, Hind Legs and Feet: Hips and thighs strong and well muscled, giving abundance of propelling power. Stifles strong and well let down. Hocks firm, symmetrical and moderately bent. Feet close and firm. *Defects:* Cow hocks or straight hocks. Lack of muscle and propelling power. Open feet.

Tail: Set moderately high; carried gaily, but not turned forward over the back. With slight curve; short as compared with size of the dog; with brush. *Defects:* A long tail. Teapot curve or inclined forward from the root. Rat tail with absence of brush.

Coat: A close, hard, hound coat of medium length. *Defects:* A short, thin coat, or coat of soft quality.

Height: Not to exceed 15 inches measured across the shoulders at the highest point, the hound standing in a natural position with his feet well under him.

Color: Any true hound color.

General Appearance: A miniature foxhound, solid and big for his inches, with the wear-and-tear look of the hound that can last in the chase and follow his quarry to the death.

SCALE OF POINTS

Skull	5
Ears	10
Eyes	5

Muzzle	5	
Head		25
Neck	5	
Chest and shoulders	15	
Back, loin and ribs	15	
Body		35
Forelegs	10	
Hips, thighs and hind legs	10	
Running gear		30
Coat	5	
Stern	5	
		10
Total		100

DACHSHUND

The German name for this breed means "badger dog," for its ancestors that fought the fierce badger in underground burrows. Long highly popular in all countries. Average weight 20 pounds; height 9 inches; also in miniature variety. Coat smooth, long- or wire-haired, solid red-brown, black, with tan markings, dappled, tiger and chocolate-colored.

Although his ancestors were larger dogs, weighing about 35 pounds, and fierce fighters, the modern dachshund has long been among the leading half dozen most popular breeds as a show dog and pet.

Stubborn and independent, every dachshund has a mind of his own. He decides for himself where he will sleep or rest and what and when he will eat. In fact, one problem with many dachshunds (or *dachshunde,* to be exact) is feeding them. If they do not like the meals offered them they just refuse to eat and may have to be force-fed or even kept alive by intravenous feeding.

As a rule, the dachshund is not a quiet dog. He greets callers with his loud-hound bark, and views casual visitors with noisy suspicion. When he greets a friend, however, his habitual response is to roll over on his back and wave his legs wildly, waiting to have his belly scratched.

One of the more active hound breeds, the dachshund is almost always at play when he is not sleeping, and fits in well with a family of active small children. He is always ready to run over with one of his toys for a game of catch or other sport, and his small, fast-moving legs provide him with plenty of exercise indoors.

Dachshund
Ch. De Sangpur Wee Lancelot
Owner: Mrs. William Burr Hill. Hicksville, New York

Wire-haired, Long-haired and Smooth Dachshunds
Owner: Mrs. William Burr Hill. Hicksville, New York

Long-haired Dachshund
Ch. De Sangpur Traveler's Trix
Owners: Mrs. William Burr Hill, Hicksville, New York and
Mrs. Harland W. Meistrell. Long Island, New York

Wire-haired Dachshund
Ch. Fir Trees Coco
Owner: Stanley Orne. Kirkland, Washington

An unusually clean breed, the dachshund almost never has any doggy odor, and except for the long-haired variety, he requires little grooming aside from an occasional brushing or nail clipping. However, many dachshunds object to being handled—except when they want to be—and grooming them or taking them to the veterinarian may be a bit of a problem.

Affectionate with his human family, the dachshund usually selects one person as his master, who gets the full measure of his loyalty.

Standard of the Breed

General Appearance: Low to ground, short-legged, long-bodied, but with compact figure and robust muscular development; with bold and confident carriage of the head and intelligent facial expression. In spite of his shortness of leg, in comparison with his length of trunk, he should not appear crippled, awkward, or cramped in his capacity for movement, nor slim and weasel-like.

Qualities: He should be lively, clever and courageous to the point of rashness, persevering in his work both above and below ground; with all the senses well developed. His build and disposition qualify him especially for hunting game below ground. Added to this, his hunting spirit, good nose, loud tongue and small size render him especially suited for beating the bush. His figure and his fine nose give him a special advantage over most other breeds of sporting dogs for trailing.

Conformation of Body: Head, viewed from above or from the side, should taper uniformly to the tip of the nose and should be clean cut. The skull is only slightly arched and should slope gradually without stop (the less stop the more typical) into the finely formed slightly arched muzzle (ram's nose). The ridge bones over the eyes should be strongly prominent. The nasal cartilage and the tip of the nose are long and narrow, lips tightly stretched, well covering the lower jaw, but neither deep nor pointed. Corner of the eye not very marked. Nostrils well open. Jaws opening wide and hinged well back of the eyes, with strongly developed bones and teeth.

Teeth: Powerful canine teeth should fit closely together, and the outer side of the lower incisors should lightly touch the inner side of the upper (scissors bite).

Eyes: Medium size, oval, situated at the side, with a clear, energetic, though pleasant expression, not piercing. Color, lustrous dark reddish brown to brownish black for all coats and colors. Wall (fish or pearl) eyes in gray or dapple-gray dogs, are not a very bad fault, but also are not desirable.

Ears: Should be set near the top of the head, and not too far forward; long but not too long; beautifully rounded; not narrow, pointed or folded. Their carriage should be animated, and the forward edge should just touch the cheek.

Neck: Fairly long, muscular, clean cut, not showing any dewlap on the throat, slightly arched in the nape, extending in a graceful line into the shoulders, carried proudly but not stiffly.

Front: To endure the arduous exertion underground, the front must be correspondingly muscular, compact, deep, long and broad. In detail, the forequarters: (a) shoulder blades—long, broad obliquely and firmly placed upon the fully developed thorax, furnished with hard and plastic muscles; (b) upper arm—of the same length as the shoulder blade, and at right angles to the latter, strong of bone and hard of muscle, lying close to the ribs, capable of free movement; (c) forearm—this is short in comparison with other breeds, slightly turned inward; supplied with hard but plastic muscles on the front and outside, with tightly stretched tendons on the inside and at the back; (d) joint between forearm and foot—these are closer together than the shoulder joints, so that the front does not appear absolutely straight; (e) paws—full, broad in front and a trifle inclined outward, compact with well-arched toes and tough pads; (f) toes—there are five of these, although only four are in use. They should be close together, with a pronounced arch, provided on top with strong nails, and underneath with tough toe pads.

Trunk: The whole trunk should be long and fully muscled. The back, with sloping shoulders and short, rigid pelvis, should lie in the straightest possible line between withers and the very slightly arched loins—the latter being short, rigid and broad.

Chest: The breast bone should be strong, and so prominent in front that on either side a depression (dimple) appears. When viewed from the front, the thorax should appear oval, and should extend downward to the midpoint of the forearm. The enclosing structure of ribs should appear full and oval, full-volumed, so as to allow by its ample capacity, complete development of heart and lungs. Well ribbed, and gradually merging into the line of the abdomen. If the length is correct, and also the anatomy of the shoulder and upper arm, the front leg when viewed in profile should cover the lowest point of the breast line.

Abdomen: Slightly drawn up.

Hindquarters: The hindquarters viewed from behind should be of completely equal width, with croup long, round, full, robustly muscled, but plastic, only slightly sinking toward the tail. The pelvic bones not too short, rather strongly developed and moderately sloping. The thigh bones robust and of good length, set at right angles on the pelvic bones. The hind legs robust and well-muscled, with well-rounded buttocks. The knee joint broad and strong.

The calf bone, in comparison with other breeds, short; perpendicular to the thigh bone and firmly muscled. The bones at the base of the foot should present a flat appearance, with a strongly prominent hock and broad Achilles tendon. The central foot bones should be long, movable toward the calf bone, slightly bent toward the front, but perpendicular when viewed from behind. The hind paws should be compactly closed and arched. The whole foot should be posed equally on the ball and not merely on the toes; nails short.

Tail: Set in continuation of the spine and extending without very pronounced curvature, and should not be carried too gaily.

Special Note: Inasmuch as the dachshund is a hunting dog, scars from honorable wounds are not considered a fault.

Special Characteristics of Three Varieties of Coat

The dachshund is bred with three varieties of coat: short-haired or smooth; wire-haired; long-haired. All varieties must conform to the standard. While the long-haired and smooth are old, well-fixed varieties, the blood of other breeds has been purposely introduced to create the wire-haired.

The following qualities are sought in the three varieties:

Short-haired or Smooth: Thick, short, smooth and shiny hair; no bald patches. Faults are too fine or thin hair, leathery ears, bald patches, too coarse or too thick hair. *Tail:* Gradually tapered to a point, well but not too richly haired; long, sleek bristles on the underside are permissible; brush tail or partly or wholly hairless tail are faults.

Color of hair, nose and nails: The one-colored group includes red (often called tan), red-yellow, and yellow, with or without a shading of interspersed black hairs A clean color is preferable and red is considered more desirable than red-yellow or yellow. Dogs strongly shaded with interspersed black hairs belong to this class and not to the other color groups. White is undesirable, but a solitary small spot is not exactly disqualifying. Nose and nails should be black. Red is admissible but not desirable.

The two-colored group includes deep black, chocolate, gray, and white; each with rust-brown or yellow marks over the eyes, on the sides of the jaw and underlip, on the inner edge of the ear, front, breast, inside and behind the front legs, on the paws and around the anus, and from there to about one-third to one-half the length of the tail of the under side. (The most common two-color dachshund is the black-and-tan.) Except in white dogs, white is undesirable. Absence or undue prominence of tan markings is undesirable. In the case of black-and-tan dogs, black toes are desired; for chocolate, black or brown; for gray or white dogs, gray or even flesh color, with gray preferred;

in the case of white dogs, black nose and nails are preferred.

The dappled or striped dachshund is a clear brownish or grayish color, or even a white ground with dark irregular patches of dark gray, brown, red-yellow or black (large areas of one color not desirable). It is desirable that neither the light nor the dark color should predominate. The color of the striped (brindle) dachshund is red or yellow with a darker streaking. Nose and nails are black, as in the two-colored dachshund.

The Wire-haired Dachshund: Has the same general appearance as the short-haired, but without being long in the legs; it is permissible for the body to be somewhat higher off the ground. With the exception of the jaw, eyebrows, and ears, the whole body is covered with a perfectly uniform, tight, short, thick, rough, hard coat, but with finer shorter hairs (undercoat) everywhere distributed among the coarser hairs, resembling the coat of the German spike-haired pointer. There should be a beard on the chin. The eyebrows are bushy; on the ears the hair is shorter than on the body, almost smooth, but in any case conforming to the rest of the coat. The general arrangement of the hair should be such that the wire-haired dachshund, seen from a distance, should resemble the smooth-haired. Any sort of soft hair in the coat is faulty, whether short or long, or wherever found on the body; the same is true of long, curly or wavy hair, or hair that sticks out irregularly in all directions; a flag tail is also objectionable. The tail should be robust, as thickly haired as possible, gradually coming to a point, and without any tuft. All colors of hair, nose and nails are permissible. White patches on the chest, although allowable, are not desired.

The Long-haired Dachshund: The distinctive characteristic differentiating the long-haired dachshund from the other varieties is the rather long silky hair. This soft, sleek, glistening, often slightly wavy hair should be longer under the neck, on the underside of the body, and especially on the ears and behind the legs, becoming there a pronounced feather. The hair should attain its greatest length on the underside of the tail. The hair should fall beyond the lower edge of the ear. Short hair on the ear—the so-called "leather" ear is not desirable. Too luxuriant a coat causes the long-haired dachshund to appear coarse, and masks the type.

The coat should remind one of the Irish setter, and should give the dog an elegant appearance. Hair too thick on the paws—so-called "mops"—is inelegant and renders the dog unfit for use. It is faulty for the dog to have equally long hair over all the body, if the coat is too curly or too scrubby, or if a flag tail or overhanging hair on the ear is lacking; or if there is a very pronounced parting on the back, or a vigorous growth between the toes. The tail should be carried gracefully in prolongation of the spine; the hair here attains its greatest growth and forms a veritable flag. The color of hair, nose and nails is exactly as for the smooth-haired dachshund.

Miniature Dachshunds are bred in all three coats and in all colors. They are not undersized or underdeveloped specimens of full-sized dogs, but have been purposely produced to work in burrows smaller than the regular-sized dachshund can enter. The limits set on their size have inevitably resulted in a more slender body structure, as adherence to the proportions of the larger dogs would have produced an animal impractical for hunting use.

In Germany the miniatures are divided into two classes according to their chest circumference. In the United States, miniature dachshunds have not been given separate classification. A division of the open class for "under nine pounds and twelve months old or older" permits class competition as miniatures.

General Faults—All Types. Serious faults (which may prevent a dog from receiving any show rating): over- or undershot jaws, knuckling over, very loose shoulders. *Secondary faults* (which may prevent a dog from receiving a high show rating): Weak, long-legged, or dragging figure, body hanging between the shoulders; sluggish, clumsy, or waddling gait; toes turned inward or too obliquely outward; splayed paws, sunken back, roach- (or carp-) back; croup higher than withers; short-ribbed or too weak chest; excessively drawn up flanks like those of a greyhound; narrow, poorly muscled hindquarters; weak loins; bad angulation in front or hindquarters; cow hock; bowed legs; "glass" eyes, except for gray or dappled dogs; poor coat. *Minor faults:* Ears wrongly set, sticking out, narrow or folded; too marked a stop; pointed or weak jaw; too wide or too short a head; goggle eyes; "glass" eyes in the case of gray or dappled dogs; insufficiently dark eyes in the case of all other coat colors; dewlaps; short neck; too fine or too thin hair.

NORWEGIAN ELKHOUND

This breed is practically unchanged from the Vikings' hunting dogs of 6,000 years ago, and it is still used as a hunter in its native land. Average weight 50 pounds; height 20 inches. Coat thick, gray, with shadings.

If your plans include moose hunting, a small pack of Norwegian elkhounds will help you bag that game. Working on the moose or their native elk, these dogs with a superlative sense of scent will locate the prey, then intercept it and hold it at bay until the hunter arrives.

In their native land, these dogs have been used as hunters, guard dogs, sled dogs, shepherds, and as pets. Brought to England in the late 1880's, they proved

Norwegian Elkhound
Gladjac Royal Oslo
Owner: Mrs. Susan D. Phillips. South Royalton, Vermont

adaptable otter hounds, gun dogs and show dogs. In the United States they have been mainly pets, and on a very small scale farm dogs.

As a family pet, the Norwegian elkhound is a remarkably clean dog who quickly becomes a member of the family circle. However, his bark is an important asset of this dog and he uses it. During the hunt, he barks to call his master in for the kill; barks to announce visitors, whom he will escort into the house; and barks when he detects a stranger outside.

He learns easily to walk alongside his master off lead, and although he may roam a bit to show his independence, he will trot back to heel on command.

Many cross- or mixed breeds with a Norwegian elkhound parent will show the traits of this breed, since it has what breeders call a "high prepotency" and they transmit their characteristics strongly even when the pure blood strain is diluted. This may be due to the fact that through long isolation in Scandinavia the breed is purer than many others which are termed "purebred."

Standard of the Breed

General Description: The Norwegian elkhound is a typical northern dog of medium size, with a compact, proportionately short body, with a thick and rich but not bristling coat of gray, with prick ears and a tail that is curled and carried over the back. His temperament is bold and energetic.

Head: "Dry" (without any loose skin), broad at the ears; the forehead and back of the head only slightly arched; the stop not large, yet clearly defined. The muzzle is of medium length, thickest at the base, and seen from above or from the side, tapers evenly without being pointed. The bridge of the nose is straight; the lips are tightly closed.

Ears: Set firm, high and erect, they are higher than they are wide at the base, pointed (not rounded) and very mobile. When the dog is listening, the orifices are turned forward.

Eyes: Not protruding; brown in color; preferably dark, lively, with a fearless energetic expression.

Neck: Of medium length, "dry" (without any loose skin, strong and well set up).

Body: Powerful, compact and short, with broad deep chest, well-sprung ribs, straight back, well-developed loins, and stomach very little drawn up.

Legs: Firm, straight and strong; elbows closely set on; hind legs with little angulation at knees and hocks. Seen from behind they are straight.

Feet: Comparatively small, somewhat oblong, with tightly closed toes, not turned out. There should be no dewclaws on hind legs.

Tail: Set high, short, thickly and closely haired, but without brush; tightly curled, not carried too much to one side.

Coat: Thick, rich and hard, but rather smooth-lying. On head and front of legs, short and even; longest on neck and chest, on buttocks, on hindside of forelegs and on underside of tail. It is made up of longer and harder covering hairs, dark at the tips, and a tight, soft, woolly undercoat.

Color: Gray, with black tips to the long covering hairs; somewhat lighter on chest, stomach, legs, underside of tail and around anus. The color may be lighter or darker, with a slight shading toward yellow; but a pronounced variation from gray color disqualifies. Too dark or too light individuals should be avoided; also yellow markings or uneven coloring. There should be no pronounced white markings.

Height at Shoulder: Males about 20½ inches; bitches about 18 inches.

WORKING DOGS

Perhaps the most "educable" of dogs, the members of the "working dog" breeds have long served man as shepherds, guard dogs, sled dogs, and in recent year as guide dogs to the blind. In war they have done sentry duty and have fought alongside their masters, and many have been trained for police work. In return they ask only praise and appreciation.

With their capacity to respond to training, these breeds make the perfect companion for the master who takes the effort to give them the training that allows them a real purpose in life—and work is part of their life. The untrained "working" dog can give only a small part of the true companionship that training brings out in these breeds.

BOXER

Native of Germany. First bought to United States in early 1930's, rose to popularity in 1930's. Has held a place among the ten most popular breeds for a number of years. Average weight 64 pounds, height 23 inches. Fawn or brindle color; white markings desirable. Short, smooth coat.

The boxer is classified by the American Kennel Club as a "working" dog and many have been used by the Army Canine Corps and as guide dogs for the blind. However, in both these fields it has been overshadowed by the German shepherd.

Although the boxer's origin is traced back by some authorities to bulldog-type dogs which were used as bull baiters, the modern boxer is notable for a friendly, in fact affectionate, disposition; boxers rarely are vicious, even in old age. As a rule, boxers are excellent with children and will submit to ear-pulling and tail-snatching by a young child without resentment. The boxer is ideal for the city dweller who wants a larger dog that will adapt himself to apartment or small-house life. But the boxer is seldom a "showy" dog when walking on leash. Most boxers insist on walking along with head down and tail drooping. In fact the boxer's "street" appearance is one of his drawbacks. But he makes up for this by showing a high degree of intelligence in home living. He easily adapts himself to the routine of the family that owns him, is readily house-broken and trained. Even adult boxers spend long hours playing contentedly with their toys.

With a bit of training a grown boxer can be left alone in a house or apartment for as long as ten hours daily, with no fear of his doing any damage or annoying the neighbors by barking.

Boxer
Int. Ch. Eldic's Darius
Owners: Mr. and Mrs. Richard Haeberle, Jr. Basking Ridge, New Jersey

As a dog for the suburbs or country, the boxer must be accepted with some reservations. If allowed to run free, some boxers become cat killers and most fail to develop the road sense that keeps many mongrels alive on trafficked roads.

Unless specially trained for the job, most boxers fail miserably as watchdogs. They will run with tails wagging to greet the person who comes in through the window as avidly as they do one who comes in through the door.

On the credit side, the boxer is a naturally clean dog, seldom has a doggy odor, and his short coat requires a minimum of grooming except for an occasional brushing; many go through life without ever being bathed. The boxer responds to training in obedience and is always eager to play or to go out for a walk or a ride in the family car. He is not a noisy dog and gets along well with other dogs and other pets.

Although a sturdy dog, the boxer is prone to several ailments. Because of the shape of the jaw, many develop tumors on the jaw and they show a high incidence of malignant skin and internal growths.

Some boxers, especially those with wider heads and long flews, drool saliva at certain times, and many boxers will sometimes throw up their meals for no apparent reason.

In colder climates the boxer should be protected with a sweater or coat during the winter months, especially if he is in and out of a heated apartment. The boxer is not one of the longer-lived breeds. At the age of eight or nine, he usually has grayed and gives the impression of being an old dog.

However, balancing his virtues and faults, the boxer is a highly desirable pet and there are many who, having once known his companionship, prefer him above all other dogs.

Standard of the Breed

General Appearance: The Boxer is a medium-sized, smooth-haired, sturdy dog of short, square figure and strong limbs. The musculature is very clean and powerfully developed, standing out plastically from under the skin. His movements are alive with energy; the gait, although firm, is elastic, the stride free and roomy, the carriage proud and noble. As a service and guard dog, he must combine with substance and ample power that considerable degree of elegance absolutely essential to his further duties—those of enduring escort dog with horse, bicycle or car, and as a splendid jumper. Only a body whose limbs are built to withstand the most strenuous effort, assembled as a complete and harmonious whole, can respond to such demands, Therefore, to be at his highest-developed efficiency, he must never be plump or heavy, and while equipped for great speed, he must not be racy.

The head imparts to the boxer a unique individual stamp peculiar to him alone. It must be in perfect proportion to his body, and above all, it must never be too light. His muzzle is his most distinctive feature, and the greatest value is to be placed on its being of correct form and in absolutely proper proportion to the skull.

In judging the boxer, the first thing to be considered is general appearance and the relation of substance to elegance, and of the desired proportions of the individual parts of the body in relation to each other. Consideration is to be given to an attractive color, after which the individual parts are to be examined for their correct constructions and functions. Special attention is to be devoted to the head.

Faults: Head not typical; plump, bulldoggy appearance; light bone; lack of proportion; bad condition; deficiency in nobility.

Head: The beauty of the head depends upon the harmonious proportion of muzzle and skull. From whatever direction you view the head, whether from the front, from the top, or from the side, the muzzle must always appear in proper relation to the skull. That means it must never appear too small. The head should be clean showing neither deep wrinkles nor dewlap. Normally, deep folds will appear on the top of the skull when the ears are held erect. And they are always indicated from the root of the nose running downward on both sides of the muzzle. The dark mask confines itself to the muzzle and must be in distinct relief to the color of the head, so that the face will not have a somber expression. The muzzle must be powerfully developed in length, breadth, and height. It must not be pointed or narrow, short or shallow. Its shape is influenced, first, through the formation of both jawbones; second, through the placement of teeth; and third, through the quality of the lips.

The two jawbones do not terminate in a normal perpendicular level in front, but the lower jaw protrudes beyond the upper and bends slightly upward. The boxer is normally undershot. The upper jaw is broad where it is attached to the skull and maintains this breadth except for a very slight tapering to the front. The canine teeth should be as widely separated from each other as possible. The six incisors are all in one row, the middle teeth not projecting. In the upper jaw they are slightly concave, in the lower they are in a straight line. Thus both jaws are very wide in front. The bite is powerful and sound, the teeth set in the most normal possible arrangement. The lips complete the formation of the muzzle. The upper lip is thick and padded; it fills out the hollow space in front formed by the projection of the lower jaw and is supported by the fangs. Therefore, these fangs must stand as far apart as possible and be of good length so that the entire front surface of the muzzle is broad and square and forms an obtuse (rounded) angle with the top line of the muzzle. The lower edge of the upper lip rests on the edge of the lower lip. The repandous (bent upward) part of the underjaw with the lower lip (the chin) must not rise above the front of the upper lip, but much less may it disappear under it. It must, however, be plainly perceptible when viewed from the front as well as the side without protruding and bending upward in the manner of the English bulldog. The teeth of the underjaw must not be seen when the mouth is closed; nor may the boxer show his tongue when his mouth is closed.

The top of the skull is slightly arched. It must not be so short that it is rotund, not too flat, nor too broad, and the occiput must not be too pronounced. The forehead forms a distinct stop with the top line of the muzzle, which should not be forced back into the forehead like that of a bulldog, nor should it slope away (appear downfaced). The tip of the nose lies somewhat higher than the root of the muzzle. The forehead shows a suggestion of furrow which, however, must never be too deep, especially between the eyes. Corresponding with the powerful set of teeth, the cheeks are accordingly well developed without protruding from the head with too bulgy an appearance. Preferably they should taper into the muzzle in a slight, graceful curve. The ears are set high, clipped to a point, and are fairly long, the shell not too broad, and are carried perpendicularly. The dark-brown eyes, not too small or protruding nor deep-set, disclose an expression of energy and intelligence, but must never appear gloomy, threatening, or piercing. The eye must have a dark rim. The nose is broad and black, very slightly turned up; the nostrils are broad with the nasolabial line running between them.

Faults: Lack of nobility and expression, somber face, unserviceable bite. Pinscher or bulldog head; driveling, badly trimmed ears, visible haw. Showing teeth or tongue. Light or "bird of prey" eye. Sloping top line of muzzle. Too pointed or too light a bite.

Neck: Round, not too thick and short, but of ample length, yet strong and muscular and clean cut throughout, without dewlap, running with a distinctly marked nape in an elegant arch down to the back. *Fault:* Dewlap.

Body: Build is square. Of the profile lines, one is horizontal over the back, with two vertical lines—one touching the shoulder tip in front, the other a hip protuberance in the rear, forming with the ground level a square. The torso rests on trunklike straight legs with strong bones.

Chest and Front Leg Measurements: The chest is deep, reaching down to the elbows; the depth of the chest amounts to half of the height of the dog at the withers. The ribs are well arched but are not barrel-shaped, extending far to the rear. The loins are short, close and taut and lightly tucked up. The lower stomach line blends into an elegant curve to the rear. The shoulders are long and sloping, close-lying but not excessively covered with muscle. The upper arm is long, forming a right angle to the shoulder blade. The forelegs when seen from the front must be straight, stand parallel to each other and have strong, firmly joined bones. The elbows must not press too closely to the chest well nor stand off too far. The underarm is perpendicular, long and firmly muscled. The pastern joint of the forelegs is clearly defined, but not distended. The pastern is short, slightly slanting, but standing almost perpendicular to the ground. Feet are small, with tightly arched toes and hard soles (cat's paws).

Faults: Too broad and low in front, loose shoulders, chest hanging between the shoulders, hare's feet, hollow flanks, hanging stomach, turned legs and toes.

Back: The withers should be clearly defined, the whole back short, straight, broad and very muscular. *Faults:* Carp- (roach-) back; sway-back; thin, lean back; long, narrow, sharp sunken-in loins. Weak union with the croup.

Hindquarters: Strongly muscled, the musculature hard as a board and standing out very plastically through the skin. The thighs are not narrow and flat but are broad and curved; the breech musculature is also strongly developed. The croup slightly sloped, flat-arched, broad. Tail attachment high rather than too deep. Tail clipped, carried upward. The pelvis should be long and especially broad in females. Upper and lower thigh long, hip and knee joint with as much angle as possible. In standing position the knee should reach so far forward that it would meet a line drawn from the hip protuberance to the floor. The hock angle should be about 140 degrees, the lower part of the foot at a slight slope of about 95 to 100 degrees from the hock joint to the floor; that is, not completely vertical. Seen from behind, the hind legs are straight. The hocks clean, not distended, supported by powerful rear pads, the rear toes just a little longer than the front toes, but similar in all other respects.

Faults: Falling off or too arched or narrow croup. Low-set tail, higher in back then in front; steep, stiff or too little angulated hindquarters; light thighs; cow hocks; bowlegs and crooked legs; dewclaws; soft hocks; narrow heel; tottering, waddling gait; hare's feet; hindquarters too far under or too far behind.

Height: Males, 22 to 24 inches at the withers; females, 21 to 23 inches at the withers. Males should not go under and females should not go over these dimensions.

Weight: Males around 23 inches should weigh over 66 pounds. Females of about 22 inches should weigh around 62 pounds.

Coat: Short, shiny, lying smooth and tight to the body.

Color: The colors are fawn and brindle, fawn in various shades from light yellow to dark, deer red. The brindle variety should have black stripes on a golden yellow or red-brown background. The stripes should be clearly defined and above all must not be gray or dirty. Stripes that do not cover the whole back are not desirable. White markings in fawn and brindle are often attractive.

The black mask is absolutely required and it is desirable to have an even distribution of head color. Boxers with white or black ground color or entirely black or white are not considered desirable and are disqualified from the show ring. The rule is that white markings may not exceed one-third of the ground color.

COLLIE

The famed herding dog of Scotland has been one of the most popular breeds for many years. Average weight 65 pounds; height 24 inches. Sable, white, tricolor and

*blue merle. The long-coated (rough) variety is most popular in the United States;
the smooth-coated collie is more rare.*

The herding instincts of the collie make him an ideal guard dog for children.
Many of these dogs seem to have an almost uncanny sense of protection and
drag or push small children away from dangerous situations.

Long used by the Scottish shepherds the collie is considered by many to be
the most intelligent of the working dogs and there is considerable dissension
among fanciers of the breed as to the merits of the modern show-type collie.
Some feel that the long-muzzled light-headed type that wins ribbons at the
shows is far inferior to the shorter-headed working-type collie whose brains,
stamina and courage make him the ideal companion for hard-working shepherds.

Lassie of the TV screen has done much to ensure the popularity of the breed
among youngsters, much as the stories by Albert Payson Terhune did with
readers a few decades ago.

One of the easiest dogs to train, most collies have one exasperating habit.
When they have just performed a routine or trick, they will often refuse to go
through it again perhaps feeling that if they have done what was demanded of
them, there is no logical reason to repeat it.

Although active in an outdoor environment the collie can readily adapt to
quieter life in a city apartment and can even be trained to subdue his watchdog
habits and not bark at any passing stranger. Traditionally, the bark of the collie
is not followed by a bite.

The long-haired collie with his double coat requires fairly constant grooming
for the best appearance and to cut down the amount hair that will be shed in
the house.

Standard of the Breed

General Character: The collie is a lithe, strong, responsive, active dog, standing naturally straight and firm. The deep, moderately wide chest shows
strength, the sloping shoulders and well-bent hocks indicate speed and grace,
and the face shows high intelligence. The collie presents an impressive, proud
picture of true balance, each part being in harmonious proportion to every
other part and to the whole. Except for the technical description that is essential to this standard and without which no standard for the guidance of
breeders and judges is adequate, it may be stated simply that no part of the
collie ever seems to be out of proportion to any other part. *Faults:* Timidity;
frailness; sullenness; viciousness; lack of animation; cumbersome appearance
and lack of over-all balance impair the general character.

Collie
Ch. Cadet of Noranda
Owners: Mr. and Mrs. William H. Long, Jr. Long Island, New York

Head: The head characteristics are of great importance. When considered in proportion to the size of the dog the head is inclined to lightness and never appears massive. A heavy-headed dog lacks the necessary bright, alert, full-of-sense look that contributes so greatly to expression. Both in front and profile view the head bears a general resemblance to a well-blunted lean wedge, being smooth and clean in outline and nicely balanced in proportion. On the sides it tapers gradually and smoothly from the ears to the end of the black nose, without being flared out in occiput (cheeky) or pinched in muzzle (snipy). In profile view the top of the occiput and the top of the muzzle lie in two approximately parallel, straight lines of equal length, divided by a very slight but perceptible stop or break.

Midpoint between the inside corners of the eyes (which is the center of a correctly placed stop) is the center of balance in length of head.

The end of the smooth, well-rounded muzzle is blunt but not square. The underjaw is strong, clean cut, and the depth of skull from the brow to the underpart of the jaw is not excessive.

The teeth are of good size, meeting in a scissors bite. Overshot or undershot jaws are undesirable, with the latter being more severely penalized.

There is a very slight prominence of the eyebrows. The occiput is flat, without receding either laterally or backward, and the occipital bone is not highly peaked. The proper width of occiput necessarily depends upon the combined length of skull and muzzle, and the width of the occiput is less than its length. Thus the correct width varies with the individual and is dependent upon the extent to which it is supported by length of muzzle.

Because of the importance of the head characteristics, prominent head faults are severely penalized.

Eyes: Because of the combination of the flat skull, the arched eyebrows, the slight stop and the rounded muzzle, the foreface must be chiseled to form a receptacle for the eyes, and they are necessarily placed obliquely to give them the required forward outlook. Except for the blue merles, they are required to be matched in color. They are almond-shaped, of medium size, and should never appear to be large or prominent. The color is dark and the eye does not show a yellow ring or a sufficiently prominent haw to affect the dog's expression.

The eyes have a clear, bright appearance, expressing intelligent inquisitiveness, particularly when the ears are drawn up and the dog is on the alert.

In blue merles, dark-brown eyes are preferable, but eyes may be merle or china in color without specific penalty.

A large, round, full eye seriously detracts from the desired "sweet" expression. Eye faults are heavily penalized.

Ears: The ears are in proportion to the size of the head and, if they are carried properly and unquestionably "break" naturally, are seldom too small. Large ears usually cannot be lifted correctly off the head, and even if lifted they will be out of proportion to the size of the head. In repose, the ears are folded lengthwise and thrown back into the frill. On the alert, they are drawn well up on the backskull and carried about three-quarters erect, with about one-fourth of the ear tipping or "breaking" forward. A dog with prick ears or low ears cannot show true expression and is penalized accordingly.

Neck: The neck is firm, clean, muscular, sinewy and heavily frilled. It is fairly long, is carried upright with a slight arch at the nape, and imparts a proud, upstanding appearance showing off the frill.

Body: The body is firm, hard and muscular, a trifle long in proportion to the height. The ribs are well rounded behind the well-sloped shoulders and the chest is deep, extending to the elbows. The back is strong and level, supported by powerful hips and thighs and the croup is sloped to give a well-rounded finish. The loin is powerful and slightly arched. Noticeably fat dogs or dogs in poor flesh or with skin disease or with no undercoat are out of condition and are moderately penalized accordingly.

Legs: The forelegs are straight and muscular, with a fair amount of bone, depending on the size of the dog. A cumbersome appearance is undesirable. Both narrow and wide placement are penalized. The forearm is moderately fleshy and the pasterns are flexible but without weakness. The hind legs are less fleshy, are muscular at the thighs, very sinewy, and the hocks and stifles are well bent. A dog with cow-hocked or straight stifles is penalized. The comparatively small feet are approximately oval in shape. The soles are well-padded and tough and the toes are well arched and close together. When the collie is not in motion, the legs and feet are judged by allowing the dog to come to a natural stop in a standing position so that both the forelegs and the hind legs are placed well apart, with the feet extending straight forward. Excessive "posing" is undesirable.

Gait: The gait or movement is distinctly characteristic of the breed. A sound collie is not out at the elbows, but he does, nevertheless, move toward an observer with his front feet tracking comparatively close together at the ground. The front legs do not "cross over" nor does the collie move with a pacing or rolling gait. Viewed from the front, one gains the impression that the dog is capable of changing direction of travel almost instantaneously, as indeed he is. When viewed from the rear, the hind legs, from the hock joint to the ground, move in comparatively close-together, parallel, vertical planes. The hind legs are powerful and propelling. Viewed from the side, the gait is not choppy but smooth. The reasonably long "reaching" stride is even, easy, light and seemingly effortless.

Tail: The tail is moderately long, the bone reaching to the hock joint or below. It is carried low when the dog is quiet, the end having an upward twist or "swirl." When gaited or when the dog is excited it is carried gaily, but not over the back.

Coat: The well-fitting, proper-textured coat is the crowning glory of the rough variety of collie. It is abundant except on the head and legs. The outer coat is straight and harsh to the touch. A soft, open outer coat or a curly outer coat, regardless of quantity, is penalized. The undercoat, however, is soft, furry and so close together that it is difficult to see the skin when the hair is parted. The coat is very abundant on the mane and frill. The face or mask is smooth. The forelegs are smooth and well feathered to the back of the pasterns. The hind legs are smooth below the hock joints. Any feathering below the hocks is removed for the show ring. The hair on the tail is profuse and on the hips is long and bushy. The texture, quantity and the extent to which the coat "fits the dog" are important points.

Color: The four recognized colors are sable and white, tricolor, blue merle, and white. There is no preference among them. The sable-and-white is predominantly sable (a fawn sable color of varying shades from light golden to dark mahogany) with white markings usually on the chest, neck, legs, feet and the tip of the tail. A blaze may appear on the foreface or occiput or both.

The tricolor is predominantly black, carrying white markings as in a sable-and-white, and has tan shadings on and about the head and legs.

The blue merle is a mottled or "marbled" color, predominantly blue-gray and black with white markings as in the sable-and-white, and usually has tan shadings as in the tricolor.

The white is predominantly white, preferably with sable or tricolor markings. Blue merle coloring is undesirable in whites.

Size: Males are 24 to 26 inches at the shoulder and weigh 60 to 75 pounds. Bitches are 22 to 24 inches at the shoulder, weighing 50 to 65 pounds. An undersized or an oversized collie is penalized accordingly.

Expression: Expression is one of the most important points in considering the relative value of collies. "Expression," like the term "character," is difficult to define. It is not a fixed point as in color, weight or height, and is something the uninitiated can properly understand only by visual illustration. In general, however, it may be said to be the combined product of the shape and balance of the skull and muzzle; the placement, size, shape and color of the eyes; and the position, size and carriage of the ears. An expression that shows sullenness or which is suggestive of any other breed is entirely foreign. The collie cannot be judged properly until its expression has been carefully evaluated.

Smooth Collie: The smooth variety of collie is judged by the same standard as the rough variety, except that references to the quantity and the distribution of the coat are not applicable to the smooth variety, which has a hard, dense, smooth coat.

DOBERMAN PINSCHER

The official war dog of the U.S. Marine Corps, the breed was developed in Germany in the 1890's. Average weight 70 pounds, height 27 inches. Smooth, short coat, black or red with rust color.

The Doberman pinscher is a perfect example of an "artificial" breed. In the early 1870's, a German, Louis Dobermann of Thuringia, set out to create a new breed of dog that would be a giant terrier with the strength of a working dog such as the German shepherd, and with the sleek appearance of the miniature pinscher. In disposition, he was seeking a "sharp" dog. In the German

Doberman Pinscher
Ch. Elfred's Christel
Owner: Mrs. Mayson H. Tucker. Long Island, New York

breeder's terminology it meant one that could be trained to attack man or any animal.

In some twenty years he achieved his goal and his dogs rapidly became popular as police and guard dogs. However, in the years since then the dogs have become gentler than the original Dobermans, and the strains found today generally have little of the ferocity of their German progenitors.

A number of Dobermans have been used as guide dogs for the blind with good success, and many have performed well in the obedience ring.

As a rule, Dobermans are highly amenable to training and their disposition can be molded to a considerable extent by their upbringing. One of the most famous teams of Dobermans are those used by R. H. Macy's department store in New York City to guard the premises at night. They are trained not to attack, but to corner and hold any intruder and to summon human assistance by barking.

Raised as a house pet, the Doberman is friendly and quiet, but novice owners should be warned against trying to train their Doberman as a watchdog. That is a job for someone who knows the breed. However, there is some possibility of purchasing a Doberman that is just too "sharp" to make a safe pet, so the puppy's disposition should be watched carefully as he grows up; and if possible, a Doberman should be purchased with a "trade-in" agreement if the dog proves unsatisfactory.

Standard of the Breed

General Conformation and Appearance: The appearance is that of a dog of good middle size, with a body that is square, the height measured vertically from the ground to the highest point of the withers, equaling the length, measured horizontally, from the forechest to the rear projection of the upper thigh. Height, at the withers—males, 26 to 28 inches; bitches, 24 to 26 inches. Compactly built, muscular and powerful, for great endurance and speed. Elegant in appearance, of proud carriage, reflecting great ability and temperament. Energetic, watchful, determined, alert, fearless and obedient. *Faults:* Coarseness. Fine greyhound build. Undersized or oversized. Shyness or viciousness.

Head Shape: Long and dry, resembling a blunt wedge, both in frontal and profile views. When seen from the front, the head widens gradually toward the base of the ears in practically an unbroken line. Top of skull flat, turning with slight stop to bridge of muzzle, with muzzle line extending parallel to the top line of the skull. Cheeks flat and muscular. Lips lying close to jaws and not drooping. Jaws full and powerful, well filled under the eyes. Nose solid black in black dogs, dark brown in brown ones, and dark gray in blue ones. *Faults:* Head out of balance in proportion to body. Ram's, dish-faced, cheeky or snipy head.

Eyes: Almond-shaped, not round, moderately deep-set, not prominent, with vigorous, energetic expression. Iris of uniform color, ranging medium to darkest brown in black dogs, the darker shade being the more desirable. In reds or blues, the color of the iris should blend with that of the markings, but not be of a lighter hue than that of the markings. *Faults:* Slit eyes; glassy eyes.

Teeth: strongly developed and white. Lower incisors upright and touching inside of upper incisors, a true scissors bite. Forty-two teeth (22 in lower jaw, 20 in upper). Distemper-stained teeth not penalized. *Faults:* Overshot more than $\frac{3}{16}$ of an inch; undershot more than $\frac{1}{8}$ of an inch.

Ears: Well trimmed and carried erect. (Ear-trim waived in states where prohibited.) Upper attachment of the ear, when carried erect, should be on a level with the top of the skull.

Neck: Carried upright, well muscled and dry. Well arched, with nape of neck widening gradually toward body. Length of neck proportionate to body and head.

Body: Back short, firm, of sufficient width, and muscular at the loin extending in a straight line from withers to the slightly rounded croup. Withers pronounced and forming the highest point of body. Brisket full and broad, reaching deep to the elbow. Chest broad, and forechest well defined. Spring of ribs pronounced. Belly well tucked up, extending in a curved line from chest. Loins wide and well muscled. Hips broad in proportion to body, breadth of hips being approximately breadth of body at rib spring. Tail docked at second joint, should appear to be a continuation of the spine, without definite drop.

Forequarters: Shoulder blade and upper arm should meet at an angle of 90 degrees. Relative length of shoulder and upper arm should be as one to one, excess length of upper arm being much less desirable than excess length of shoulder blade. Legs, seen from the front and side, perfectly straight and parallel to each other from elbow to pastern; muscled and sinewy, with round, heavy bone. In a normal position, and when gaiting, the elbow should lie close to the brisket. Pasterns firm with an almost perpendicular position to the ground. Feet well arched, compact, and catlike, turning neither in nor out.

Hindquarters: In balance with forequarters. Upper shanks long, wide and well muscled on both sides of thigh, with clearly defined stifle. While the dog is at rest, hock to heel should be perpendicular to the ground. Upper shanks, lower shanks and hocks parallel to each other and wide enough apart to fit in with a properly built body. The hip bone should fall away from the spinal column at an angle of about 30 degrees. The upper shank should be at right angles to the hip bone. Croup well filled out. Catlike feet as on hind legs, turning neither in nor out.

Gait: The gait should be free, balanced and vigorous, with good reach in the forequarters and good driving power in the hindquarters. When trotting there should be a strong rear-action drive, with rotary motion of hindquarters. Each rear leg should move in line with the foreleg on the same side. Rear and front legs should be thrown neither in nor out. Back should remain strong, firm and level.

Coat, Color, Markings: Coat smooth-haired, short, hard, thick, and close-lying. Invisible gray undercoat on neck permissible. Allowed colors: black, brown or blue. Markings: rust red, sharply defined, and appearing above each eye and on muzzle, throat, and forechest, and on all legs and feet and below tail. White on chest, not exceeding one-half square inch, permissible.

SCALE OF POINTS

General Appearance and Conformation

Proportions	8	
Bone		
Substance	8	
Temperament		
Expression	8	
Nobility		
Condition	5	
		29

Head

Shape	6	
Teeth	5	
Eyes	3	
Ears	1	
		15

Neck	3	
		3

Body

Backline		
Withers		
Loins	8	
Tail placement		
Chest		
Brisket		
Rib spring	8	
Tuck-up		
Shape and proportions	4	
		20

Forequarters

Shoulders		
Upper arms		
Legs	5	
Pasterns		
Angulation	4	
Paws	2	
		11

Hindquarters		
Upper thigh		
Stifle	*5*	
Hocks		
Angulation	*4*	
Paws	*2*	
		11
Gait	*6*	
		6
Coat, color, markings	*5*	
		5
Total		*100*

GERMAN SHEPHERD

The famed "war dog" already known in England, popularized by Rin Tin Tin in movies, became the most popular breed in the United States until 1926. Then indiscriminate breeding and the introduction of vicious strains from Germany caused a fast decline in popularity. In recent years has again become desirable and now ranks about fifth among breeds in the United States. Average weight 75 pounds, height 25 inches. Dense coat, black, black-and-tan or gray.

Basically a working dog, the German shepherd is an ideal choice for the person who is seriously interested in training his dog. In obedience trials, these dogs work superbly and their performance as guide dogs for the blind indicates their adaptability for training and their high intelligence. But the family whose children clamor for a "police dog" should consider carefully before buying a German shepherd.

Even skilled amateur dog handlers and some professionals find these dogs—especially many of the imports from Germany—just too hot to handle. In Germany the breeders still train their sheperds for attack work and deliberately breed for dogs with a belligerent disposition rather than for the steady temperament that makes a good house pet. On the other hand, some domestic strains have been bred down to the point where they may cringe from strangers and snap from sheer timidity.

As dogs generally inherit the traits of their immediate parents, a German shepherd whose sire and dam are good-natured should be a safe bet for a family pet, and a reliable breeder will be familiar with the nature of his litters.

On the credit side, these dogs are highly protective to children and are

German Shepherd
Ch. Servie v. Alexyrvo Hof
Owner: Dr. Leo C. Clauss. New York, New York

sturdy enough to take the mauling that the dog in a family with young children must undergo. The shepherd's double coat makes him comfortable in any weather and he can take the transition from a heated house or apartment to stormy outdoor weather with no ill effects (one reason why he is so often chosen to be trained as a guide dog for the blind).

To a considerable extent, you can mold your German shepherd's behavior by the manner in which he is raised. Try to avoid playing any "games" that lead him to think aggressive behavior is desirable and give him enough varied human companionship as a puppy to make him feel that all people are his friends. The German shepherd is naturally aloof with persons outside his immediate human family circle, but he can be trained to accept other people.

If you want him trained as a watchdog, it might be worth the expense to have him trained by a professional who knows the breed. If your German shepherd turns out to be the vicious type it may still be possible to have him retrained by an expert; otherwise he can be a hazardous pet.

However, the fact that there are so many of these dogs that are highly satisfactory pets shows that fanciers of the breed may be justified in their plea that the many should not suffer for the sins of the few.

Standard of the Breed

General Appearance: The first impression of a German shepherd is that of a strong, agile, well-muscled animal, alert and full of life. He should both be and appear to be well balanced, with harmonious development of the forequarter and hindquarter. The dog should appear to the eye—and actually be—longer than tall; deep-bodied, and presenting an outline of smooth curves rather than corners. He should look substantial and not spindly, giving the impression, both at rest and in motion, of muscular fitness and nimbleness without any look of clumsiness or soft living.

Height and Weight: The ideal height for males is 25 inches at the shoulder; bitches, 23 inches. This height is established by taking a perpendicular line from the top of the shoulder blade to the ground with the coat parted or so pushed down that this measurement will show the actual height of the dog's frame. The working value of dogs above or below the indicated heights is proportionately lessened, although variations of an inch above or below the ideal height are acceptable, while greater variations must be considered as faults. Weights of males of desirable size in proper flesh and condition average between 75 and 85 pounds; and of bitches, between 60 and 70 pounds.

Traits: The German shepherd should be stamped with a look of quality and nobility—difficult to define, but unmistakable when present. The good shepherd dog never looks common. The breed has a distinct personality marked by a direct and fearless, but not hostile, expression; self-confidence and a certain aloofness which does not lend itself to immediate and indiscriminate friendships.

Secondary sex characteristics should be strongly marked, and every animal should give a direct impression of masculinity or femininity, according to its sex. Males should be definitely masculine in appearance and deportment; bitches unmistakably feminine without weakness of structure or apparent softness of temperament.

Coat: The shepherd is normally a dog with a double coat, the amount of undercoat varying with the season of the year and the proportion of time the dog spends out of doors. The undercoat should, however, always be present to a sufficient degree to keep out water, to insulate against temperature extremes, and as a protection against insects. The outer coat should be as dense as possible, hair straight and harsh and lying close to the body. A slightly wavy outer coat, often of wiry texture, is equally acceptable. The head, including the inner ear, foreface and legs and paws are covered with short hair, and the neck with longer and thicker hair. The rear of forelegs and hind legs has somewhat longer hair extending to the pastern and hock, respectively. Faults in coat include complete lack of undercoat; soft, silky or too long outer coat, and curly or open coat.

Body Structure: A German shepherd is a trotting dog and his structure has been developed to best meet the needs of his work in herding. That requires a long, effortless trot which covers the maximum amount of ground with the minimum number of steps, consistent with the size of the animal. The proper body proportions, firmness of back and muscles and the proper angulation of the forequarters and hindquarters serve this end. They enable the dog to propel himself forward by a long step of the hindquarter and to compensate for this stride by a long step of the forequarter. The high withers, the firm back, the strong loin, the properly framed croup, even with the tail as balance and rudder, all contribute to this purpose.

Proportion: The German shepherd is normally longer than tall, the most desirable proportion being 10 to 8½. The length is established by taking a dog standing naturally and foursquare, measured on the horizontal line from the point of the breastbone to the rear edge of the pelvis, commonly called the sitting bone.

Angulation: Forequarters—the shoulder blade should be long, laid flat against the body with its rounded upper end in a vertical line above the elbow, and sloping well forward to the point where it joins the upper arm. The withers should be high, with shoulder blades meeting closely at the top, and the upper arm set on at an angle approaching as nearly as possible a right angle. Such an angulation permits the maximum forward extension of the foreleg without binding or effort. Shoulder faults include too steep or straight a position of either blade or upper arm; too short a blade or upper arm; lack of sufficient angle between these two members; looseness through lack of firm ligamentation, and loaded shoulders with prominent pads of flesh or muscles on the outer side. Construction in which the whole shoulder assembly is pushed too far forward also restricts the stride and is faulty.

Hindquarters—the angulation of the hindquarters also consists ideally of a series of sharp angles as far as the relation of the bones to each other is concerned, and the thigh bone should parallel the shoulder blade while the stifle bone parallels the upper arm. The whole assembly of the thigh, viewed from the side, should be broad and with both thigh and stifle well muscled and of proportionate length, forming as nearly as possible a right angle. The metacarpus (the unit between the hock joint and the foot, commonly called the hock) is strong, clean and short, the hock joint clean cut and sharply defined.

Head: Clean cut and strong, the head of the shepherd is characterized by nobility. It should seem in proportion to the body and should not be clumsy, although a degree of coarseness of head, especially in dogs, is less of a fault than overrefinement. A round or domy skull is a fault. The muzzle is long and strong, with lips firmly fitted, its top line usually parallel with an imaginary elongation of the line of the forehead. Seen from the front, the forehead is only moderately arched and the skull slopes into the long, wedge-shaped muzzle without abrupt stop. Jaws are strongly developed. *Faults:* Weak and too narrow underjaws, snipy muzzles, and no stop.

Ears: The ears should be moderately pointed, open toward the front, and are carried erect when at attention, the ideal carriage being one in which the center lines of the ears, viewed from the front, are parallel with each other and perpendicular to the ground. Puppies usually do not permanently raise their ears until the fourth or sixth month, and sometimes not until later. Ears should not be cropped. The well-placed and well-carried ear of a size in proportion to the skull materially adds to the general appearance of the breed. Neither too small nor too large ears are desirable. Too much stress, however, should not be laid on perfection of carriage if the ears are fully erect.

Eyes: Of medium size, almond-shaped, set a bit obliquely and not protruding. The color should be as dark as possible. Eyes of a lighter color are sometimes found and are not a serious fault if they harmonize with the general coloration, but a dark-brown eye is always to be preferred. The expression should be keen, intelligent and composed.

Teeth: The powerful teeth, 42 in number, 20 upper and 22 lower, should be strongly developed and meet in a scissors grip in which part of the inner surface of the upper teeth meets and engages part of the outer surface of the lower teeth. Overshot and undershot jaws are serious faults.

Neck: The neck is strong and muscular, clean cut and relatively long, proportionate in size to the head and without loose folds of skin. When the dog is at attention or excited, the head is raised and the neck carried high. Otherwise, typical carriage of the head is forward rather than up, and but little higher than the top of the shoulder, particularly while in motion.

Top Line: The withers should be higher than, and sloping into, the level back to provide for proper attachment of the shoulder blades.

Back: The back should be straight and very strongly developed, without sag or roach, the section from the wither to the croup being relatively short.

Loin: Viewed from the top, broad and strong; blending smoothly into the back without undue length between the last rib and the thigh, when viewed from the side.

Croup: Long and gradually sloping. Too level or flat a croup prevents the proper functioning of the hindquarter, which must be able to reach well under the body. A steep croup also limits the action of the hindquarter.

Tail: Bushy, with the last vertebra extended at least to the hock joint and usually below. Set smoothly into the croup and low rather than high. At rest the tail hangs in a slight curve like a saber. A slight hook—sometimes carried to one side—is faulty only to the extent that it mars the general appearance. When the dog is excited or in motion, the curve is accentuated and the tail raised, but it should never be lifted beyond a line at right angles with the line of the back. Docked tails are a disqualification as are those which have been operated upon to prevent curling. Tail too short or with clumpy end is a serious fault.

Body: The whole structure of the body gives an impression of depth and solidity without bulkiness.

Forechest: Commencing at the prosternum, should be well filled and carried well down between the legs with no sense of hollowness.

Chest: Deep and capacious with ample room for lungs and heart. Carried well forward, with the prosternum or breastbone showing well ahead of the shoulder when the dog is viewed from the side.

Ribs: Well sprung and long, neither barrel-shaped nor too flat, and carried down to a breastbone which reaches to the elbow. Correct ribbing allows the elbow to move freely when the dog is at a trot, while too round a rib structure causes interference and throws the elbow out. Ribbing should be carried well back so that the loin and flank are relatively short.

Abdomen: Firmly held and not paunchy. The bottom line of the shepherd is only moderately tucked up in the flank; never like that of a greyhound.

Legs: The bone of the legs should be straight, oval rather than round or flat and free from sponginess. Its development should be in proportion to the size of the dog and contribute to an over-all impression of substance without grossness. Crooked legs and malformation, as for example, that caused by rickets, should be penalized.

Pastern: Should be of medium length, strong and springy. Much more spring of pastern is desirable in the shepherd than in many other breeds, as it contributes to the ease and elasticity of the trotting gait. The upright "terrier" pastern is definitely undesirable.

Metacarpus (or hock): Short, clean, sharply defined and of great strength. This is a fulcrum upon which much of the forward motion of the dog depends. Cow hocks are a decided fault, but before penalizing for this, it should be definitely determined—with the dog in motion—whether the dog has this fault, since many dogs with exceptionally good hindquarter angulation occasionally stand so as to give the impression of cow-hockedness which is not actually present.

Feet: Rather short, compact, with toes well arched. Pads thick and hard, nails short and strong. The feet are important to the working qualities of the dog. The ideal foot is extremely strong, with good gripping power and plenty of depth of pad. The so-called cat foot or terrier foot is not desirable. The thin, spread or hare foot is, however, still more undesirable.

Color: The German shepherd dog differs widely in color and all colors are permissible. Generally speaking, strong, rich colors are to be preferred, with definite pigmentation and without the appearance of a washed-out color. White dogs are not desirable and are to be disqualified if they show albino characteristics.

Gait (general impression): The gait of the dog is outreaching, elastic, seemingly without effort, smooth and rhythmic. At a walk he covers a great deal of ground, with long step of both hind leg and foreleg. At a trot, the dog covers still more ground and moves powerfully but easily, with a beautiful coordination of limbs and back so that the gait appears to be the steady motion of a well-oiled machine. The feet travel close to the ground, and neither fore nor hind feet should reach high on either forward reach or backward push.

The hindquarter delivers through the back a powerful forward thrust which slightly lifts the whole animal and drives the body forward. Reaching far under, and passing the imprint left by the front foot, the strong, arched hind foot takes hold of the ground; then hock, stifle and upper thigh come into play and sweep back, the stroke of the hind leg finishing with the foot still close to the ground in a smooth follow-through. The overreach of the hindquarters usually necessitates one hind foot passing outside and the other inside the track of the forefeet, and such action is not faulty unless the locomotion is crabwise, with the dog's body sideways out of the normal straight line.

The typical smooth, flowing gait of the shepherd cannot be maintained without great strength and firmness (which does not mean stiffness) of back. The whole effort of the hindquarter is transmitted to the forequarter through the muscular and bony structure of the loin, back and withers. At full trot, the back must remain firm and level, without sway, roll, whip or roach.

To compensate for the forward motion imparted by the hindquarter, the shoulder should open to its full extent—the desirability of good shoulder angulation now becomes apparent—and the forelegs should reach out in a stride balancing that of the hindquarter. A steep shoulder will cause the dog to stumble or to raise the forelegs very high in an effort to coordinate with the hindquarter, which is impossible when the shoulder structure is faulty. A serious gait fault results when a dog moves too low in front, presenting an unlevel top line with the wither lower than the hips.

The shepherd does not track on widely separated parallel lines as does the terrier, but brings the feet inward toward the middle line of the body when at a trot in order to maintain balance. For this reason, a dog viewed from the front or rear while in motion will often seem to travel close. This is not a fault if the feet do not strike or cross, or if the knees or shoulders are not thrown out, but the feet and hocks should be parallel even if close together.

The excellence of gait must also be evaluated by viewing from the side the effortless, properly coordinated covering of ground.

Character: Normally, the shepherd dog is not one that fawns upon every new acquaintance. At the same time, he should be approachable, quietly standing his ground and showing confidence and a willingness to meet overtures, without making them. He should be poised, but when the occasion demands, eager and alert; both fit and willing to serve in any capacity as companion, watchdog, guide dog to the blind, herding dog or guardian, whichever the circumstances may demand.

The shepherd must not be timid, shrinking behind its master or handler; nervous, looking about or upward with anxious expression or show nervous reaction of strange sights or sounds; nor should he be lackadaisical, sluggish or manifestly disinterested in what goes on around him. Lack of confidence under any surroundings is not typical of good character; extreme timidity and nervous imbalance sometimes give the dog an apparent, but totally unreal, courage and it becomes a "fear biter," snapping for no justifiable reason but because of apprehensiveness when a stranger approaches.

In summary, it should never be forgotten that the ideal German shepherd is a working animal that must have an incorruptible character combined with body and gait suitable for the arduous work which constitutes his primary purpose. All his qualities should be weighed in respect to their contribution to such work, and while no compromise should be permitted with regard to its working potential, the dog must nevertheless possess a high degree of beauty and nobility.

Disqualifying Faults: Albino characteristics; cropped ears; hanging (hound-like) ears; docked tail.

Very Serious Faults: Major faults of temperament; undershot lower jaw.

Serious Faults: Faults of balance and proportion; poor gait; bitchy male dogs; faulty backs; too level or too short croup; long and weak loin; very bad feet; ring tail; tail too short; rickety condition; more than four missing molars or any other missing teeth (unless due to accident); lack of nobility;

badly washed-out color; badly overshot bite.

Faults: Doggy bitches; poorly carried ears; too fine head; weak muzzle; improper muscular condition; faulty coat; bad teeth.

Minor Faults: Too coarse head; hooked tail; too light, round, or protruding eyes; discolored teeth; condition of coat due to season or keeping.

GREAT DANE

Originated in Germany about 400 years ago as a boar hunter. Average weight 130 pounds, height 32 inches. Coat smooth, brindle, fawn, blue, black, and harlequin (black and white).

Despite his size, the great Dane is fairly popular with people living in apartments and small houses. Somehow this huge dog manages to move his bulk around a house without knocking things over, although a sweep of his tail may wreak havoc with bric-a-brac. Indoors, a great Dane is usually quiet and dignified and affectionate with members of his human family. One common way he has of showing that he likes people is to lean against them or even try to sit on their laps.

Historically, the Dane is a hunter and guard dog. He was used to trail and kill wild boars, and was used as a war dog by the Germans and the English. The modern Dane still has a strongly developed protective feeling for his home and his master and makes an excellent watchdog. Fanciers of the modern great Dane claim that the ferocity has been bred out of the breed, but this writer has found some of them rather unpredictable and has known several who had bitten children with no apparent provocation. During the 1880's the breed was barred from dog shows in New York City because of ferocity and bad temper.

Being a true working dog, the great Dane can be trained, and many have performed well in the obedience ring, some being put through their paces by women and children.

In acquiring a great Dane there are two important points to be considered. One is the effect on the budget, since an adult dog weighing about 130 pounds requires a substantial amount of food daily. The other is that the great Dane is comparatively short-lived. A dog's life expectancy is influenced by his size, and the larger the breed, the shorter the life span.

Standard of the Breed

General Appearance: The great Dane combines, in its distinguished appearance, dignity, strength and elegance with great size and a well-formed, smoothly muscled body. He is one of the giant breeds, but is unique in that his general

Great Dane
Ch. Heidere Devil-D of Marydane
Owner: Mary K. Johnston. Wilton, Connecticut

Harlequin Great Dane
Ch. Herold V. St. Magn Obertraubling
Owner: Robert J. Bohrer. Allentown, Pennsylvania

Brindle Great Dane
Ch. Autopilot of Kanedane
Owner: Mary K. Johnston. Wilton, Connecticut

conformation must be so well balanced that he never appears clumsy and is always a unit—the Apollo of dogs. He must be spirited and courageous— never timid. He is friendly and dependable. This physical and mental combination is the characteristic which gives the great Dane the majesty possessed by no other breed. It is particularly true of this breed that there is an impression of great masculinity in males as compared to an impression of femininity in the bitches. The male should appear more massive throughout than the female, with larger frame and heavier bone. In the ratio between length and height, the great Dane should appear as square as possible. In bitches a somewhat longer body is permissible. *Faults:* Lack of unity; timidity; bitchy dogs; poor musculature; poor bone development; out of condition; rickets; doggy bitches.

Color and Markings: In brindle Danes, the base color ranges from light golden yellow to deep golden yellow, always brindled with strong black cross stripes. The more intensive the base color and the more intensive the brindling, the more attractive will be the color. Small white marks at the chest and toes are not desirable. *Faults:* Brindle with too dark a base color; silver-blue and grayish blue base color; dull brindling; white tail tip.

Fawn Danes: Golden yellow up to deep golden yellow color with a deep black mask. The golden deep-yellow color must always be given preference. Small white spots at the toes and chest are not desirable. *Faults:* Yellowish gray, bluish yellow; grayish blue; dirty yellow (drab) color; lack of black mask.

Blue Danes: The color must be a pure steel blue as far as possible without any tinge of yellow, black or mouse gray. *Faults:* Any deviation from a pure steel-blue coloration.

Black Danes: Glossy black. *Faults:* Yellow-black, brown-black or blue-black. White markings, such as stripes on the chest, speckled chest and markings on the paws are permitted but not desirable.

Harlequin Danes: Base color, pure white with black torn patches irregularly and well-distributed over the entire body; pure white neck preferred. The black patches should never be large enough to give the appearance of a blanket nor so small as to give a stippled or dappled effect. Less desirable are coats with a few small gray spots, also pointings, where instead of a pure white base with black spots there is a white base with single black hairs showing through, which tend to give a salt-and-pepper or dirty effect. *Faults:* White base color with a few large spots; bluish gray pointed background.

Size: The male should be not less than 30 inches at the shoulder, but it is preferable that he be 32 inches or more, provided he is well proportioned to his height. The female should not be less than 28 inches at the shoulder, but it is preferable that she be 30 inches or more, also well porportioned to height.

Substance: Substance is that sufficiency of bone and muscle which rounds out a balance with the frame. *Faults:* Lightweight, whippety-like Danes; coarse, ungainly Danes; always there should be balance.

Condition of Coat: The coat should be very short and thick, smooth and glossy. *Faults:* Excessively long hair or dull hair, indicating malnutrition, worms and negligent rearing.

Movement: Gait is long, easy, springy stride with no tossing or rolling of body. The back line should move smoothly, parallel to the ground. The gait of the Dane should denote strength and power. The rear legs should have drive. The forelegs should track smoothly and straight. The Dane should track in two parallel straight lines. *Faults:* Short steps. The rear quarters should not pitch. The forelegs should not have a hackney gait (forced or choppy stride).

When moving rapidly the great Dane should not pace for the reason that it causes excessive side-to-side rolling of the body and thus reduces endurance.

Rear End; Croup, Legs, Paws: The croup must be full, slightly drooping, and must continue imperceptibly to the tail root. Hind legs, the first thighs (from hip joint to knee) are broad and muscular. The second thighs (from knee to hock joint) are strong and long. Seen from the side, the angulation of the first thigh with the body, of the second thigh with the first thigh, and the pastern root with the second thigh, should be very moderate, neither too straight nor exaggerated. Seen from the rear, the hock joints appear to be perfectly straight, turned neither toward the inside nor toward the outside. *Faults:* A croup which is too straight; a croup which slopes downward too steeply; and too narrow a croup. Hind legs: Soft, flabby, poorly muscled thighs; cow hocks which are the result of the hock joint turning outward; barrel legs, the result of the hock joints being too far apart; steep rear. As seen from the side, a steep rear is the result of angles of the rear legs forming almost a straight line; overangulation is the result of exaggerated angles between the first and second thighs and the hocks, and is very conducive to weakness. The hind legs should never be too long in proportion to the forelegs.

Paws, round and turned neither toward the inside nor outside. Toes short, highly arched and well closed. Nails short, strong and as dark as possible. *Faults:* Spreading toes (splay foot); bent, long toes (rabbit paws); toes turned toward the inside or the outside. Fifth toe appearing at a higher position on the hind legs and with wolf's claw or spur; excessively long nails; light-colored nails.

Front End, Shoulders, Legs, Paws: The shoulder blades must be strong and sloping and, seen from the side, must form as nearly as possible a right angle in its articulation with the humerus (upper arm) to give a long stride. A line from the upper tip of the shoulder to the back of the elbow joint should be as nearly perpendicular as possible. Since all dogs lack a clavicle (collar bone) the ligaments and muscles holding the shoulder blade to the rib cage must be well developed, firm and secure to prevent loose shoulders. *Faults:* Steep shoulders, which occur if the shoulder blade does not slope sufficiently; overangulation; loose shoulders which occur if the Dane is flabbily muscled, or if the elbow is turned toward the outside; loaded shoulders.

Forelegs: The upper arm should be strong and muscular. Seen from the side or the front, the strong lower arms run absolutely straight to the pastern joints. Seen from the front, the forelegs and the pastern roots should form perpendicular lines to the ground. Seen from the side, the pastern roots should slope only very slightly forward. *Faults:* Elbows in or out; a considerable bend in the pastern toward the front; a forward bow in the forearm (chair leg); an excessively knotty bulge in the front of the pastern joint.

Paws: Round and turned neither in nor out. Toes short, highly arched and well closed. Nails short, strong and as dark as possible. *Faults:* Spreading toes (splay foot); bent long toes (rabbit paws); toes turned in or out; light-colored nails.

Head: Conformation—long, narrow, distinguished, expressive, finely chiseled, especially the part below the eyes, with a strongly pronounced stop. The masculinity of the male is very pronounced in the expression and structure of head (this subtle difference should be evident in the dog's head by the massive skull and depth of muzzle); the bitch's head may be more delicately formed. Seen from the side, the forehead must be sharply set off from the bridge of the nose. The forehead and bridge of the nose must be straight and parallel to one another. Seen from the front, the head should appear narrow; the bridge of the nose should be as broad as possible. The cheek muscles show slightly, but under no condition should they be too pronounced. The muzzle part must have full flews and must be as blunt vertically as possible, in front; the angles of the lip must be quite pronounced. The front part of the head, from the tip of the nose up to the center of the stop should be as long as the rear part of the head from the center of the stop to the only slightly developed occiput. The head should be angular from all sides and should have definite flat planes, and its dimensions should be absolutely in proportion to the general appearance of the Dane. *Faults:* Any deviation from the parallel planes of skull and foreface; too small a stop; a poorly defined stop or none at all; too narrow a nose bridge; the rear of the head spreading laterally in a wedgelike manner (wedge head); an excessively round head (apple head); excessively pronounced cheek musculature; pointed muzzle; loose lips hanging over the lower jaw (fluttering lips) which create an illusion of a full, deep muzzle. The head should be shorter and distinguished rather than long and expressionless.

Teeth: Strong, well developed and clean. The incisors of the lower jaw must touch very lightly the bottoms of the inner surface of the upper incisors (scissors bite). If the front teeth of both jaws bite on top of each other they wear down too rapidly. *Faults:* Even bite; undershot or overshot; incisors out of line; black or brown teeth; missing teeth.

Eyes: Medium size, as dark as possible, with lively, intelligent expression; almond-shaped eyelids, well-developed eyebrows. *Faults:* Light-colored, piercing, amber-colored, light blue to watery blue, red or bleary eyes, eyes of different colors; eyes too far apart; Mongolian eyes; eyes with pronounced haws; eyes with excessively drooping eyelids. In blue and black Danes, lighter eyes are permitted but are not desirable. In harlequins, the eyes should be dark. Light-colored eyes, two eyes of different color, and walleyes are permitted but not desirable.

Nose: The nose must be large, and in the case of brindled and "single-colored" Danes it must always be black. In harlequins the nose should be black; a black-spotted nose is permitted; a pink-colored nose is not desirable.

Ears: Ears should be set high, not too far apart, medium in size, of moderate thickness, drooping forward close to the cheek. Top line of folded ear should be about level with skull. *Faults:* Hanging on the side, as in a foxhound. Cropped ears; high set; not set too far apart; well pointed; but always in proportion to the shape of the head and carried uniformly erect.

Torso: The neck should be firm and clean, high-set, well arched, long, muscular and sinewy. From the chest to the head it should be slightly tapering, beautifully formed, with well-developed nape. *Faults:* Short, heavy neck; pendulous throat folds (dewlaps).

Loin and Back: The withers form the highest part of the back which slopes downward slightly toward the loins, which are imperceptibly arched and strong. The back should be short and tensely set. The belly should be well shaped and tightly muscled, and, with the rear part of the thorax, should swing in a pleasing curve (tuck up). *Faults:* Receding back; sway-back; camel- or roach-back; a back line which is too high at the rear; an excessively long back; poor tuck-up.

Chest: Chest deals with that part of the thorax (rib cage) in front of the shoulders and front legs. The chest should be quite broad, deep and well muscled. *Faults:* A narrow and poorly muscled chest; protruding sternum (pigeon breast).

Ribs and Brisket: Deals with that part of the thorax back of the shoulders and front legs. Should be broad with the ribs sprung well out from the spine and flattened at the side to allow proper movement of the shoulders extending down to the elbow joint. *Faults:* Narrow (slab-sided) rib cage; round (barrel) rib cage; shallow rib cage not reaching the elbow joint.

Tail: Should start high and fairly broad, terminating slender and thin at the hock joint. At rest, the tail should fall straight. When the Dane is excited or running, the tail is slightly curved (saberlike). *Faults:* A too high- or too low-set tail (the tail set is governed by the slope of the croup); too long or too short a tail; tail bent too far over the back (ring tail); a tail which is curled; a twisted tail (sideways); a tail carried too high over the back (gay tail); a brush tail (hair too long on lower side). Cropping tails to desired length is forbidden.

SCALE OF POINTS

	Points	
General conformation		30
General appearance	10	
Color and markings	8	
Size	5	
Condition of coat	4	
Substance	3	
Movement		28
Gait	10	
Rear end (croup, legs, paws)	10	
Front end (shoulders, legs, paws)	8	
Head		20
Head conformation	12	
Teeth	4	
Eyes, nose and ears	4	
Torso		20
Neck	6	
Loins and back	6	
Chest	4	
Ribs and brisket	4	
Tail		2
Total		100

SAMOYED

This breed was named after the nomadic Arctic tribe whom it served as sled dog, reindeer herder and pet. Was brought to England 100 years ago. Average weight 55 pounds, height 22 inches. Double white coat.

The Samoyed is a happy dog. He always looks as if he is smiling and is naturally a well-mannered cheerful dog, getting along well with people and more or less ignoring other dogs.

For many generations the Samoyed lived with the tribes of the Arctic, sharing their homes and their labors. His reputation—and work—as a sled dog made him the first choice of many of the early Arctic expeditions. Unlike some

Samoyed
Ch. Pratika's Pilot
Owner: Ruth Bates Young. Medway, Ohio

of the other sled dogs, the Samoyed is not quarrelsome and makes an excellent companion for children. Another point in his favor is that he never has a doggy odor and his long white outer coat remains clean.

Like other long-haired dogs, the Samoyed will shed profusely at times, but there is a built-in bonus for the Samoyed's owner. His inner coat, when brushed out, yields a fine "wool" that can be woven into yarn that is light in weight and surprisingly warm.

Despite his Arctic origin, the Samoyed seems quite comfortable in warmer areas. The same coat that allows him to sleep outdoors in subzero weather serves as insulation against the hot sun, although he is likely to shed his inner coat during warm weather.

The Samoyed is considered by many fanciers to be one of the most beautiful breeds, and makes an impressive appearance in the show ring or trotting on lead alongside his master. A number have done well in obedience training and they seem eager to do what is expected of them and learn quickly.

Standard of the Breed

General Appearance: The Samoyed, being essentially a working dog, should be strong and active and graceful, and as he works usually in cold climates, his coat should be heavy and weather-resistant. He should not be long in the back, as a weak back would make him practically useless for his legitimate work; but at the same time, a cobby body, such as the chow's, would place him at a great disadvantage as a draught dog. Breeders should aim for the happy medium—a body not long, but muscular, allowing liberty, with a deep chest and well-sprung ribs, strong neck, straight front and exceptionally strong loins. A full-grown dog should stand 21 inches at the shoulder. On account of the depth of chest required, the legs should be moderately long; a very short-legged dog is depreciated. Hindquarters should be particularly well developed, stifles well bent, and any suggestion of unsound stifles or of cow hocks severely penalized.

Disposition: Intelligent, alert, full of action, but above all displaying marked affection for all mankind.

Coat: The body should be well covered with a thick, close, soft and short undercoat, with harsh hair growing through it, forming the outer coat, which should stand straight away from the body and be quite free from curl.

Head: Powerful and wedge-shaped with broad flat skull; muzzle of medium length, a tapering foreface, not too sharply defined; ears not too long and slightly rounded at tips, set well apart and well covered inside with hair. Eyes dark, set well apart and deep, with alert, intelligent expression. Lips black. Hair short and smooth before the ears. Nose and eye-rims black for preference, but may be brown or flesh-colored. Strong jaws with level teeth.

Back: Medium in length, broad and very muscular.

Chest and Ribs: Chest broad and deep. Ribs well sprung, giving plenty of heart and lung room.

Hindquarters: Very muscular, stifles well let down; cow hocks or straight stifles very objectionable.

Legs: Straight and muscular. Good bone.

Feet: Long, flattish and slightly spread out. Soles well padded with hair.

Tail: Long and profuse, carried over back or side when alert; sometimes dropped down when dog is at rest. Tight curl or double hook is a fault.

Size and Weight: Males, 21 to $23\frac{1}{2}$ inches at shoulder, 50 to 67 pounds; bitches, 19 to 21 inches, 36 to 55 pounds.

Color: Pure white; white and biscuit; cream. Black or black spots disqualify.

SCALE OF POINTS

General appearance	20
Head	15
Coat	10
Size	10
Chest and ribs	10
Hindquarters	10
Back	10
Feet	5
Legs	5
Tail	5
Total	100

ST. BERNARD

Descended from the huge dogs that fought in the Roman arenas, the modern St. Bernard is a peaceful, melancholy-looking animal. Average weight 165 pounds; height 28 inches. Coat long or short, white with red or brindle color.

Despite the classic pose of the St. Bernard with the flask of brandy at his throat, and the tradition that the breed has saved the lives of thousands of travelers in the Swiss mountain passes, there is little actual proof that a St. Bernard ever rescued anyone from a snow drift.

True, the dogs were bred and the breed preserved at the St. Bernard hospice high in the mountains, but so far as can be reliably established the dogs were merely used as guides over the passes and the alleged rescues can only be attributed to overzealous press-agentry.

As a rule, the St. Bernard is a gentle and placid dog and readily accepts training. In fact, one occasionally may be seen lumbering his way through the routine of an obedience training school. However, there have been occasional reports of vicious St. Bernards and an evil-tempered 165-pound dog with powerful jaws can mean real danger.

Though the breed has never been very numerous, largely because of the expense of feeding, there are enough fanciers of the breed to keep it up among the fifty most popular breeds, and it is usually well represented at the major dog shows.

While the long-coated variety is probably more popular in the United States, the short-coated variety is used in the Alps because their coats do not cake with snow.

St. Bernard (Rough)
Ch. Harvey's Zwingo Barri V Banz
Owner: Mrs. George M. Harvey. Syracuse, Indiana

St. Bernard (Smooth)
Ch. Terence of Sunny Slopes
Owner: Mrs. Alfred Wright, Jr. Darien, Connecticut

Like the other extremely large breeds, the St. Bernard is comparatively short-lived, particularly where he leads a confined life with little outdoor exercise.

Standard of the Breed

Short-Haired

General Appearance: Powerful, proportionately tall figure, strong and muscular in every part, with powerful head and most intelligent expression. In dogs with a dark mask the expression appears more stern, but never ill-natured.

Head: Like the body, very powerful and imposing. The massive skull is wide, slightly arched, and the sides slope in a gentle curve into the very strongly developed, high cheekbones. Occiput only moderately developed.

The supraorbital ridge is very strongly developed and forms nearly a right angle with the horizontal axis of the head.

Deeply imbedded between the eyes and starting at the root of the muzzle, a furrow runs over the whole skull. It is strongly marked in the first half, gradually disappearing toward the base of the occiput. The lines at the sides of the head diverge considerably from the outer corner of the eyes toward the back of the head.

The skin of the forehead, above the eyes, forms rather noticeable wrinkles, more or less pronounced, which converge toward the furrow. Especially when the dog is in action, the wrinkles are more visible without in the least giving the impression of morosity. Too strongly developed wrinkles are not desired.

The slope from the skull to the muzzle is sudden and rather steep.

The muzzle is short, does not taper, and the vertical depth at the root of the muzzle must be greater than the length of the muzzle. The bridge of the muzzle is not arched, but straight; in some dogs, occasionally, slightly broken.

A rather wide, well-marked, shallow furrow runs from the root of the muzzle over the entire bridge of the muzzle to the nose.

The flews of the upper jaw are strongly developed, not sharply cut, but turning in a beautiful curve into the lower edge, and slightly overhanging.

The flews of the lower jaw must not be deeply pendant.

The bite must be strong, and, in proportion to the conformation of the head, is only moderately developed.

A black roof to the mouth is desirable.

Nose: Very substantial, broad with wide-open nostrils, and, like the lips, always black.

Ears: Of medium size, rather high set, with very strongly developed burr at the base. They stand slightly away from the head at the base, then drop with a sharp bend to the side and cling to the head without a turn. The flap is tender and forms a rounded triangle, slightly elongated toward the point, the front edge lying firmly to the head, whereas the back edge may stand somewhat away from the head, especially when the dog is at attention. Lightly set ears, which at the base immediately cling to the head, give it an oval and too little marked exterior, whereas a strongly developed base gives the skull a squarer, broader and much more expressive appearance.

Eyes: Set moderately deep and more to the front than the sides, the eyes are of medium size, dark brown, with intelligent, friendly expression. The lower eyelids, as a rule, do not close completely and, if that is the case, form an angular wrinkle toward the inner corner of the eye. Eyelids which are too deeply pendant and conspicuously show the tear glands, or a very red, thick haw, and eyes that are too light, are objectionable.

Neck: Set high, very strong, and in action is carried erect. Otherwise horizontally or slightly downward. The junction of the head and neck is distinctly marked by an indentation. The nape of the neck is very muscular and rounded at the sides, which makes the neck appear rather short. The dewlap of the throat and neck is well-pronounced; too strong development, however, is not desirable.

Shoulders: Sloping and broad, very muscular and powerful. The withers are strongly pronounced.

Chest: Very well arched, moderately deep, not reaching below the elbows.

Back: Very broad, perfectly straight as far as the haunches, from there gently sloping to the rump, and merging imperceptibly into the root of the tail.

Hindquarters: Well developed. Legs very muscular.

Belly: Distinctly set off from the powerful loin section, only little drawn up.

Tail: Starting broad and powerful directly from the rump, the tail is long, very heavy, ending in a powerful tip. In repose it hangs straight down, turning gently upward in the lower third only, which is not considered a fault. In a great many specimens the tail is carried with the edge slightly bent and therefore hangs down in the shape of an "f." In action all dogs carry the tail more or less turned upward. However, it may not be carried too erect or by any means rolled over the back, slight curling of the tip is sooner admissible.

Forearms: Very powerful and extraordinarily muscular.

Forelegs: Straight, strong.

Hind Legs: Hocks of moderate angulation. Dewclaws are not desired; if present, they must not obstruct gait.

Feet: Broad, with strong toes, moderately closed, and with rather high knuckles. The so-called dewclaws which sometimes occur on the inside of the hind legs are imperfectly developed toes. They are of no use to the dog and are not taken into consideration in judging. They may be removed by surgery.

Coat: Very dense, short-haired, lying smooth, tough, without however feeling rough to the touch. The thighs are slightly bushy. The tail at the root has longer and denser hair which gradually becomes shorter toward the tip. The tail appears bushy, not forming a flag.

Color: White with red or red with white, the red in its various shades; brindle patches with white markings. The colors red and brown-yellow are of entirely equal value. Necessary markings are: white chest, feet and tip of tail, nose band, collar or spot on the nape; the latter and blaze are very desirable. Never of one color or without white. *Faults:* All other colors, except the favorite dark shadings on the head (mask) and ears. One distinguishes between mantle dogs and splash-coated dogs.

Height: Male, 27.56 inches minimum at shoulder; bitch, 25.59 inches. Female animals throughout are of a more delicate and finer build.

Faults: All deviations from the standard as, for instance, a sway-back and disproportionately long back; hocks too much bent; straight hindquarters; upward-growing hair in spaces between the toes; out at elbows; cow hocks and weak pasterns.

Long-Haired

Completely resembles the short-haired except for the coat, which is of medium length, plain to slightly wavy, never rolled or curly and not shaggy either. Usually on the back, especially from the region of the haunches to the rump, the hair is more wavy, a condition, by the way, that is slightly indicated in short-haired dogs.

The tail is bushy with dense hair of moderate length. Rolled or curly hair on the tail is not desirable. *Faults:* A tail with parted hair, a flag tail.

Face and ears are covered with short and soft hair; longer hair at the base of the ear is permissible. Forelegs only slightly feathered; thighs very bushy.

SHETLAND SHEEPDOG

Best known by the nickname of "sheltie," this dog is a native of the Shetland Islands, where all animals are small. Average weight 16 pounds, height 14 inches. Long, heavy coat, sable and white, tricolor or blue.

The Shetland sheepdog is an ideal solution for the family with limited space and a child who wants a "Lassie" for a pet; or for anyone who wants a collie in

Shetland Sheepdog
Ch. Pixie Bright Vision
Owner: Meadow Ridge Kennels. Stamford, Connecticut

reduced size. It is believed that the collie and the "sheltie" have a common ancestor and the breeders of the modern Shetland sheepdog have worked toward a dog which bears a great resemblance in coat and conformation to the collie.

The sheltie, also used to herd sheep, has the high intelligence of a working dog. For countless generations these dogs lived in the small cottages of their breeders and they have a strongly developed feeling for family life. However, they sometimes suffer skin ailments when kept indoors too much, and their coat requires frequent grooming to prevent skin ailments especially in warmer climates. Their real element seems to be where they can run in the snow and their lightness enables them to travel over snow where heavier dogs would founder.

Many shelties have been trained for obedience work and their herding aptitude makes them excellent guardians for young children. However, some strains show a tendency to pick fights with other dogs, and their watchdog background may lead them to excessive barking at noises outside the house or apartment.

Like the other working dogs, the Shetland sheepdog needs a lot of outdoor exercise to keep him in good physical condition and should get more than his few "walks" a day to keep him in trim and happy.

Standard of the Breed

The Shetland sheepdog, like the collie, traces to the border collie of Scotland, which, transported to the Shetland Islands and crossed with small, intelligent, long-haired breeds, was reduced to miniature proportions. Subsequently crosses were made from time to time with collies. The breed now bears the same relationship in size and general appearance to the rough collie as the Shetland pony does to some of the larger breeds of horses. Although the resemblance between the Shetland sheepdog and the rough collie is marked, there are differences which may be noted.

General Description: The Shetland sheepdog is a small, alert, rough-coated, long-haired working dog. He must be sound, agile and sturdy. The outline should be so symmetrical that no part appears out of proportion to the whole. Males should appear masculine; bitches feminine.

Size: The Shetland sheepdog should stand between 13 and 16 inches at the shoulder.

Coat: The coat should be double, the outer coat consisting of long, straight, harsh hair; the undercoat short, furry, and so dense as to give the entire coat its "stand off" quality. The hair on face, tips of ears and feet should be smooth. Mane and frill should be abundant, and particularly impressive in males. The forelegs well feathered, the hind legs heavily so, but smooth below the hock joint. Hair on tail profuse. *Note:* Excess hair on the ears, feet and hocks may be trimmed for the show ring. *Faults:* Coat short or flat in whole or part; wavy, curly, soft or silky; lack of undercoat; smooth coat.

Color: Black, blue merle, and sable (ranging from golden through mahogany); marked with varying amounts of white and/or tan. *Faults:* Rustiness in a black or a blue coat. Washed-out or degenerate colors, such as pale sable and faded blue. Self-color in the cases of blue merle, that is, without any merling or mottling and generally appearing as a faded or dilute tricolor. Conspicuous white spots. Specimens with more than 50 per cent white are severely penalized in shows; brindles are disqualified.

Temperament: The Shetland sheepdog is intensely loyal, affectionate, and responsive to his owner. However, he may be reserved toward strangers, but not to the point of showing fear or cringing in the ring. *Faults:* Shyness, timidity or nervousness. Stubborness, snappiness, or ill-temper.

Head: The head should be refined and its shape, when viewed from the top or side, be a long, blunt wedge, tapering slightly from ears to nose, which must be black.

Skull and Muzzle: Top of skull should be flat, showing no prominence at top of occiput. Cheeks should be flat and should merge smoothly into a well-rounded muzzle. Skull and muzzle should be of equal length, balance point being inner corner of eye. In profile, the top line of skull should parallel the top line of muzzle, but on a higher plane due to the presence of a slight but definite stop.

Jaws clean and powerful. The deep, well-developed underjaw, rounded at chin, should extend to base of nostril. Lips tight. Upper and lower lips must meet and fit smoothly together all the way around. Teeth level and evenly spaced. Scissors bite. *Faults:* Too-angled head. Too prominent stop or no stop. Overfull below, between, or above eyes. Prominent occiput crest. Domed skull. Prominent cheekbones. Snipy muzzle. Short, receding or shallow underjaw, lacking breadth and depth. Overshot or undershot, missing or crooked teeth. Teeth visible when mouth is closed.

Eyes: Medium size with dark, almond-shaped rims, set somewhat obliquely in skull. Color must be dark, with blue or merle eyes permissible in blue merles only. *Faults:* Light, round or too large or small eyes; prominent haws.

Ears: Small and flexible, placed high, carried three-fourths erect, with tips breaking forward. When in repose, the ears fold lengthwise and are thrown back into the frill. *Faults:* Set too low; hound ears; prick, bat or twisted ears; leather too thick or too thin.

Expression: Contours and chiseling of the head, the shape, set and use of ears, the placement and color of the eyes, combine to produce expression. Normally, the expression should be alert, gentle, intelligent and questioning. Toward strangers, the eyes should show watchfulness and reserve, but no fear.

Neck: Neck should be muscular, arched, and of sufficient length to carry the head proudly. *Faults:* Too short and thick.

Body: In over-all appearance the body should appear moderately long as measured from shoulder joint to rearmost extremity of the pelvic bone, but much of this length is actually due to the proper angulation and breadth of the shoulder and hindquarter, as the back itself should be comparatively short. Back should be level and strongly muscled.

Chest should be deep, the brisket reaching to point of elbow. The ribs should be well sprung, but flattened at their lower half to allow free play of the foreleg and shoulder. Abdomen moderately tucked up. *Faults:* Back too long; short, swayed, or roached. Barrel ribs. Slab sides, Chest narrow and/or too shallow.

Forequarters: From the withers the shoulder blades should slope at a 45-

degree angle forward and downward to the shoulder joint. At the withers they are separated only by the vertebra, but they must slope outward sufficiently to accommodate the desired spring of rib. The upper arm should join the shoulder blade as nearly as possible at a right angle. Elbow joint should be equidistant from the ground or from the withers. Forelegs straight, viewed from all angles, muscular and clean, and strong-boned. Pasterns very strong and sinewy. Dewclaws may be removed. *Faults:* Insufficient angulation between shoulder and upper arm. Upper arm too short. Lack of outward slope of shoulders. Loose shoulders. Turning in or out at elbows. Crooked legs. Light bone.

Feet (Front and Hind): Feet should be oval and compact, with the toes well arched and fitting tightly together. Pads deep and tough, nails hard and strong. *Faults:* Feet turning in or out. Splay feet, hare feet, cat feet.

Hindquarters: There should be a slight arch at the loins and the croup should slope gradually to the rear. The hipbone (pelvis) should be set at a 30-degree angle to the spine. The thigh should be broad and muscular. The thighbone should be set into the pelvis at a right angle, corresponding to the angle of the shoulder blade and upper arm. Stifle bones join the thighbone and should be distinctly angled at the stifle joint. The over-all length of the stifle should at least equal the length of the thighbone and preferably should slightly exceed it. Hock joint should be clean cut, angular, sinewy, with good bone and strong ligamentation. The hock should be short and straight, viewed from all angles. Dewclaws should be removed. *Faults:* Croup higher than withers; croup too straight or too steep; narrow thighs; cow hocks; hocks turning out; poorly defined hock joint.

Tail: The tail should be sufficiently long so that when it is laid along the back edge of the hind legs the last vertebra will reach the hock joint. Carriage of the tail at rest is straight down or in a slight upward curve. When the dog is alert, the tail is normally lifted but should not be carried forward over the back. *Faults:* Too short; twisted at end.

Gait: The trotting gait of the Shetland sheepdog should denote effortless speed and smoothness. There should be no jerkiness, nor stiff, stilted, up-and-down movement. The drive should be from the rear, true and straight, dependent upon correct angulation, musculature and ligamentation of the entire hindquarters, thus allowing the dog to reach well under his body with his hind foot and propel himself forward. Reach of the stride of the foreleg is also dependent upon correct angulation, musculature and ligamentation of the forequarters, together with correct width of chest and construction of rib cage. The foot should be raised only enough to clear the ground as the leg swings forward.

Viewed from the front, both forelegs and hind legs should move forward almost perpendicular to the ground at walk, slanting a little inward at a slow trot, until at a swift trot the feet are brought so far inward toward center line of body that the tracks left show two parallel lines of footprints actually touching a center line at their inner edges. There should be no crossing of the feet nor throwing of the weight from side to side. *Faults:* Stiff, short steps with a choppy, jerky movement. Mincing steps with a hopping up and down, or a balancing of weight from side to side. Lifting of front feet in hackney-like action, resulting in loss of speed and energy. Pacing gait.

SCALE OF POINTS

General appearance		25
Symmetry	10	
Temperament	10	
Coat	5	
Head		20
Skull and stop	5	
Muzzle	5	
Eyes, ears and expression	10	
Body		20
Neck and back	5	
Chest, ribs and brisket	10	
Loin, croup and tail	5	
Forequarters		15
Shoulders	10	
Forelegs and feet	5	
Hindquarters		15
Hip, thigh and stifle	10	
Hocks and feet	5	
Gait		5
Gait-smoothness and lack of waste motion when trotting-	5	
Total		100

WELSH CORGI (CARDIGAN AND PEMBROKE)

Cardigan: A low-slung herding dog, which is not believed to be related closely to the similar Pembroke. Average weight 21 pounds; height 12 inches. Short or medium coat, tan, black-and-tan, blue merle, may have white markings.

Pembroke: An old Welsh breed. Its longer legs and docked tail distinguish it from the Cardigan. Average weight 21 pounds; height 11 inches. Short coat, any color except white.

Smallest of the working dogs, these breeds met the needs of the hard-working Welsh farmers for a small, economical dog that could help herd their cattle, keep vermin off the farm, and indulge in a bit of rabbit poaching after hours.

Their names comes from the Welsh: *cor* (dwarf) and *gi* (dog), and they both work cattle in the same manner, driving the herd by nipping at their heels and then dropping flat to avoid the expected kick.

Although there was much cross-breeding at different times the two corgis have different ancestry. The Cardigan is believed to come from the dachshund family, while the Pembroke appears to be more of a spitz-wolf type, and both probably contain some collie and other herding-dog strains.

Both types of corgi are lively, alert, intelligent dogs that make fine house pets. However, although they are ranked among the twelve most popular breeds in England, and have been bred and exhibited in America since 1925, they are still down near the end of the most popular fifty breeds in the United

Cardigan Welsh Corgi
Swansea Jimm Dandy
Owner: Mrs. Margaret S. Douglas. Perkasie, Pennsylvania

Welsh Corgi (Pembroke)
Ch. Stormerbanks Tristam of Cote de Neige
Owner: Cote de Neige Kennels. Bedford Village, New York

States, with the dock-tailed Pembroke the more popular of the two. The dog owner who falls in the category of "status seeker" might follow the trend of the British royal family, which adopted the Pembroke as the favorite family pet in 1933.

Standard of the Breed

Welsh Corgi (Cardigan)

Head: Foxy in shape and appearance. Skull is fairly wide between the ears and flat, tapering toward the eyes. Muzzle about 3 inches in length (or in proportion to skull as 3:5) and tapering toward the snout. Nose rather pointed. Teeth strong, level and sound.

Eyes: Medium size, but giving a sharp and watchful expression, preferably dark in color but clear. Silver eyes permissible in blue merles.

Ears: Proportionate to size of dog and prominent; preferably pointed at the tips; moderately wide at the base; carried erect and set about 3½ inches apart and well back so that they can be laid flat along neck, sloping forward slightly when erect.

Neck: Fairly long and without throatiness, sitting into well-sloped and strong muscular shoulders.

Front: Slightly bowed, with strong bones; chest moderately broad with prominent breastbone.

Body: Fairly long and strong, with deep brisket, well-sprung ribs and clearly defined waist. Hindquarters strong, with muscular thighs.

Feet: Round and well-padded. Legs short and strong. Forelegs slightly bowed or straight; dewclaws removed.

Tail: Moderately long and set in line with body (not curled over back) and resembling that of a fox.

Coat: Short or medium, of hard texture. Any color except pure white. Other points being equal, preference to be given in the following order: red (sable, fawn or golden); brindle; black-and-tan; black-and-white; blue merle. White markings are considered to enhance the general appearance.

Height: As near as possible to 12 inches at the shoulder.

Weight: Males 18 to 25 pounds; bitches 15 to 22 pounds.

General Appearance and Expression: Foxy as possible; alertness essential; the body measuring about 34 to 36 inches from point of nose to tip of tail.

Faults (Examples): Overshot or undershot mouth; high, peaked occiput; prominent cheeks; low, flat forehead; expressionless eyes; crooked forearms; splayed feet; tail curled over; silky coat.

SCALE OF POINTS

Head	*15*
Eyes	*5*
Ears	*10*
Neck	*5*
Front	*10*
Body	*10*
Feet	*10*
Tail	*5*
Coat	*10*
Height	*10*
General appearance and expression	*10*
Total	*100*

Welsh Corgi (Pembroke)

General Appearance: Low-set, strong, sturdily built, alert and active, giving an impression of stamina and substance in a small space; outlook bold, expression intelligent and workmanlike. The movement should be free and active, elbows fitting closely to the side, neither loose nor tied. Forelegs should move well forward, without too much lift, in unison with the thrusting action of the hind legs.

Head and Skull: Head should be foxy in shape and appearance, with alert and intelligent expression, skull fairly wide and flat between the ears; moderate amount of stop. Length of foreface in proportion to the skull as 3:5. Muzzle slightly tapering; nose black.

Eyes: Well set, medium size, hazel in color and blending with color of coat.

Ears: Pricked, medium sized, slightly pointed. A line drawn from the tip of the nose through the eye should, if extended, pass through, or close to, the tip of the ear.

Mouth: Teeth level, or with inner side of the upper front teeth resting closely on the front of the under ones.

Neck: Fairly long.

Forequarters: Legs short and straight as possible, which means straight as soundness and deep chest will permit. It does not mean terrier-straight. Ample bone carried right down to the feet. Elbows should fit closely to the side, neither loose nor tied. Forearm should curve slightly round the chest.

Body: Of medium length, with well-sprung ribs. Not short-coupled or terrier-like. Level top line. Chest broad and deep, well let down between the forelegs.

Hindquarters: Strong and flexible, slightly tapering. Legs short. Ample bone carried right down to the feet. Hocks straight when viewed from behind.

Feet: Oval. The two center toes slightly in advance of the two outer toes, pads strong and well arched. Nails short.

Tail (a distinguishing feature): Short, preferably natural.

Coat: Of medium length and dense, not wiry.

Color: Solid colors in red, sable, fawn, black-and-tan, or with white markings on legs, chest and neck. Some white on head and foreface is permissible.

Weight and Size: Males 20 to 24 pounds; bitches 18 to 22 pounds. Height 10 to 12 inches at shoulder.

TERRIERS

Historically the dog of the peasant and farmer, these smaller breeds enjoyed hunting foxes and badgers and kept the farm and home free of rodents. Spunky and full of fire, they all have fighting hearts and fierce loyalty. Their breed name comes from *terra*—the earth—into whose burrows they would plunge after their prey.

AIREDALE TERRIER

Largest of the terriers, was one of the most popular dogs in the United States from 1905—1920; now regaining its place as a pet. Average weight 50 pounds; height 23 inches. Coat harsh and wiry, tan with black back and sides.

The largest of the twenty-one terrier breeds, the Airedale has the typical spunky "fire" of the terriers and the protective and hunting instincts that come from his old English ancestors. The larger terriers have been used since the Middle Ages as hunters of otter and other game, and the smaller terriers have long enjoyed fame as "ratters."

The distinctive traits of the Airedale make him strongly a one-man dog and he will almost invariably attach himself to one member of the family and show extremely strong protective tendencies. In fact, if anyone even speaks harshly to the Airedale's master the dog will rise with a growl and show every readiness to take prompt action. On the other hand, the Airedale does not readily attach himself to people and many spend a lifetime with a person without really forming any strong attachment to his master.

Aloof to strangers, the Airedale may attack a person coming into the home or on his master's property, and some are ready to pick a fight with any strange dog. While some of the American strains of Airedale have been "gentled," the owner of an Airedale should keep him under control at all times and should be especially careful not to allow younger members of the family to encourage the dog's belligerent tendencies.

The Airedale is one of the most sturdy breeds. In fact, many Airedale owners claim that they are practically indestructible and it is common for an Airedale to jump from a fast-moving automobile, shrug himself and take off after the car.

The fall in the breed's popularity may stem from the fact that they are not a "pretty" breed—except to their fanciers—and that the Airedale requires fairly constant grooming to keep him looking presentable.

In many parts of the country the Airedale is used in hunting bear, mountain lion and wolves, where their job is to move in for the kill. Although training an Airedale is a job that will call for persistent work and much patience, they have been used for police work in Germany and England and will respond to a persistent and firm trainer.

Airedale
American and Canadian Ch. Airline Star Monarch
Owners: Mr. and Mrs. Charles W. Marck. El Cajon, California

Standard of the Breed

Head: Should be well balanced with little apparent difference between the length of skull and foreface.

Skull: Long and flat, not too broad between the ears and narrowing very slightly to the eyes. Scalp should be free from wrinkles, stop hardly visible, and cheeks level and free from fullness.

Ears: V-shaped with carriage rather to the side of the head, not pointing to the eyes; small, but not out of proportion to the size of the dog. The top line of the folded ear should be above the level of the skull.

Foreface: Deep, powerful, strong and muscular. Should be well filled up before the eyes.

Eyes: Dark, small, not prominent, full of terrier expression, keenness and intelligence.

Lips: Tight.

Nose: Black and not too small.

Teeth: Strong and white, free from discoloration or defect. Bite either level or viselike. A slightly overlapping or scissors bite is permissible, without preference.

Neck: Of moderate length and thickness, gradually widening toward the shoulders. Skin tight, not loose.

Shoulders and Chest: Shoulders long and sloping well into the back. Shoulder blades flat. From the front, chest deep not broad. The depth of the chest should be approximately on a level with the elbows.

Body: Back should be short, strong and level. Ribs well sprung. Loins muscular and of good width. There should be but little space between the last rib and the hip joint.

Hindquarters: Strong and muscular with no droop.

Tail: The root of the tail should be set well up on the back. It should be carried gaily, but not curled over the back. Should be of good substance and of fair length.

Legs: Forelegs should be perfectly straight, with plenty of muscle and bone.

Elbows: Perpendicular to the body, working free of sides.

Thighs: Long and powerful, with muscular second-thigh stifles well bent, not turned either in or out, hocks well let down, parallel with each other when viewed from behind.

Feet: Small and compact, round, with good depth of pad, well cushioned toes moderately arched, not turned in or out.

Coat: Hard, dense and wiry, lying straight and close, covering the dog well over the body and legs. Some of hardest hairs crinkling or just slightly waved. At the base of the hard stiff hair should be a shorter coat of softer hair termed the undercoat.

Color: Head and ears, tan; the ears a darker shade than the rest. Dark markings on either side of the skull are permissible. The legs up to the thighs and elbows and the underpart of the body and chest are also tan, and the tan frequently runs into the shoulder. The sides and upper parts of the body should be black or dark grizzle. A red mixture is often found in the black and is not objectionable. A small white blaze on the chest is a characteristic of certain strains of the breed.

Size: Males should measure about 23 inches at the shoulder; bitches slightly less. Both sexes should be sturdy, well muscled and well boned.

Movement: Movement or action is the crucial test of conformation. Movement should be free. As seen from the front the forelegs should swing perpendicular from the body free from the sides, the feet the same distance apart as the elbows. Seen from the rear, the hind legs should be parallel with each other, neither too close nor too far apart, but so placed as to give a strong, well-balanced stance and movement. The toes should not be turned in or out.

Faults: Yellow eyes, hound ears, white feet, soft coat, over- or undersize, poor movement.

Note: Use of foreign substances to improve the appearance of the dog in the show ring, such as coloring, dilating the pupils or stiffening of the coat is a violation of show rules.

SCALE OF POINTS

Head	*10*
Neck, shoulders and chest	*10*
Body	*10*
Hindquarters and tail	*10*
Legs and feet	*10*
Coat	*10*
Color	*5*
Size	*10*
Movement	*10*
General characteristics and expression	*15*
Total	*100*

BEDLINGTON TERRIER

This dog that looks like a lamb was named for the English mining region where they were used as ratters in the nineteenth century. Average weight 23 pounds; height 16 inches. Thick coat, trimmed to smoothness, blue-gray, tan or liver color.

This terrier's disposition and temperament completely belie his appearance. His breed was originated by the tough coal miners of Bedlington, Northumberland, England, for their after-hour crude sports. An inbreeding of whippet gave him his roached back and his speed. Many a day's pay was won and lost in informal dog races by the miners. From the Dandie Dinmont terrier, the Bedlington inherited a fighting temperament that made him a fierce vermin killer and a tough opponent in a dog fight.

The spirited appearance of the Bedlington, which does not show on a

Bedlington Terrier
Ch. Jo-Fran's Ensign
Owner: John Howland. Clearwater, Florida

photograph, but must be actually seen makes him an excellent choice for the person who wants a dog that is full of life. Although the Bedlington is still fairly new to the United States—the first were brought over in the early 1900's —the breed has made a big impact in the show ring, winning "best of show" at some of the most important breed shows.

As a house pet, the Bedlington becomes devoted to his own family, and has a strong protective feeling toward young children. Like most of the terriers, however, he may regard any other dog as a natural enemy, although he can be trained to tolerate them.

Of the different color varieties, the blue-gray is the most popular.

Standard of the Breed

Skull: Narrow, but deep and rounded, high at the occiput, wedge-shaped, covered with profuse topknot, which should be nearly white, and, when trimmed, should give a Roman-nose appearance.

Jaws: Long and tapering. There must be no stop, and the line from occiput to nose end should be straight and unbroken. Well filled up beneath the eye. Close-fitting lips, no flews.

Teeth: Level or pincer-jawed. The teeth should be large and strong.

Nose: Nostrils large and well-defined. Blues and blue-and-tans have black noses; livers and sandies have brown noses.

Eye: Small, bright and well sunken. The ideal eyes have the appearance of being triangular. Blue should have a dark eye; blue-and-tans have light eyes with amber lights; livers and sandies have a light hazel eye.

Ears: Moderate-sized, filbert-shaped; set on low and hanging flat to the cheek. They should be covered with short, fine hair, with a fringe of silky hair at the tip.

Legs and Feet: Muscular and moderate length. The hind legs, by reason of the roach-back and arched loin, have the appearance of being longer than the forelegs. The forelegs should be straight, with a moderately wide chest and hare feet.

Body: Muscular, yet markedly flexible. Flat-ribbed and deep through the brisket, well ribbed. The chest should be deep and fairly broad. The back should be roached and the loin markedly arched. Light, muscular, galloping quarters, which are also fine and graceful.

Neck: Long, tapering, arched, deep at the base. The neck should spring well from the shoulders, which should be flat, and the head should be carried high.

Coat: The coat is distinctive and unlike that of other terriers; should be thick and linty (not wiry), and when in show condition, should not exceed one inch in length.

Tail: Of moderate length, thick at the root, tapering to a point and gracefully curved, slightly feathered, 9 to 11 inches long, scimitar-shaped, carried elevated but not over the back.

Color: Blue, blue-and-tan, liver, liver-and-tan, sandy, sandy-and-tan.

Height: About 15 to 16 inches.

Weight: Males about 24 pounds; bitches about 22 pounds.

Action: Very distinctive. Rather mincing, light and springy, must gallop like a greyhound, with the whole body.

General: A graceful, lithe but not shelly, muscular dog, with no sign of coarseness or weakness. The whole head should appear pear-shaped or wedge-shaped. When roused, the eyes should sparkle and the dog look full of temper and courage.

SCALE OF POINTS

Head	*20*
Size	*10*
Teeth	*10*
Color	*5*
Legs and feet	*10*
Ears	*5*
Nose	*5*
Body	*15*
Coat	*10*
Tail	*5*
Eyes	*5*
Total	*100*

CAIRN TERRIER

This rugged working terrier was named after the cairns, or rocky piles, into which it burrows after game. Average weight 14 pounds; height 10 inches. Harsh outer coat and soft inner coat; wheaten, tan or grizzle color.

Smallest of the Scottish terriers, the cairn is believed to be the ancestor of many of the other popular small terriers. Since his first appearance in this country about 1913, he has gradually moved up the popularity scale, although he is still rare enough for his owner to be asked, "What is it?"

In disposition, the cairn is definitely a one-man dog, always lively and eager to please his master, somewhat aloof with strangers, and an excellent watchdog with a shrill, loud bark to attract attention or give the alarm.

The double coat of the cairn, similar to that of the sled dogs and German shepherd, keeps him comfortable in all weather and he can be kenneled out-doors with no ill effects. The naturally shaggy coat of this breed requires little care, although his shedding may pose a problem for the overly fastidious house-wife.

A quick way for the novice to distinguish the cairn from some of the similar small terriers is to look at the head. The cairn's head has a definitely catlike appearance, with a shorter, wider muzzle than in the other terriers.

Standard of the Breed

General Appearance: An active, game, hardy, small working terrier of the short-legged class; very free in its movements, strongly but not heavily built, standing well forward on its forelegs; deep in the ribs, well coupled with

Cairn Terrier
English and American Ch. Thistleclose MacGregor of Caithness
Owner: Mrs. Ralph E. Stone. Cross River, New York

strong hindquarters and presenting a well-proportioned build with a medium length of back. It has a weather-resistant coat. The head is shorter and wider than in any other terrier, and is well furnished with hair, giving a general foxy expression.

Skull: Broad in proportion to length, with a decided stop, top of the head well furnished with hair, which may be somewhat softer than the body coat.

Muzzle: Strong, but not too long or heavy.

Teeth: Large; mouth neither overshot nor undershot.

Nose: Black.

Eyes: Set wide apart, rather sunken, with shaggy eyebrows, medium in size, hazel or dark hazel in color, depending on body color, with a keen terrier expression.

Ears: Small, pointed, carried well erect, set wide apart on the side of the head. Free from long hairs.

Tail: In proportion to head, well furnished with hair, but not feathery. Carried gaily but must not curl over back. Set on at back level.

Body: Well-muscled, strong, active, with well-sprung, deep ribs, coupled to strong hindquarters, with a level back of medium length, giving an impression of strength and activtity without heaviness.

Shoulders, Legs and Feet: A sloping shoulder, medium length of leg, good but not too heavy bone; forelegs should not be out at elbows, and be perfectly straight, but forefeet may be slightly turned out. Forefeet larger than hind feet. Legs must be covered with hard hair. Pads should be thick and strong and the dog should stand well up on its feet.

Coat: Hard and weather-resistant. Must be double-coated with profuse harsh outer coat and short, soft, close furry undercoat.

Color: May be any color except white. Dark ears, muzzle and tail tip are desirable.

Ideal Size: Involves the weight, the height at the withers and the length of body. Weight for bitches 13 pounds; for males, 14 pounds. Height at withers: bitches $9\frac{1}{2}$ inches; males, 10 inches. Length of body $14\frac{1}{4}$ to 15 inches from the front of chest to back of hindquarters. The dog must be of balanced proportions and appear neither leggy nor too low to ground; and neither too short nor too long in body. Weight and measurements are for mature dogs at two years of age. Older dogs may weigh slightly more, and growing dogs may be under these weights and measurements.

Condition: Dogs should be shown in good, hard flesh, well muscled, neither too fat nor too thin. Should be in full, good coat with plenty of head furnishings, be clean, combed, brushed and tidied up on ears, tail, feet and general outline. Should move freely and easily on a loose lead, should not cringe on being handled, should stand up on their toes and show marked terrier characteristics.

Faults

Skull: Too narrow.

Muzzle: Too long and heavy a foreface; mouth overshot or undershot.

Eyes: Too large, prominent, yellow or ringed.

Ears: Too large, round at points, set too close together, set too high on the head, heavily covered with hair.

Legs and Feet: Too light or too heavy bone. Crooked forelegs or out at elbows. Thin, ferrety feet; feet let down on the heel or too open and spread. Too high or too low on the leg.

Body: Too short back and compact body. Too long, weedy and snaky body. Tail set on too low. Back not level.

Coat: Open coat, blousy coat, too short or dead coat, lack of sufficient undercoat, lack of head furnishings, lack of hard hair on the legs; silkiness or curliness. A slight wave is permissible.

Nose: Flesh or light-colored nose.

Color: White on chest, feet or other parts of body.

FOX TERRIER

In England the fox terrier was used to dig foxes from their burrows, being carried by the horse-borne riders in a basket and released when the fox was run to earth. Average weight 17 pounds; height 15 inches. Coat smooth or wiry, white with black-and-tan markings.

First brought to the United States in 1875, the fox terrier has become the most popular terrier according to American Kennel Club registrations. (The Boston terrier, which outranks him, is not considered a terrier.)

An ideal size for a family pet, the fox terrier that we know today is a lively, highly sociable and affectionate dog and one of the most attractive of the terriers. Drawings of the early fox terriers show a rougher-looking dog, but when the English fanciers began entering the breed in shows they bred for a more refined dog with a longer head and legs, which has carried over into the American strains.

The modern fox terrier represents a mingling of various older breeds. His ancestory includes beagle, bull terrier, greyhound, and black-and-tan working terriers which contributed the smooth- and wire-haired coats. And he seems to have acquired the most desirable character traits from his different ancestors.

The breed has distinguished itself in shows in the country. The records of the Westminster Kennel Club show that more fox terriers have taken "best in show" than any other breed. During the 1920's the fox terriers were at the peak of their popularity among purebred registrations and they are still among the top fifth. In addition, a large number of mixed-breed dogs have a good proportion of fox terrier and their actual popularity is probably greater than is indicated by the A.K.C. registrations.

Standard of the Breed

Smooth-haired

Head: The skull flat and moderately narrow, gradually decreasing in width to the eyes. Not much stop should be apparent, but there should be more dip in the profile between the forehead and the top jaw than is seen in a greyhound. The cheeks must not be full. The ears should be V-shaped, small, of moderate

Wire Fox Terrier
Ch. Copper Beech Storm
Owner: Mrs. Frederick H. Dutcher. Stamford, Connecticut

Smooth Fox Terrier
Ch. Top Brass of Andely
Owner: William J. Holdebrandt, Jr. Jacksonville, Florida

thickness, drooping close to the cheek, not hanging by the side of the head as do a foxhound's. The top line of the folded ear should be well above the level of the skull.

The jaws, upper and lower, should be strong and muscular and of fair punishing strength, but not so as in any way to resemble the greyhound or modern English terrier. There should not be much falling away below the eyes. This part of the head, however, should be moderately chiseled out so as not to go down in a straight slope like a wedge.

The nose, toward which the muzzle must gradually taper, should be black. Although the foreface should gradually taper from eye to muzzle and should tip slightly at its juncture with the forehead, it should not "dish" or fall away quickly below the eyes, where it should be full and well up, but relieved from "wedginess" by a little delicate chiseling.

The eyes and the rims should be dark in color, moderately small and rather deep-set, full of fire, life and intelligence and as nearly as possible circular in shape. Anything approaching a yellow eye is most objectionable.

The teeth should be as nearly as possible together with the points of the upper incisors on the outside of, or slightly overlapping the lower teeth.

There should be apparent little difference in length between the skull and foreface of a well-balanced head.

Neck: Should be clean and muscular, without throatiness, of fair length, and gradually widening to the shoulders.

Shoulders: Should be long and sloping, well laid back, fine at the points, and clearly cut at the withers.

Chest: Deep and not broad.

Back: Should be straight (level) and strong, with no appearance of slackness. Brisket should be deep, yet not exaggerated.

Loin: Should be very powerful, muscular and very slightly arched. The fore ribs should be moderately arched, the back ribs deep and well sprung and the dog well ribbed up.

Hindquarters: Should be strong and muscular, free from droop or crouch; the thighs long and powerful; stifles well curved and turned neither in nor out; hocks well bent and near the ground, perfectly parallel and upright when viewed from the rear, the dog standing well up on them like a foxhound, and not straight in the stifle. The worst possible form of hindquarters consists of a short second thigh and a straight stifle.

Tail: Should be set on rather high and carried gaily, but not over the back or curled. It should be of good length, anything approaching a "pipe-stopper" tail being especially objectionable.

Legs: The forelegs viewed from any direction must be straight, with bone strong right down to the feet, showing little or no appearance of ankle in front, and short and straight in pasterns. Both forelegs and hind legs should be carried straight forward in traveling, the stifles not turning outward. The elbows should hang perpendicular to the body, working free of the sides.

Feet: Should be compact, round and not large; the soles hard and tough; the toes moderately arched and turned neither in nor out.

Coat: Should be smooth, flat but hard, dense and abundant. The belly and underside of thigh should not be bare.

Color: White should predominate; brindles, red or liver markings are objectionable. Otherwise this point is of little or no importance.

Symmetry, Size and Character: The dog must present a generally gay, lively and active appearance. Bone and strength in a small compass are essentials, but the fox terrier should not be cloddy or in any way coarse. Speed and endurance must be looked to as well as power and the symmetry of the foxhound he takes as a model. The terrier, like the hound, must never be leggy, nor should he be too long in the leg. He should stand like a cleverly made hunter, covering a lot of ground, yet with a short back. He will then attain the highest degree of propelling power, together with the greatest length of stride that is compatible with the length of his body. Weight is not a certain criterion of a terrier's fitness for his work—general size, contour, shape are the main points; and if a dog can gallop and stay, and if he can follow a fox up a drain, it matters little what his weight is to a pound or so.

According to present requirements, a full-sized, well-balanced male should not exceed 15½ inches at the withers, the bitch being proportionately lower—nor should the length of back from withers to root of tail exceed 12 inches; while, to maintain the relative proportions, the head should not exceed 7¼ inches or be less than 7 inches. A male with these measurements should scale 18 pounds in show condition—a bitch weighing some two pounds less, with a margin of one pound either way.

Balance: This may be defined as the correct proportions of a certain point or points, when considered in relation to certain other point or points. It is the keystone of the terrier's anatomy. The chief points for consideration are the relative proportions of skull and foreface; head and back; height at withers and length of body from shoulder-point to buttock—the ideal of proportion being when the last two measurements are the same. It should be added that, although the head measurements can be taken with absolute accuracy, the height at withers and length of back and coat are approximate and are included for the information of breeders and exhibitors rather than as a hard-and-fast rule.

Movement: Movement or action is the crucial test of conformation. The fox terrier's legs should be carried straight forward while traveling, the forelegs hanging perpendicular and swinging parallel with the sides, like the pendulum of a clock. The principal propulsive power is furnished by the hind legs, perfection of action being found in the terrier possessing long thighs and muscular second thighs well bent at the stifles, which admit of a strong forward thrust or "snatch" of the hocks. When approaching, the forelegs should form a continuation of the straight line of the front, the feet being the same distance apart as the elbows. When stationary, it is often difficult to determine whether a dog is out at the shoulder, but directly he moves, the defect—if it exists— becomes apparent, the forefeet having a tendency to cross, "weave" or "dish." When, on the contrary, the dog is tied at the shoulder, the tendency of the feet is to move wider apart, with a sort of paddling action. When the hocks are turned in (cow hocks), the stifles and feet are turned outward, resulting in a serious loss of propulsive power. When the hocks are turned inward, the tendency of the hind feet is to cross, resulting in an unsightly waddle.

Old scars or injuries, the result of work or accident, should not prejudice a terrier's chances in the show ring, unless they interfere with his movement or with his utility for work or stud.

Wire-haired

This variety of the breed should resemble the smooth sort in every respect except the coat. The harder and more wiry the texture of the coat is, the better. On no account should the dog feel or look woolly; and there should be no silky hair about the poll or elsewhere. The coat should not be too long, so as not to give the dog a shaggy appearance, but, at the same time, it should show a marked and distinct difference all over from the smooth species.

SCALE OF POINTS

Head and ears	*15*
Neck	*5*
Shoulders and Chest	*10*
Back and loin	*10*
Hindquarters	*15*
Stern (tail)	*5*
Legs and feet	*15*
Coat	*15*
Symmetry, size and character	*10*
Total	*100*

Disqualifications: Nose: White, cherry, or spotted to a considerable extent with either of these colors. *Ears:* Prick, tulip or rose. *Mouth:* Much undershot or much overshot.

IRISH TERRIER

A smaller version of the huge Irish wolfhound, the Irish terrier has been used as messenger dog in wartime. It is a reckless and courageous breed. Average weight 25 pounds; height 18 inches. Wiry, red coat.

Patriotic Irishmen trace the origin of this breed to the Emerald Isle where it appeared in the early 1800's. Like most of the other terriers its early parentage was mixed, but for about 150 years it has been a distinct breed.

Strictly a working terrier, the dog is hardy and able to work in any weather, with good endurance, and won its keep by killing rats for the Irish farmers. In addition, the Irish terrier can be trained as a sporting dog and can learn to retrieve on land and from water or go after badgers or other ground game.

Its wiry coat is protection against brush and brambles and it has even been used in Africa by lion hunters. Fortunately, this powerful-jawed breed confines its hostile attitude to four-legged adversaries. Toward humans, he has a strongly protective attitude, and while young is a good playmate for children. As he matures, however, the Irish terrier takes on a quiet dignity and reserve.

Like other Irish dogs (and Irish horses) the Irish terrier may suffer from cracked and horny pads, especially in dry and hot weather, and this tendency seems to be inherited. If possible, try to acquire an Irish terrier bred from parents with sound feet.

Standard of the Breed

Head: Long, but in nice proportion to the rest of the body; the skull flat, rather narrow between the ears, and narrowing slightly toward the eyes; free from wrinkle, with the stop hardly noticeable except in profile. The jaws must be strong and muscular, but not too full in the cheek and of good punishing length. The foreface must not fall away appreciably between or below the eyes; instead, the modeling should be delicate and in contradistinction, for example, to the fullness of foreface of the greyhound. An exaggerated foreface which is out of proportion to the length of skull from the occiput to the stop, disturbs the proper balance of the head and is not desirable. Also, the head of exaggerated length usually accompanies oversize or disproportionate length of body, or both, and such conformation is not typical. On the other

Irish Terrier
Ch. Derg Mr. Tipperary
Owner: Elizabeth Gillespie. New York, New York

hand, the foreface should not be noticeably shorter than is the skull from occiput to stop. Excessive muscular development of the cheeks, or bony development of the temples, conditions which are described by the fancier as "cheeky," or "strong in head," or "thick in skull" are objectionable. The "bumpy" or "alligator" head, sometimes described as the "taneous" head, in which the skull presents two lumps of bony structure with or without indentations above the eyes, is unsightly and to be faulted. The hair on the upper and lower jaws should be similar in quality and texture to that on the body, and only of sufficient length to present an appearance of additional strength and finish to the foreface. The profuse, goatlike beard is unsightly and undesirable, and almost invariably it betokens the objectionable linty and silken hair in the coat.

Teeth: Strong and even, white and sound, neither overshot nor undershot.
Nose: Black.
Eyes: Dark hazel in color; small, not prominent; full of life, fire and intelligence. Light or yellow eye most objectionable.

Ears: Small, V-shaped, of moderate thickness, set well on head, dropping forward closely to the cheek. The ear must be free of fringe, and the hair much shorter and somewhat darker than on the body. A "dead" ear, houndlike in appearance, must be severely penalized as it is not characteristic of the Irish terrier. An ear which is too slightly erect is undesirable.

Neck: Should be of fair length and gradually widening toward the shoulders, well and proudly carried. Free from throatiness. Generally there is a slight frill in the hair at each side of neck, extending almost to the corner of the ear.

Shoulders and Chest: Shoulders must be fine, long and sloping well into the back. The chest, deep and muscular, but neither full nor wide.

Back and Loin: The body should be moderately long—neither too long nor too short. The short back, so coveted and so appealing in the fox terrier is *not* characteristic of the Irish terrier. The back must be symmetrical, strong and straight, and free from an appearance of slackness or "dip" behind the shoulders. The loin strong and muscular, and slightly arched. The ribs fairly sprung, deep rather than round, with a well-ribbed back. The bitch may be slightly longer in appearance than the male.

Hindquarters: Strong and muscular; powerful thighs; hocks near the ground; stifles moderately bent.

Stern: Should be docked, and set on rather high, but not curled. It should be of good strength and substance; of fair length and well-covered with harsh, rough hair, and free from fringe or feather. The three-quarters dock is about right.

Feet and Legs: The feet should be strong, tolerably round, and moderately small; toes arched and turned neither in nor out, with black toenails. The pads should be deep but not hard, with a pleasing velvety quality, and perfectly sound; they must be entirely free from cracks or horny excrescences. "Corny feet," so called, are a serious blemish. Legs are moderately long, well set from the shoulders, perfectly straight, with plenty of bone and muscle; the elbows working clear of the sides; pasterns short, straight and hardly noticeable. Forelegs and hind legs should move straight forward when traveling; the stifles should not turn outward. Cow hocks are a serious fault. Legs should be free from feather and covered, like the head, with hair of similar texture to that on body, but not as long.

Coat: Dense and wiry in texture, rich in quality, having a broken appearance, yet lying fairly close to the body, the hair growing so closely and strongly together that when parted with the fingers the skin is hardly visible; free of softness, and not so long as to alter the outline of the body, particularly in the hindquarters. At the base of the stiff outer coat there should be a growth of finer and softer hair, differing in color, termed the undercoat. Single coats which are without any undercoat, and wavy coats, are undesirable; the curly coat is most objectionable. On the sides of the body, the coat is never as harsh as on the back and quarters, but it should be plentiful and of good texture.

Color: Whole-colored; the bright red, red wheaten, or golden red colors are preferable. A small patch of white on the chest, frequently encountered in all whole-colored strains, is permissible but not desirable. White on any other part of the body is faulted.

Size, Symmetry: The most desirable weight for showing is 27 pounds for the male and 25 pounds for the bitch. The shoulder height should be about 18 inches. The Irish terrier must be active, lithe and wiry in movement, with great animation. He should be sturdy and strong in substance and bone structure but at the same time free from clumsiness, for speed, power and endurance are desired. He must be neither "cobby" nor "cloddy," but should be built on lines of speed, with a graceful, racing outline.

Temperament: The Irish terrier is game and asks no quarter. He is of good temper, most affectionate and absolutely loyal. Tender and forebearing with those he loves, this rugged, stout-hearted terrier will guard his master, his mistress, children in his charge, or their possessions, with unflinching courage and with utter contempt of danger or hurt. His life is one continuous and eager offering of loyal and faithful companionship and devoted, loving service. He is ever on guard, and stands between his house and all that threatens.

SCALE OF POINTS

Head, ears, expression	*20*
Legs and feet	*15*
Neck	*5*
Shoulder and chest	*10*
Back and loin	*5*
Hindquarters and stern	*10*
Coat	*15*
Color	*10*
Size, symmetry	*10*
Total	*100*

Negative Points

White nails, toes and feet	*—10*
Much white on chest	*—10*

Dark shadings on face	— 5
Mouth undershot or cankered	—10
Coat shaggy, curly or soft	—10
Uneven in color	— 5
Total	—50

Disqualifications: Nose any color other than black. Mouth much undershot or overshot. Cropped ears. Any disallowed color or parti-color.

KERRY BLUE TERRIER

Known in Ireland as the Irish blue, this is the national dog of the Irish Republic. Has been known for about 200 years as a farm dog and hunter. Average weight 35 pounds; height 18 inches. Dense, wavy coat; gunmetal to steel blue in color.

This bushy-browed breed is more adaptable than many of the terriers. In Ireland, he is still used as a working terrier, and there he may not win a bench championship without first qualifying in a field trial.

In England and America, he has proved superb as a companion dog, becoming an affectionate family member and a conscientious watchdog, and fitting equally well into city or country life.

He responds well to training and a number of Kerries have won their obedience degrees. In England, being widely used in hunting, he has proved himself a good trailer and retriever as well as being willing to go "to earth" after rodents. In a number of English cities he has been used successfully in police work.

For breed or show purposes, the color of the Kerry's coat is important; black or greenish blue shading being considered serious faults. However, the Kerry is usually black at birth and the color gradually clears until the age of eighteen months when the adult colors should be evident.

Some of the old-time Kerry breeders were known to prefer dogs with a black roof of the mouth and black gums as indications of proper pigmentation in the strain.

Standard of the Breed

Head: Long but not exaggerated, and in good proportion to the rest of the body. Well balanced, with little apparent difference between the length of the skull and foreface—20 points.

Kerry Blue Terrier
Ch. Gered's Bean Admarach
Owner: Mrs. Edward Loebe. Glencoe, Illinois

Skull: Flat, with very slight stop, of but moderate breadth between the ears and narrowing very slightly to the eyes.

Cheeks: Clean and level, free from bumpiness.

Ears: V-shaped, small but not out of proportion to the size of the dog, of moderate thickness, carried forward close to the cheeks with the top of the folded ear slightly above the level of the skull. A "dead" ear, houndlike in appearance, is undesirable.

Nose: Black, nostrils large and wide.

Teeth: Strong, white and either level or with the upper teeth (incisors) slightly overbiting the lower teeth. An undershot mouth is severely penalized.

Eyes: Dark, small, not prominent, well placed and with a keen terrier expression. Anything approaching a yellow eye is very undesirable.

Neck: Clean and moderately long, gradually widening to the shoulders upon which it should be well set and carried proudly—5 points.

Shoulders and Chest: Shoulders fine, long and sloping, well laid back and well knit. Chest deep and of but moderate length—10 points.

Legs and Feet: Legs moderately long with plenty of bone and muscle. The forelegs should be straight from both front and side view, with the elbows hanging perpendicular to the body and working clear of the sides in movement. Pasterns short, straight and hardly noticeable. Both forelegs and hind legs should move straight out when traveling. Stifles turning neither in nor out—10 points.

Feet should be compact, strong, fairly round and moderately small, with good depth of pad, free from cracks, toes arched, turned neither in nor out, with black toenails.

Body: Back short, strong and straight (level), with no appearance of slackness. Loin short and powerful with a slight tuck-up, the ribs fairly well sprung, deep rather than round—10 points.

Hindquarters and Stern: Hindquarters strong and muscular with full freedom of action, free from droop or crouch; thighs long and powerful; stifles well bent and turned neither in nor out; hocks near the ground, and, when viewed from behind, upright and parallel with each other, the dog standing well up on them. Tail should be set on high, of moderate length and carried gaily erect, the straighter the tail the better—10 points.

Color: The correct mature color is any shade of blue-gray or gray-blue, from deep slate to light blue-gray, of a fairly uniform color throughout, except that distinctly darker to black parts may appear on the muzzle, head, ears, tail and feet—10 points.

Kerry blue color, in its process of "clearing" from an apparent black at birth to the mature gray-blue or blue-gray, passes through one or more transitions— involving a very dark blue (darker than deep slate), shades or tinges of brown, and mixtures of these, together with a progressive infiltration of the correct mature color.

Up to eighteen months, such deviations from the correct mature color are permissible without preference and without regard for uniformity. Thereafter, deviation from it to any significant extent must be severely penalized.

Solid black is never permissible in the show ring. Up to eighteen months any doubt whether a dog is black or a very dark blue should be resolved in favor of the dog, especially in the case of a puppy. Black on the muzzle, head, ears, tail and feet is permissible at any age.

Coat: Soft, dense and wavy. A harsh, wire or bristle coat should be severely penalized. In show trim, the body should be well covered but tidy, with the head (except for whiskers) and the ears and cheeks clear—15 points.

General Conformation and Character: The typical Kerry blue terrier should be upstanding, well knit and in good balance, showing a well-developed and muscular body with definite terrier style and character throughout. A low-slung Kerry is not typical—10 points.

Height: The ideal height for a Kerry blue is 18½ inches at the withers for the male, slightly less for the bitch. Acceptable limits are 17½–20 inches for the male; 17–19½ for the bitch.

Weight: The most desirable weight for a fully developed male is 33 to 40 pounds, bitches weighing proportionately less.

SCALE OF POINTS

Head	*20*
Neck	*5*
Shoulders and chest	*10*
Legs and feet	*10*
Body	*10*
Hindquarters and stern	*10*
Color	*10*
Coat	*15*
General conformation and character	*10*
Total	*100*

Disqualifications: Solid black color. Faking or dyeing. Dewclaws on hind legs.

MINIATURE SCHNAUZER

An old German breed, has been noted as ratters and pets since the 1400's. The miniature is the smallest of the three types of schnauzer. Average weight 15 pounds, height 12 inches. Coat wiry with colors varying from pepper-and-salt to black.

Although classed as a terrier by the American Kennel Club, the schnauzer is actually a dog of mixed ancestry containing some poodle in his background, which may account for his mixed disposition. Terrier-like in many ways, the schnauzer is much more adaptable to training than the other terriers and has a strong desire to do what his master wants. In recent years, many miniature schnauzers have done remarkably well in obedience training and in obedience trials, and their happy appearance in the show ring and obvious enjoyment of working with their handler has done much to spur the popularity of the breed.

Like the other terriers, he is often aloof with strangers, but is more likely

Miniature Schnauser
Ch. Jonaire Pocono Rock 'n Roll
Owner: Jonaire Kennels. Mt. Pocono, Pennsylvania

to fit in with the family group, besides picking out one family member as his "person." However, he is always able to combine the characteristics of a family pet with his ingrained "ratting" ability. In Germany some of the breed clubs still hold "ratting" trials, and the miniature often surpasses the giant and medium schnauzers in rat-catching.

In many respects, he is an ideal city dog, although he may become bored if left alone in an apartment too long and become destructive and noisy. His compact size and proportions make him one of the better-looking terrier-type dogs, and the distinctive whiskers on his muzzle from which he gets his name (*Schnauze* means muzzle) give him an especially appealing look. With a little training he will trot along at his master's side without a leash even on a crowded city sidewalk.

Standard of the Breed

The miniature schnauzer is a robust, active dog of the terrier type, resembling his larger cousin, the medium schnauzer, in general appearance, and of an alert, active disposition. He should be sturdily built, nearly square in proportion of body length to height, with plenty of bones, less racy in outline than a fox terrier, and without any suggestion of toyishness.

Head: Should be strong and rectangular, diminishing slightly from the ear to the eyes, and again to tip of the nose. The skull should be fairly broad between the ears, its width not exceeding two-thirds of its length, the forehead flat and unwrinkled, the nose straight and almost parallel to the extension of the forehead (neither dish-faced nor down-faced) with a moderate stop. The muzzle should be strong, in proportion to the skull, and should end in a moderately blunt manner, with wiry whiskers, accentuating the rectangular shape of the head. The tip of the nose should be black, the lips tight and not overlapping, with well-developed fangs, healthy and pure white. The jaws should meet in a scissors bite, the upper teeth passing just outside the lower, with no space between. The eyes should be medium-sized, dark brown, oval, turned forward, with the brow arched and wiry. Ears should be evenly shaped, set high, and carried erect when cropped. If uncropped, they should be small and V-shaped, of moderate thickness, folding forward close to the skull. *Faults:* Too long and narrow a skull; soft silky whiskers and topknot; light yellow, large or protruding eyes; low-set houndlike ears; undershot or overshot mouth.

Neck: Strong and slightly arched, set cleanly on the shoulders and with the skin fitting closely at the throat. Too short and thick, long and light, or too throaty a neck is undesirable.

Forequarters: Flat, strongly muscled, somewhat sloping shoulders, without the deep-set "terrier front." The forelegs straight and vertical when seen from all sides. Chest moderately broad, reaching at least to the elbows, and extending well back. Back strong and straight, with well-developed withers. Length should equal height at the withers. Belly should be well drawn up toward the flank, but should not give a tucked-up appearance. *Faults:* Too narrow or too broad a chest; loose shoulders or elbows; weak back; shallow body.

Hindquarters: Strongly muscled, slanting thighs, and should never appear overbuilt or higher than the shoulders. When standing naturally, the line from hip to knee should be vertical, from knee to hock should be parallel to the upper neckline, and from the hock to the ground should be vertical.

Tail: Set moderately high and carried erect. It is cut down to three joints and should not be longer than one inch.

Feet: Short and round, with the toes well arched (cat's feet), with dark nails and hard pads.

Coat: Should be hard and wiry, neither smooth nor long, but giving a slightly rough appearance when seen against the grain. The outer coat should be harsh to the touch, the undercoat close and soft. It should be trimmed only enough to accentuate the body outline, and should be not less than three-quarters of an inch long, except on the ears and skull.

Size: From 11½ to 13½ inches for males and females. Dogs over 14 inches tall should be disqualified for oversize. The ideal size approximates 12½ inches. Too small, toyish-appearing dogs are not typical and should be penalized.

Color: Pepper-and-salt or similar equal mixtures, light or dark, and including the "red pepper," pure black and black-and-tan. *Faults:* Solid colors other than black; very light, whitish, spotted or tiger colors. A small white spot on the breast is not a fault.

Faults: Dogs too low- or high-legged; too heavy in head; with badly cut or carried ears; too steep or too level croup; straight shoulders; low shoulders; cow hocks; toed-in, long or spreading feet; weak pasterns; light bones; coat too long and soft or curly, and too short or smooth, or too closely trimmed; shy, savage, or highly nervous temperament.

SCOTTISH TERRIER

This highland terrier is believed to be the ancestor of all Scottish terriers. It was established as a distinct breed in 1879, but its ancestry goes far back into history. Average weight 20 pounds; height 10 inches. Thick and wiry coat, black, sandy or grizzle.

From the many different types of Scottish terriers the present-day type emerged, and once the breed was recognized and stabilized by selective breeding, it rapidly became popular.

A highly independent animal, the Scottie is generally described as having the "dour" traits of the Scottish people. He usually ignores outsiders and bestows his affection on his own family circle. His alert, intelligent appearance and his appealing rolling gait account in part for his popularity, aided to some extent by the predilection of advertisers of Scottish whisky to use the Scottie on their billboards and in their advertisements.

The most famous of the breed, Fala, shared the White House and his travels with President Franklin D. Roosevelt; and during the 1930's and early 1940's the Scottie appeared in the annual list of the ten most popular breeds.

Today he is down to about twentieth in popularity, but the active members of the Scottish Terrier Club of America are working to keep the breed standards high and expect him to move up on the list. A number of Scottish terriers have been trained in obedience work and have turned in almost perfect scores in obedience trials, and the jaunty-tailed little terriers always draw an appreciative audience in the show ring.

Scottish Terrier
English and American Ch. Reanda Rheola
Owners: Mr. and Mrs. T. Howard Snethen. Dewittville, New York

Standard of the Breed

Skull: Long, of medium width, slightly domed and covered with short, hard hair. It should not be quite flat; there should be a slight stop or drop between the eyes.

Muzzle: In proportion to the length of skull, with not too much taper toward the nose. Nose should be black and of good size. The jaws should be level and square. The nose projects somewhat over the mouth, giving the impression that the upper jaw is longer than the lower. The teeth should be evenly placed, having a scissors or level bite, with the former preferable.

Eyes: Set wide apart, small and of almond shape, not round. Color, dark brown or nearly black. Bright, piercing and set well under the brow.

Ears: Small, prick, set well up on the skull, rather pointed, but not cut. The hair on them should be short and velvety.

Neck: Moderately short, thick and muscular, strongly set on sloping shoulders, but not so short as to appear clumsy.

Chest: Broad and very deep, well let down between the forelegs.

Body: Moderately short and well ribbed up with strong loin, deep flanks and very muscular hindquarters.

Legs and Feet: Both forelegs and hind legs should be short and very heavy in bone in proportion to size of the dog. Forelegs straight or slightly bent, with elbows close to the body. Scottish terriers should not be out at the elbows. Stifles should be well bent and legs straight from hock to heel. Thighs very muscular. Feet round and thick with strong nails, forefeet larger than the hind feet. *Note:* The gait of the Scotty is peculiarly its own—very characteristic of the breed. It is not the square trot or walk that is desirable in the long-legged breeds. The forelegs do not move in exact parallel planes—rather in reaching out incline slightly inward. This is due to the shortness of leg and width of chest. The action of the rear legs should be square and true, and at the trot both the hocks and stifles should be flexed with a vigorous motion.

Tail: Never cut and about 7 inches long, carried with a slight curve, but not over the back.

Coat: Rather short, about two inches, dense undercoat with outer coat intensely hard and wiry.

Size and Weight: Equal consideration must be given to height, length of back and weight. Height at shoulder for either sex should be about 10 inches. Generally, a well-balanced Scottish terrier male of correct size should weigh 19 to 22 pounds, and a bitch 18 to 21 pounds. The principal objective must be symmetry and balance.

Color: Steel or iron gray, brindled or grizzled black, sandy or wheaten. White markings are objectionable and can be allowed only on the chest, and that to a slight extent only.

General Appearance: The face should wear a keen, sharp and active expression. Both head and tail should be carried well up. The dog should look very compact, well muscled and powerful, giving the impression of immense power in a small size.

Faults: Soft coat; round or very light eye; overshot or undershot jaw; oversize or undersize; shyness, timidity or failure to show with head and tail up.

SCALE OF POINTS

Skull	5
Muzzle	5
Eyes	5
Ears	10
Neck	5
Chest	5
Body	15

Legs and feet	*10*
Tail	*2½*
Coat	*15*
Size	*10*
Color	*2½*
General appearance	*10*
Total	*100*

WELSH TERRIER

Established as a pure breed in Wales about 100 years ago, the breed is descended from the black-and-tan terrier and is closely related to the Airedale and fox terrier. Average weight 20 pounds; height 15 inches. Dense, wiry coat, black-and-tan, red, mustard or wheaten color.

Very much like an Airedale in miniature, the Welsh terrier is perhaps the calmest, best-natured and friendliest of the terriers.

In their native land they performed the all-around job of the typical terriers. On the farm they rounded up livestock, and for the hunters they ran with the hounds and went underground after the fox when he was cornered.

In this country since about 1890, the breed has won many friends as a companion dog and watchdog. Despite his somewhat dour look, the Welshie is a lively, active playmate and gets along fairly well with dogs of other breeds. He is much easier to train and handle than many of the other terriers, and the person who might have a problem in managing a 50-pound Airedale could probably get along very well with his smaller Welsh cousin.

Also, the Welsh terrier is somewhat less of a one-man dog than other terriers and will spread his affections among members of the family and their friends.

Standard of the Breed

Head: The skull should be flat and rather wider between the ears than the wire-haired fox terrier. The jaw should be powerful, clean cut, rather deeper and more punishing—giving the head a more masculine appearance than that usually seen on a fox terrier. Stop should not be too defined, fair length from stop to end of nose, the latter being black.

Ears: Ears should be V-shaped, small and not too thin, set on fairly high, carried forward and close to the cheek.

Eyes: The eyes should be small, not too deeply set in, nor protruding out of the skull; of a dark hazel color, expressive and showing abundant spunk.

Welsh Terrier
Ch. Patty's Fancy Lady of Dorian
Owners: Mr. and Mrs. Sloan Colt. Westhampton, New York

Neck: The neck should be of moderate length and thickness, slightly arched and sloping gracefully into the shoulders.

Body: The back should be short and well ribbed up, the loin strong, with good depth, and the chest moderately wide. The shoulders should be long, sloping and well set back. Hindquarters should be strong, thighs muscular and of good length, with the hocks moderately straight, well let down and with fair amount of bone. The stern should be set on moderately high, but not too gaily carried.

Legs and Feet: The legs should be straight and muscular, possessing fair amount of bone, with upright and powerful pasterns. Feet should be small, round and catlike.

Coat: The coat should be wiry, hard, very close and abundant.

Color: Desired color is black-and-tan, or black grizzle and tan, free from black penciling on toes.

Height and Weight: The height at shoulder should be 15 inches for males; bitches proportionately less. Twenty pounds is considered a fair average weight in working condition, but variance of a pound or so in either direction is allowed.

SCALE OF POINTS
Head and jaws   *10*

Eyes	*5*
Ears	*5*
Body	*10*
Neck and shoulders	*10*
Loins and hindquarters	*10*
Legs and feet	*10*
Coat	*15*
Color	*5*
Stern	*5*
General appearance	*15*
Total	*100*

Disqualifications: White, cherry, or spotted nose showing either of these colors to a considerable extent; prick, tulip or rose ears; undershot jaw or pig-jawed mouth; black below hocks or white to an appreciable extent.

WEST HIGHLAND WHITE TERRIER

Originated by the Malcolm family of Poltalloch, Scotland, this breed is closely related to the cairn and Scottish terriers. Average weight 16 pounds; height 10 inches. Double coat, hard, thick and pure white.

Often mistaken for a "white Scottie," the West Highland white terrier has an unusual history. As a rule the old Scottish terrier breeders of cairn and Scottie-type dogs destroyed white puppies. However, the Malcolm family began to gather these "culls" and bred them, disposing of any that were not pure white. After many generations of breeding they produced this strain of terrier which bred true to type, giving a heavy-coated white dog with a jet black nose.

In addition to the distinct coat, the new strain showed characteristics different from those of his progenitors. This breed, although as good at ratting as any of his cousins, proved to be much more fun-loving and playful and less of a watchdog than the other terriers.

Another point in his favor for the person who wants a white dog is that he is easy to keep white. He has a dry skin, with no doggy odor, and a good, brisk brushing will keep him sleek and clean. Like the cairn, he has a woolly under-coat of thick fur which keeps him warm in the coldest weather. In this country less than sixty years, the West Highland white has won many dog fanciers over to his breed.

West Highland White Terrier
Ch. Wolvey Piper's Son
Owner: Mrs. Chester C. Caldwell, Honolulu, Hawaii

Standard of the Breed

General Appearance: A small, game, hardy-looking terrier exhibiting good showmanship, possessed of no small amount of self-esteem, with dashing appearance, strongly built, deep in chest and back ribs, straight back and powerful hindquarters on muscular legs, exhibiting in a marked degree a combination of strength and activity. The coat should be about two inches long, white, hard, with plenty of soft undercoat and no tendency to wave or curl. The tail should be as straight as possible and carried not too gaily, and covered with hard hair but not bushy. The skull should be not too broad, being in proportion to the terribly powerful jaws. The ears should be as small and sharp-pointed as possible and carried tightly up, and must be absolutely erect. The eyes of moderate size, as dark as possible, widely placed, with a sharp, bright, intelligent expression. The muzzle should not be too long, powerful and gradually tapering toward the nose. The roof of mouth and pads of feet are usually black.

Color: Pure white; any other color objectionable.

Coat: Very important and seldom seen to perfection. Must be double-coated. The outer coat consists of hard hair, about two inches long and free from any curl. The undercoat, which resembles fur, is short, soft and close. Open coats are objectionable.

Size: Males, about 11 inches at the withers; bitches, about one inch smaller.

Skull: Should not be too narrow, being in proportion to the powerful jaw, not too long, slightly domed and gradually tapering to the eyes, between which there should be a slight indentation or stop. Eyebrows heavy. There should be little apparent difference in length between the muzzle and skull.

Eyes: Widely set apart, medium in size, as dark as possible in color, slightly sunken, sharp and intelligent, and which, looking from under the heavy eyebrows give a piercing look. *Faults:* Full eyes and light-colored eyes.

Muzzle: Should be nearly equal in length to the rest of the skull, powerful and gradually tapering toward the nose, which should be fairly wide. The nose itself should be black. The jaws level and powerful, the teeth square or evenly met, well set and large for the size of the dog. *Faults:* Teeth much overshot or undershot; muzzle longer than the skull and not in proportion.

Ears: Small, carried tightly erect and never dropped, set wide apart and terminating in a sharp point. The hair on them should be short, smooth and velvety and they should never be cut. Ears should be free from fringe on top. *Faults:* Round-pointed, broad and large ears; ears set too closely together or heavily covered with hair.

Neck: Muscular and nicely set on sloping shoulders.

Chest: Very deep, with breadth in proportion to size of the dog.

Body: Compact, straight back, ribs deep and well arched in the upper half of rib, presenting a flattish side appearance, loins broad and strong, hindquarters strong, muscular and wide across the top.

Legs and Feet: Both fore- and hind legs should be short and muscular. The shoulder blades should be comparatively broad and well sloped backward. The points of the shoulder blades should be closely knitted into the backbone, so that very little movement of them should be noticeable when the dog is walking. The elbow should be close into the body when moving or standing, thus causing the foreleg to be well placed in under the shoulder. The forelegs should be straight and thickly covered with short, hard hair. The hind legs should be short and sinewy. The thighs very muscular and not too wide apart. The hocks bent and well set in under the body, so as to be fairly close to each other when standing, walking or trotting. The forefeet are larger than the hind feet, are round, proportionate in size, strong, thickly padded, and covered with short, hard hair. The hind feet are smaller and thickly padded. Cow hocks detract from the general appearance. *Faults:* Straight or weak hocks.

Tail: Five or 6 inches long, covered with hard hairs, no feather, as straight as possible, carried gaily, but not curled over back. *Fault:* Tail longer than 6 inches.

Movement: Should be free, straight and easy all around. In front the leg should be freely extended forward by the shoulder. The hind movement should be free, strong and close. The hocks should be freely fixed and drawn close in under the body, so that when moving off on the foot, the body is thrown or pushed forward with some force. Stiff, stilty movement behind is objectionable.

SCALE OF POINTS

General appearance	*15*
Color	*7½*
Coat	*10*
Size	*7½*
Skull	*5*
Eyes	*5*
Muzzle	*5*
Ears	*5*
Neck	*5*
Chest	*5*
Body	*10*
Legs and feet	*7½*
Tail	*5*
Movement	*7½*
Total	*100*

NONSPORTING DOGS

Neither hunters nor workers, the different breeds that have been classified as "nonsporting dogs" have been developed in different parts of the world as companions for man in his leisure hours. Among these breeds, although they are fairly small in number, a man or woman can find the dog to fill the need for canine companionship, matching the personality of the person to the dog.

BOSTON TERRIER

A true American, this breed was developed around Boston in the 1870's, purely as a companion dog. Average weight 17 pounds; height 16 inches. Coat smooth and glossy, black or brindle with white markings.

Although the blood of pit fighters runs in his veins, the modern Boston terrier is small, neat, friendly and the perfect dog for a city dog lover. His many favorable traits have made him the most popular American dog for many years, although he has had some fall from popularity in the past decade.

When young, the Boston may be destructive around the house, although he will outgrow this phase of his growing-up, but he is not much of an outdoor dog and has a great facility for getting lost if he wanders around the corner from his home.

Mainly because of his popularity—which has spread to other countries—the

Boston Terrier
Ch. Chappie's Little Man
Owner: Mrs. Charles D. Cline. Los Angeles, California

Boston has been much overbred and the purchaser of this breed should be cautious in selecting his Boston. The best guide is to follow the advice of someone who knows Bostons. Lacking that aid, there are a few points to be checked before choosing a Boston puppy.

The Boston has a naturally stubby tail and docking of the tail is sometimes practiced. This can be detected by the rounded tip left by docking.

Occasionally puppies are born with a harelip and this defect is sometimes repaired by simple surgery—although it may be accompanied by a deformed palate which is not visible to the novice. Rubbing a finger over the edge of the lip will disclose the scar and slight ridge left by the operation.

Particular attention should be paid to the puppy's eyes. The natural color of the Boston's eye is black, and the blue eye is a serious fault. At times, some sellers have been known to apply eyedrops to make the eyes appear dark. One way to check, if possible, is to see the parents of the puppy; one of them will usually have the undesirably colored eye, as the condition is hereditary. Also, opaque or cloudy eyes should be avoided as they may indicate a condition similar to the human cataract, which can lead to blindness.

Some strains carry a tendency to deafness and the six- or eight-week-old puppy should both hear and see well. As to the ears themselves, they will usually be "floppy" until the age of $4\frac{1}{2}$ to 7 months. At that age, the puppy should have finished teething and the ears should be erect if the ear cartilage has not been broken.

The purchaser of a bitch puppy for breeding purposes should be particularly careful, as a high proportion of Boston whelpings require caesarians—estimated as 75 per cent by some veterinarians—and only the larger-boned specimens may be capable of "free" whelping.

Standard of the Breed

General Appearance: A lively, highly intelligent, smooth-coated, short-headed, compactly built, short-tailed, well-balanced dog of medium station, of brindle color and evenly marked with white. The head should indicate a high degree of intelligence and should be in proportion to the size of the dog; the body rather short and well knit, the limbs strong and neatly turned; tail short; and no feature so prominent that the dog appears badly proportioned. The dog should convey an impression of determination, strength and activity, with style of a high order; carriage easy and graceful. A proportionate combination of "color" and "ideal markings" is a particularly distinctive feature of a representative specimen, and a dog with a preponderance of white on body, or without the proper proportion of brindle and white on head, should possess sufficient merit otherwise to counteract its deficiencies in these respects.

The ideal Boston terrier expression as indicating a high degree of intelligence is also an important characteristic of the breed.

"Color and markings" and "expression" should be given particular consideration in determining the relative value of "general appearance" to other points.

Skull: Flat on top, free from wrinkles; cheeks flat; brow abrupt, stop well defined.

Eyes: Wide apart, large and round, dark in color, expression alert, but kind and intelligent. The eyes should set squarely in the skull, and the outside corners should be on a line with the cheeks as viewed from the front.

Muzzle: Short, square, wide and deep, and in proportion to skull; free from wrinkles; shorter in length than in width and depth, not exceeding in length approximately one-third of length of skull; width and depth carried out well to end; the muzzle from stop to end of nose on a line parallel to the top of skull; nose black and wide, with well-defined line between nostrils. The jaws broad and square, with short regular teeth. Bite even or sufficiently undershot to square muzzle. The chops of good depth, but not pendulous, completely covering the teeth when mouth is closed.

Ears: Carried erect; small and thin; situated as near corners of skull as possible.

Head Faults: Skull domed or inclined; furrowed by a medial line; skull too long for breadth or vice versa; stop too shallow; brow and skull too slanting. Eyes small or sunken; too prominent; light color or walleye; showing too much white or haw. Muzzle wedge-shaped or lacking depth; down-faced; too much cut out below the eyes; pinched or wide nostrils; butterfly nose; protruding teeth; weak lower jaw; showing turn-up; layback or wrinkled. Ears poorly carried or out of proportion in size to head.

Neck: Of fair length, slightly arched and carrying the head gracefully; setting neatly into shoulders. *Faults:* Ewe-necked; throatiness; short and thick.

Body: Deep, with good width of chest; shoulders sloping; back short; ribs well sprung, carried well back to loins; loins short and muscular; rump curving slightly to set-on of tail; flank very slightly cut up. The body should appear short but not chunky. *Faults:* Flat sides; narrow chest; long or slack loins; roach-back; sway-back; too much cut up in flank.

Elbows: Standing neither in nor out.

Forelegs: Set moderately wide apart and on a line with the point of the shoulders; straight in bone and well muscled; pasterns short and strong.

Hind Legs: Set true; bent at stifles; short from hocks to feet; hocks turning neither in nor out; thighs strong and well muscled.

Feet: Round, compact, small, turned neither in nor out; toes well arched.

Leg and Foot Faults: Loose shoulders or elbows; hind legs too straight at stifles; hocks too prominent; long or weak pasterns; splay feet.

Gait: The gait of a Boston terrier is that of a sure-footed, straight-gaited dog, forelegs and hind legs moving straight ahead in line with perfect rhythm, each step indicating grace with power. *Faults:* Rolling, paddling or weaving when gaited and any crossing movement, either front or rear.

Tail: Set on low; short, fine, and tapering; straight or screw; devoid of fringe or coarse hair and not carried above horizontal. *Faults:* Long or gaily carried tail; extremely gnarled or curled against body. The preferred tail should not exceed in length approximately half the distance from set-on to hock.

Ideal Color: Brindle with white markings. The brindle to be evenly distributed and distinct. Black with white markings permissible but brindle with white markings preferred.

Ideal Markings: White muzzle, even white blaze over head, collar, breast, part or whole of forelegs, and hind legs below hocks. *Faults:* All white; absence of white markings; preponderance of white on body; without the proper proportion of brindle and white on head; or any variations detracting from the general appearance.

Coat: Short, smooth, bright and fine in texture. *Faults:* Long or coarse; lacking luster.

Weight: Divided by class as follows: lightweight, under 15 pounds; middleweight 15 and under 20 pounds; heavyweight, 20 and not exceeding 25 pounds.

SCALE OF POINTS

General appearance	*10*
Skull	*10*
Eyes	*5*
Muzzle	*10*
Ears	*2*
Neck	*3*
Body	*15*
Elbows	*4*
Forelegs	*5*

Hind legs	5
Gait	10
Feet	5
Tail	5
Color	4
Ideal markings	5
Coat	2
Total	100

BULLDOG

Adopted by the British as the symbol of courage and tenacity, the bulldog is descended from dogs bred to bait bulls. Average weight 50 pounds; height 15 inches. Short, flat coat, brindle, white or tan color.

The outward grimness of the bulldog hides an interior as full of love and gentleness as any other breed. Given a friendly scratch on the neck, the average bulldog wiggles his whole stubby body in appreciation.

An ideal pet for children, whom he loves, the modern bulldog is a far cry from his ancestors—larger dogs weighing about 100 pounds—that were trained to fight bulls by clinging to the creature's nose or an ear until the bull went down. The pushed-in face of the bulldog is the result of breeding to produce a head that would allow the dog to breathe while hanging onto the bull.

While modern breeding has removed all traces of viciousness it has also done much harm to the breed. As a rule, the modern bulldog is short-lived, short-winded, unable to stand much exertion, and subject to blindness and loss of hearing at a fairly early age.

Bitches are often sterile and many require caesarians when whelping.

On the credit side, this good-hearted tough-looking dog has a personality all its own and one which made him the official mascot of the U.S. Marine Corps and of Yale University. One of his charms is his swaggering gait, which has been compared to that of a tough seaman on shore leave. He has contributed much in courage and disposition to other breeds that include some bulldog in their ancestral background.

Standard of the Breed

General Appearance, Attitude, Expression: The perfect bulldog must be of medium size with smooth coat; and heavy, thickset body, massive short-faced head, wide shoulders and sturdy limbs. The general appearance and attitude should suggest stability, vigor and strength. The disposition should be equable

Bulldog
Ch. Vardonna Frosty Snowman
Owner: Dr. E. M. Vardon. Detroit, Michigan

and kind, resolute and courageous (not vicious or aggressive) and the demeanor should be pacific and dignified. These attributes should be apparent by the expression and behavior.

Gait: The style and carriage are peculiar, the gait being a loose-jointed shuffling, sidewise motion, giving the characteristic "roll." The action must, however, be unrestrained, free and vigorous.

Proportion and Symmetry: The "points" should be well distributed and bear good relation one to the other, no feature being in such prominence from either excess or lack of quality that the animal appears deformed or ill-proportioned.

Influence of Sex: In comparison of specimens of different sex, due allowance should be made in favor of bitches, which do not bear the characteristics of the breed to the same degree of perfection and grandeur as do the males.

Size: The size for mature males is about fifty pounds; for mature bitches about forty pounds.

Coat: The coat should be straight, short, flat, close, of fine texture, smooth and glossy. (No fringe, feather or curl.)

Color of Coat: The color of coat should be uniform, pure of its kind and brilliant. The various colors found in the breed are to be preferred in the following order: (1) red brindle, (2) all other brindles, (3) solid white, (4) solid red, fawn or fallow, (5) piebald, (6) inferior qualities of all the foregoing. A perfect piebald is preferable to muddy brindle or defective solid color.

Solid black is very undesirable, but not so objectionable if occurring to a moderate degree in piebald patches. The brindles to be perfect should have a fine, even and equal distribution of the composite colors. In brindles and solid colors a small white patch on the chest is not considered detrimental. In piebalds the color patches should be well defined, of pure color and symmetrically distributed.

Skin: The skin should be soft and loose, especially at the head, neck and shoulders.

Wrinkle and Dewlap: The head and face should be covered with heavy wrinkles, and at the throat from jaw to chest there should be two loose pendulous folds, forming the dewlap.

Skull: The skull should be very large, and in circumference, in front of the ears, should measure at least the height of the dog at the shoulders. Viewed from the front it should appear very high from the corner of the lower jaw to the apex of the skull, and also very broad and square. Viewed at the side, the head should appear very high, and very short from the point of the nose to occiput. The forehead should be flat (not rounded or domed), not too prominent or overhanging the face.

Cheeks: The cheeks should be well rounded, protruding sideways and outward beyond the eyes.

Stop: The temples, or frontal bones, should be very well defined, broad, square and high, causing a hollow or groove between the eyes. This indentation, or "stop," should be both broad and deep and extend up the middle of the forehead, dividing the head vertically, being traceable to the top of the skull.

Eyes and Eyelids: The eyes, seen from the front, should be situated low down on the skull as far from the ears as possible, and their corners should be in a straight line at right angles with the stop. They should be quite in front of the head, as wide apart as possible, provided their outer corners are within the outline of the cheeks when viewed from the front. They should be quite round in form, of moderate size, neither sunken nor bulging, and in color should be very dark. The lids should cover the white of the eyeball when the dog is looking directly forward, and the lid should show no haw.

Ears: The ears should be set high in the head, the front inner edge of each ear joining the outline of the skull at the top corner of the skull, so as to place them as wide apart, and as high and as far from the eyes as possible. In size they should be small and thin. The shape termed "rose ear" is the most desirable. The "rose ear" folds inward at its back lower edge, the upper front edge curving over, outward and backward, showing part of the inside of the burr. (The ears should not be carried erect or prick-eared or "buttoned," and should never be cropped.)

Face: The face, measured from the front of the cheek bone to the tip of the nose, should be extremely short, the muzzle being very short, broad, turned upward and very deep from the corner of the eye to the corner of the mouth.

Nose: The nose should be large, broad and black, its tip set back deeply between the eyes. The distance from the bottom of stop, between the eyes to the tip of the nose, should be as short as possible and not exceed the length from the tip of the nose to the edge of underlip. The nostrils should be wide, large and black. Any nose other than black is objectionable, and Dudley (flesh-colored) nose absolutely disqualifies from competition.

Chops: The chops, or flews, should be thick, broad, pendant and very deep, completely overhanging the lower jaw at each side. The underlip in front should almost or quite cover the teeth, which should be scarcely noticeable when the mouth is closed.

Jaws: The jaws should be massive, very broad, square and undershot, the lower jaw projecting considerably in front of the upper and turning up.

Teeth: The teeth should be large and strong, with the canine teeth, or tusks, wide apart; and the six small teeth in front, between the canines, in an even, level row.

Neck: The neck should be short, very thick, deep and strong and well arched at the back.

Shoulders: The shoulders should be very broad, deep and full.

Brisket and Body: The brisket and body should be very capacious, with full sides, well-rounded ribs and very deep from the shoulders down to its lowest part where it joins the chest. It should be well let down between the shoulders and forelegs, giving the dog a broad, low, short-legged appearance. The body should be well ribbed up behind with the belly tucked up and not rotund.

Back: The back should be short and strong, very broad at the shoulders and comparatively narrow at the loins. There should be a slight fall in the back, close behind the shoulders (its lowest part), from which the spine should rise to the loins (the top of which should be higher than the top of the shoulders), and then curving up again more suddenly to the tail, forming an arch (a very distinctive feature of the breed), termed "roach-back," or, more correctly, "wheel-back."

Forelegs: The forelegs should be short, very stout, straight and muscular, set wide apart, with well-developed calves, presenting a bowed outline, but the bones of the legs should not be curved or bandy, nor should the feet be too close together.

Elbows: The elbows should be low and stand well out and loose from the body.

Hind legs: The hind legs should be strong and mucular and longer than the forelegs, so as to elevate the loins above the shoulders. Hocks should be slightly bent and well let down, so as to give length and strength from loins to hock. The lower leg should be short, straight and strong, with the stifles turned slightly outward and away from the body. The hocks are thereby made to approach each other, and the hind feet to turn outward.

Feet: The feet should be moderate in size, compact and firmly set. Toes compact, well split up, with high knuckles and with short and stubby nails. The forefeet may be straight or slightly out-turned, but the hind feet should be pointed outward.

Tail: The tail may be either straight or "screwed" (but never curved or curly) and in any case must be short, hung low, with decided downward carriage, thick root and fine tip. If straight, the tail should be cylindrical and of uniform taper. If "screwed," the bends or kinks should be well defined, and they may be abrupt and even knotty, but no portion of the member should be elevated above the base or root.

SCALE OF POINTS

General properties	22	
Properties and symmetry		5
Attitude		3
Expression		2
Gait		3
Size		3
Coat		2
Color of coat		4

Head	39	
Skull		5
Cheeks		2
Stop		4
Eyes and eyelids		3
Ears		5
Wrinkle		5
Nose		6
Chops		2
Jaws		5
Teeth		2
Body, legs, etc.	39	
Neck		3
Dewlap		2
Shoulders		5
Chest		3
Ribs		3
Brisket		2
Belly		2
Back		5
Forelegs and elbows		4
Hind legs		3
Feet		3
Tail		4
Total		100

CHOW CHOW

This breed has been used as a hunting dog in China for over 2,000 years. Has been bred in the United States for about 70 years. Average weight 60 pounds; height 20 inches. Abundant coat, usually red or black, but may be any solid color.

An antisocial person wanting a dog that shares a dim view of other humans will find a soul mate in the bearlike chow chow. Most chows are playful and protective toward their masters and family, but sternly aloof toward strangers. And the dog's usual look, a perpetual scowl, helps to keep strangers at arm's length.

Like the Pekingese, the first chows were brought to England during Queen

Chow Chow
Ch. Pandees Red Rufs II
Owner: Imogene P. Earle. Laurel, Maryland

Victoria's reign, and by the 1920's they were at the height of their popularity both in Britain and the United States. All-around dogs, they have served as hunters, guard dogs, sled dogs and pets.

Despite their sturdy, bearlike appearance, most chows are high-strung and sensitive, although they can be trained for show-ring appearance and for obedience work.

One unusual feature of the breed is that the purebred specimens have a blue-black tongue and mouth, and this has led to much theorizing as to the basic origin of the breed. Some authorities hold that it is descended from a different ancestor than other Western dogs. Some attribute the tongue and mouth coloring and the breed's sure-footedness to a heavy infusion of bear blood. Others find a close relationship to the Eskimo, keeshond and elkhound, but there, conflict arises as to whether the chow chow is the result of intermixing of these breeds or the pure remnant of one of the basic breeds.

While dogs have been used as foods in many parts of China, the breed's name has no connection with chow mein. In pidgin English the words "chow chow" were used to describe bric-a-brac and curios, and masters of sailing vessels listed the dogs under this heading on their manifests and so the name became attached to the breed.

Standard of the Breed

General Appearance: A massive, cobby, powerful dog, active and alert, with strong muscular development and perfect balance. Body squares with height of leg at shoulder; head, broad and flat, with short, broad, and deep muzzle, accentuated by a ruff; the whole supported by straight, strong legs. Clothed in a shining, offstanding coat, the chow chow is a masterpiece of beauty, dignity and perfect naturalness.

Head: Large and massive in proportion to size of the dog, with broad, flat skull; well filled under the eyes; moderate stop; proudly carried.

Expression: Essentially dignified, lordly, scowling, discerning, sober, and snobbish—one of independence.

Muzzle: Short in comparison to length of skull; broad from eyes to end of nose, and of equal depth. The lips somewhat full and overhanging.

Teeth: Strong and level, with a scissors bite; should neither be overshot nor undershot.

Nose: Large, broad and black in color. *Disqualification:* Nose spotted or distinctly other color than black; except in blue chows which may have solid blue or slate noses.

Tongue: Blue-black. The tissues of the mouth should approximate black. *Disqualification:* Tongue red, pink, or obviously spotted with red or pink.

Eyes: Dark, deep-set, of moderate size, and almond-shaped.

Ears: Small, slightly rounded at tip, stiffly carried. They should be placed wide apart on top of skull, and set with as slight forward tilt. *Disqualification:* Drop ear or ears. (A drop ear is one which is stiffly carried or stiffly erect, but which breaks over at any point from its base to its tip.)

Body: Short, compact, with well-sprung ribs, and let down in the flank.

Neck: Strong, full, set well on shoulders.

Shoulders: Muscular, slightly sloping.

Chest: Broad, deep and muscular. *Serious Fault:* A narrow chest.

Back: Short, straight and strong.

Loins: Broad, deep and powerful.

Tail: Set well up and carried closely to the back, following line of spine at start.

Forelegs: Perfectly straight, with heavy bone and upright pasterns.

Hind Legs: Straight-hocked, muscular and heavy-boned.

Feet: Compact, round, catlike, with thick pads.

Gait: Completely individual. Short and stilted because of straight hocks.

Coat: Abundant, dense, straight and offstanding; rather coarse in texture with a soft, woolly undercoat. It may be any clear color, solid throughout, with lighter shadings on ruff, tail and breechings.

DALMATIAN

Originally from the Adriatic province of Dalmatia, this spotted coach or fire dog was trained to run with horses or carriages and was the favorite mascot of the horse-drawn firemen. Average weight 45 pounds, height 21 inches. Coat short and sleek, black or liver spots on a white background.

He might have been a casualty of the automobile age, but the Dalmatian, thanks to a number of dedicated breeders, is still a popular dog, and has been increasing in popularity in recent years.

For centuries this dog has been associated with the horse, keeping pace with a rider or trotting along under the axles of a carriage; and some fanciers affirm that even a puppy will break away and try to follow a horse he sees on the street.

As a pet, the Dalmatian trains readily, and many have done well in obedience trials. Not a persistent barker, the Dalmatian is an excellent watchdog and gets along well with children. However, some are a bit too enthusiastic as guardians and may not discriminate between visitors and intruders.

The sleek Dalmatian seldom looks as sturdy as he really is and his smooth coat requires little care. However, one handicap in owning a Dalmatian is that the breed requires far more exercise than most house pets receive, and may sicken from lack of outdoor running. In fact, many fire companies have lost their dogs because they did not receive enough exercise to keep them healthy.

Deafness is a defect that has shown up among some strains of Dalmatians in recent years and a hearing test should be part of the pre-purchase examination of any Dalmatian. Also, if the purchase of the Dalmatian is for show or breeding purposes, it should be kept in mind that the spotted coat is of primary importance and that even distribution of coin-sized dots is the most desirable coloring.

Dalmatian
Ch. Roadcoach Roadster
Owner: Mrs. S. K. Allman, Jr. Doylestown, Pennsylvania

Although the puppies are born pure white, the color develops quickly and a young dog will soon give a good indication of what his adult coloring will show.

Standard of the breeds

General Appearance: A strong, muscular and active dog, symmetrical in outline and free from coarseness and lumber, capable of great endurance combined with a fair amount of speed.

Head: Of a fair length, the skull flat, rather broad between the ears, and moderately well defined at the temple—exhibiting a moderate amount of stop, and not in one straight line from the nose to the occiput bone, as required in a bull terrier. It should be entirely free from wrinkle.

Muzzle: Long and powerful; lips clean, fitting the jaws moderately close.

Eyes: Set moderately well apart, and of medium size, round, bright and sparkling, with an intelligent expression, their color greatly depending on the markings of the dog. In the black-spotted variety the eyes should be dark (black or brown); in the liver-spotted variety they should be light (yellow or light brown). Walleyes are permissible. The rim around the eyes in the black-spotted variety should be black; in the liver-spotted variety, brown—never flesh-colored in either.

Ears: Set on rather high, of moderate size, rather wide at the base and gradually tapering to a rounded point. They should be carried close to the head, be thin and fine in texture, and always spotted, the more profusely the better.

Nose: In the black-spotted variety the nose should always be black; in the liver-spotted variety, always brown.

Neck and Shoulders: The neck should be fairly long, nicely arched, light and tapering, and entirely free from throatiness. The shoulders should be moderately oblique, clean and muscular, denoting speed.

Body, Back, Chest and Loins: The chest should not be too wide, but very deep and capacious, ribs moderately well sprung, never rounded like barrel hoops (which would indicate want of speed); back powerful; loin strong, muscular and slightly arched.

Legs and Feet: (Of great importance.) The forelegs should be perfectly straight, strong and heavy in bone; elbows close to the body; feet compact with well-arched toes, and tough, elastic pads. In the hind legs, the muscles should be clean, though well defined; the hocks well let down.

Nails: In the black-spotted variety, black and white; in the liver-spotted variety, brown and white.

Gait: Length of stride should be in proportion to the size of the dog; steady in rhythm of 1-2-3-4, as the cadence count in military drill. Front legs should not paddle, nor should there be a straddling appearance. Hind legs should neither cross nor weave; judges should be able to see each leg move with no interference of another leg. Drive and reach are most desirable.

Tail: Should not be too long, strong at the insertion, and gradually tapering toward the end, free from coarseness. It should not be inserted too low down, but carried with a slight curve upward, and never curled. It should be spotted, the more profusely the better.

Coat: Short, hard, dense and fine, sleek and glossy in appearance, but neither woolly nor silky.

Color and Markings: (These are most important points.) The ground color in both varieties should be pure white, very decided and not intermixed. The color of spots in the black-spotted variety should be black, the deeper and richer the black, the better. In the liver-spotted variety they should be brown. The spots should not intermingle, but should be as round and well defined as possible, the more distinct the better. They should be from dime to half-dollar size. The spots on the face, head, ears, and legs should be smaller than those on the body.

Size: Height of males and bitches between 19 and 23 inches; weight between 35 and 50 pounds.

SCALE OF POINTS

Head and eyes	*10*
Ears	*5*
Neck and shoulders	*10*
Body, back, chest and loins	*10*
Legs and feet	*10*
Gait	*10*
Coat	*5*
Color and markings	*25*
Tail	*5*
Size, symmetry, etc.	*10*
Total	*100*

KEESHOND

This is one of the "coming" breeds that is rapidly gaining favor. Was used as a watchdog and pet on canal barges by the Dutch. Average weight 40 pounds; height 18 inches. Thick, double coat, shaded gray in color.

A medium-sized dog with an extremely attractive long coat that is waterproof, requires little grooming and does not mat; an excellent watchdog, good with children, highly intelligent and a fast learner, the keeshond has been promoted by an active group of fanciers during the past thirty-five years.

Related to the elkhound, spitz, and probably the Eskimo from whom he may have inherited the double coat—the keeshond is a dog of many abilities. Almost always reliable with children, he can be used to keep rodents under control and is a natural rabbit dog. He trains readily, and some have shown considerable ability in the obedience ring.

Although he has a long background as a watchdog, the keeshond is not at all aggressive. In fact, one of the minor faults of the breed is that many of them are extremely sensitive and if they are not handled properly may become rather timid.

Long known in their native Holland as a definite breed, these dogs were first recognized by English dog fanciers in 1900 as the "Dutch barge dog," and received formal acceptance of the name keeshond in 1926. At that time

Keeshound
Ch. Ruttkay Heir Apparent
Owner: Pat Marcmann. Limerick, Pennsylvania

the first specimens were brought to the United States where they won fast acceptance because of their personality and beauty. Strangely enough, after the dogs won the hearts of dog fanciers in the United States and England, the breed regained popularity in their native Holland, where a number of breeders set up kennels and revived local interest in the one-time popular barge dogs.

Standard of the Breed

General Appearance and Conformation: The keeshond (plural keeshonden) is a handsome dog, of well-balanced, short-coupled body, attracting attention not only by his alert carriage and intelligent expression, but also by his luxuriant coat, his richly plumed tail, well curled over his back, and by his foxlike face and head, with small pointed ears. His coat is very thick round the neck, forepart of the shoulders and chest, forming a lionlike mane. His rump and hind legs, down to the hocks, are also thickly coated, forming the characteristic "trousers." His head, ears and lower legs are covered with thick, short hair.

Height: The ideal height of fully mature dogs (over two years old), measured from top of withers to ground, is: males, 18 inches; bitches, 17 inches. However, size consideration should not outweight that of type. When dogs are judged equal in type, the dog nearest the ideal height is preferred. Length of back from withers to rump should equal height, as measured above.

Expression: Expression is largely dependent on the distinctive characteristic called "spectacles"—a delicately penciled line slanting slightly upward from the outer corner of each eye to the lower corner of the ear, coupled with distinct markings and shadings forming short but expressive eyebrows. Markings (or shadings) on the face and head must present a pleasing appearance, imparting to the dog an alert and intelligent expression. *Fault:* Absence of "spectacles."

Skull: The head should be well proportioned to the body, wedge-shaped when viewed from above. Not only the muzzle, but the whole head should give this impression when the ears are drawn back by covering the nape of the neck and the ears with one hand. Head in profile should exhibit a definite stop. *Faults:* Apple head or absence of stop.

Muzzle: The muzzle should be dark in color and of medium length, neither coarse nor snipy, and well proportioned to the skull.

Mouth: The mouth should be neither overshot nor undershot. Lips should be black and closely meeting, not thick, coarse or sagging; and with no wrinkle at the corner of the mouth. *Fault:* Overshot or undershot.

Teeth: The teeth should be white, sound and strong (but discoloration from distemper not to penalize severely); upper teeth should just overbite the lower teeth.

Eyes: Eyes should be dark brown in color, of medium size, rather oblique in shape, and not set too wide apart. *Faults:* Protruding round eyes or eyes light in color.

Ears: Small, triangular in shape, mounted high on head and carried erect; dark in color and covered with thick, velvety short hair. Size should be proportionate to the head—length approximating the distance from the outer corner of the eye to the nearest edge of the ear. *Fault:* Ears not carried erect when at attention.

Neck and Shoulders: The neck should be moderately long, well shaped and well set on shoulders; covered with a profuse mane, sweeping from under the jaw and covering the whole of the front part of the shoulders and chest, as well as the top part of the shoulders.

Chest, Back and Loin: The body compact, with a short straight back sloping slightly downward toward the hindquarters; well ribbed, barrel well rounded, belly moderately tucked up, deep and strong of chest.

Legs: Forelegs straight as seen from any angle, and well feathered. Hind legs profusely feathered down to the hocks, not below, with hocks only slightly bent. Legs must be of good bone and cream in color. *Fault:* Black markings below the knee, penciling excepted.

Feet: Compact, well rounded, catlike and cream in color. Toes nicely arched, with black nails. *Fault:* White foot or feet.

Tail: Set on high, moderately long, and well feathered, tightly curled over the back. It should lie flat and close to the body, with a very light gray plume on top where curled, but the tip of the tail should be black. The tail should form a part of the silhouette of the dog's body, rather than give the appearance of an appendage. *Fault:* Tail not lying close to the back.

Action: Dogs should show boldly and keep tails curled over the back. They should move cleanly and briskly; and the movement should be straight and erect, not a lope like a German shepherd. *Fault:* Tail not carried over back when moving.

Coat: The body should be abundantly covered with long, straight, harsh hair standing well out from a thick, downy undercoat. The hair on the legs should be smooth and short, except for a feathering on the front leg and the "trousers" as previously described on the hind legs. The hair on the tail should be profuse, forming a rich plume. Head, including muzzle, skull and ears, should be covered with smooth, soft, short hair, velvety in texture on the ears. *Fault:* Silky, wavy or curly coat; coat parted down the back.

Color and Markings: A mixture of gray and black. The undercoat should be very pale cream or gray, not tawny. The hair of the outer coat is black-tipped, the length of the black tips producing the characteristic shading of color. The color may vary from light to dark, but any pronounced deviation from the gray color is not permissible. The plume of the tail should be very light gray when curled on back, and the tip of the tail should be black. Legs and feet should be cream. Ears should be very dark—almost black.

Shoulder-line markings (light gray) should be well defined. The color of the ruff and the "trousers" is generally lighter than that of the body. "Spectacles" and shadings, as previously described, are characteristic of the breed and must be present to some degree. There should be no pronounced white markings. *Very Serious Faults:* Entirely black or white or any other solid color; any pronounced deviation from the gray color.

SCALE OF POINTS

General conformation and appearance			*20*
Head			
	Shape	*6*	
	Eyes	*5*	
	Ears	*5*	
	Teeth	*4*	*20*
Body			
	Chest, back and loin	*10*	
	Tail	*10*	
	Neck and shoulders	*8*	
	Legs	*4*	
	Feet	*3*	*35*
Coat			*15*
Color and markings			*10*
	Total		*100*

POODLE

Although the national dog of France, the poodle is actually a German dog, originally a retriever and circus dog. Poodles are found in any solid color from white to black. In size they range from the standard 55 pounds and 23 inches high; the miniature (most popular),16 pounds, 13 inches high; to the toy, 7 pounds, 9 inches high.

In recent years the poodles have been challenging the beagle for top place in the registration books of the American Kennel Club. Fanciers of this breed claim that a combination of brains and beauty make the breed's popularity natural.

Since the first obedience trails were held in this country, poodles have consistently outnumbered other breeds in earning top scores, and poodle people assert that the brain structure of the poodle is superior to that of other dogs, and that the shape of the head provides for a larger brain surface than that of other breeds.

When it comes to learning tricks or obedience routines, the poodle has an almost human capacity to understand what is required of him. But he is a natural clown and will often purposely misperform if it seems to draw applause or laughter from his audience.

Maintaining a poodle in style in the city can be rather expensive, with a monthly "beauty parlor" bill of ten dollars or more for his clippings and trims,

Toy Poodle
American and Canadian Ch. Thornlea Silver Souvenir
Owner: Mrs. George W. Dow. Whatley, Massachusetts

Standard Poodle
Ch. Ivardon Paris
Owner: William H. Ivens, Jr., V.D. Doylestown, Pennsylvania

Miniature Poodle
Ch. Summercourt Square Dancer of Fircot
Owners: Mr. and Mrs. Lewis J. Garlick. Woodmere, New York

and the accessories for the well-dressed poodle running to whatever the budget can bear.

There is no such breed as the "French poodle," although that is a term often applied to poodles by pet shops and some kennels. The fancy clips in which poodles appear can be traced back to the days when the poodle was generally used as a retriever and his coat was clipped to allow for a freer swimming motion and to reduce the amount of hair that might become waterlogged.

All three of the poodle varieties are similar in intelligence and behavior. The standard, however, is a far stronger dog than might be gathered from his appearance and might be a bit too much dog for a woman or a child to manage.

Standard of the Breed

General Appearance, Carriage and Condition: That of a very active, intelligent, smart and elegant-looking dog, squarely built, well proportioned and carrying himself proudly. Properly clipped in the traditional fashion and carefully groomed, the poodle has about him an air of distinction and dignity peculiar to himself.

Head and Expression: Skull should be slightly full and moderately peaked, with a slight stop. Cheekbones and muscles flat. Eyes set far enough apart to indicate ample brain capacity. Muzzle long, straight and fine, but strong without lippiness. The chin definite enough to preclude snipiness. Teeth white, strong and level. Nose sharp with well-defined nostrils. Eyes oval, very dark, full of fire and intelligence. Ears set low and hanging close to the head. The leather long, wide and heavily feathered—when drawn forward almost reaches the nose.

Neck: Well proportioned, strong and long enough to admit of the head being carried high and with dignity. Skin snug at throat.

Shoulders: Strong, muscular, angulated at the point of the shoulder and the elbow joint, sloping well back.

Body: The chest deep and moderately wide. The ribs well sprung and braced up. The back short, strong and very slightly hollowed, with the loins broad and muscular. (Bitches may be slightly longer in back than males.)

Tail: Set on rather high, docked and carried gaily. Never curled or carried over the back.

Legs: The forelegs straight from the shoulders with plenty of bone and muscle. Hind legs very muscular, stifles well bent, and hocks well let down. Hindquarters well developed, with the second thigh showing both width and muscle.

Feet: Rather small and of good oval shape. Toes well arched and close, pads thick and hard.

Coat: Quality—Curly poodles, very profuse, of harsh texture, even length, frizzy or curly, not at all open; corded poodles, very thick, hanging in tight, even cords. Clip—Clipping in either the traditional "continental" or "English saddle" style is correct. (See pages 262–265 for details of poodle clips.)

Color: Any solid color. All but the browns have black noses, lips and eyelids. The browns and apricots may have liver noses and dark amber eyes. In all colors toenails are either black or the same color as the dog. Gray poodles whose coats have not cleared to an even solid color may be shown up to the age of eighteen months. The degree of clearing shall count in judging two or more gray poodles under the age of eighteen months when all other points are equal, in which case the more completely cleared dog shall be judged superior.

Gait: A straightforward trot with light springy action. Head and tail carried high.

Size: The standard poodle is fifteen inches or more at the shoulder.

The Ideal Miniature Poodle: Judged the same as large poodle, except its size, which is from 10 to 15 inches at shoulder. So long as the dog is definitely a miniature, diminutiveness is the deciding factor only when all other points are equal. Soundness and activity are every whit as necessary in a miniature or toy as they are in a large poodle, and as these traits can only be seen when the dog is in action, it is imperative that the miniature and toy poddles be moved in the show ring as fully and decidedly as large poodles.

Major Faults: Bad mouth—either under- or overshot. Cow hocks, flat or spread feet, thin pads, very light eyes, excessive shyness. *Disqualifications:* Parti-colors or unorthodox clip.

SCALE OF POINTS

General appearance, carriage and condition	*20*
Head, ears, eyes and expression	*20*
Neck and shoulders	*10*
Body and tail	*15*
Legs and feet	*10*
Coat, color and texture	*15*
Gait	*10*
Total	*100*

SCHIPPERKE

This breed has been used as mascot and watchdog on Belgian barges since the 1600's. His name means "little captain." He has been bred in the United States for some 25 years. Average weight 15 pounds; height 12 inches. Thick coat of solid black, with naturally bobbed tail.

This pint-sized watchdog companion fitted ideally into the cramped living quarters of the barges that plied the waters of the Belgian and Dutch canals three hundred years ago. Unchanged over the years, the small spitz-type dog makes a fine apartment-sized pet.

Watchful, he is naturally gentle with children, full of energy and intensely loyal to his family. His thick coat needs little care and makes him a good all-climate dog.

Another favorable feature as a companion is the usual long life of this breed. Schipperkes fifteen and sixteen years of age are not at all unusual and they

Schipperke
Maggie of Kelso
Owner: Beatrice Palmer. Sayre, Pennsylvania

have been known to live into their twenties.

For the person seeking an unusual-looking dog, the schipperke is ideal. A foxlike face and keen, intelligent expression give him a unique appearance, not quite like any other breed. His tail is naturally stubby, and many are born tailless.

In disposition, perhaps his outstanding trait is curiosity. Any closed door represents a challenge to him and any moving object arouses his immediate attention. In addition to his watchdog abilities, he has been used in hunting rabbits and he is terrier-like with rodents.

Standard of the Breed

Appearance and General Characteristics: An excellent and faithful little watchdog, suspicious of strangers. Active, agile, indefatigable, continually occupied with what is going on around him, careful of things that are given him to guard, very kind with children, knows the ways of the household; always curious to know what is going on behind closed doors or about any object that has been moved, betraying his impressions by his sharp bark and upstanding ruff, seeking the company of horses, a hunter of moles and other vermin; can be used to hunt; good rabbit dog.

Color: Solid black.

Head: Foxlike, fairly wide, narrowing at the eyes; seen in profile, slightly rounded; tapering muzzle not too elongated nor too blunt; not too much stop.

Nose: Small and black.

Eyes: Dark brown, small, oval rather than round, neither sunken nor prominent.

Expression: Should have a questioning expression: sharp and lively, not mean or wild.

Ears: Very erect, small, triangular, placed high, strong enough not to be capable of being lowered except in line with the body.

Teeth: Meeting evenly. A tight scissors bite is acceptable.

Neck: Strong and full, slightly arched, rather short.

Shoulders: Muscular and sloping.

Chest: Broad and deep in brisket.

Body: Short, thickset and cobby. Broad behind the shoulders, seeming higher in front because of ruff. Back strong, short, straight and level or slightly sloping down toward rump. Ribs well sprung.

Loins: Muscular and well drawn up from the brisket, but not to such an extent as to cause a weak and leggy appearance of the hindquarters.

Forelegs: Straight under body, with bone in proportion, but not coarse.

Hindquarters: Somewhat lighter than the foreparts, but muscular, powerful, with rump well rounded, tail docked to not more than one inch in length.

Feet: Small, round and tight (not splayed), nails straight, strong and short.

Coat: Abundant and slightly harsh to the touch, short on the ears, on the front of legs and on the hocks; fairly short on the body but longer around neck beginning back of the ears and forming a ruff and a cape; the jabot extending down between the front legs, also longer on rear where it forms a culotte, the points turning inward. Undercoat dense and short on body, very dense around neck making ruff stand out. Culotte should be as long as the ruff.

Weight: Up to 18 pounds.

Faults: Light eyes, large round prominent eyes, ears too long or too rounded, narrow head and elongated muzzle, muzzle too blunt, domed skull, smooth short coat with short ruff and culotte, lack of undercoat, curly or silk coat, body coat more than three inches long, jaw slightly overshot or undershot, sway-back, bull-terrier-shaped head, straight hocks. Straight stifles and shoulders, cow hocks, feet turning in or out, legs not straight when viewed from front. Lack of distinction between length of coat, ruff and culotte.

Disqualifications: Any color other than solid black. Drop or semi-erect ears. Badly overshot or undershot.

TOY DOGS

Long the favorite of the aristocrat, these toy breeds have never been so popular in the past as they are today. They seem to fit the modern way of life. Small apartments, compact cars, travel . . . and everywhere the soprano barks of these tiny dogs whose only function is to repay with affection the attention they receive.

CHIHUAHUA

Smallest of all breeds, these dogs are believed to be descended from Aztec dogs that disappeared from history after the destruction of Montezuma's empire. Smooth (most popular) and long-coated. Average weight 4 pounds. Colors range from fawn, red, black-and-tan through splashed and blue.

In recent years, four breeds have been vying for the coveted number one place in American Kennel Club registrations—the blue book of American dogdom. The beagle, dachshund, poodle and the tiny Chihuahua are currently the most popular purebred dogs, with the Chihuahua holding firmly onto second place.

Purse- or pocket-sized, this breed is perfect for the dog owner who has to travel and faces the problem of "No Dogs Allowed" signs. The visitor to a dog show who sees the Chihuahuas on exhibition in glass cages to protect them against drafts, or wrapped in flannel in their owners' arms, may think they are extremely delicate, but this is not the case.

While the Chihuahua may need a coat to protect him from cold weather, he is as sturdy as any other toy breed and is one of the more intelligent and alert breeds. Many owners find it advisable to keep a pair of Chihuahuas, as these dogs have a close affinity for other Chihuahuas but seem to resent other breeds.

The Chihuahua can be paper-trained, which eliminates the need for walks several times a day. As with other toys, care should be exercised in breeding

Smooth Chihuahua
Farriston My Little Margie
Owner: Mrs. Homer V. Farris. New Hartford, Connecticut

the tinier females that may weigh as little as one pound; and a bitch bought for breeding should weigh at least five pounds and can be bred to a smaller sire for tiny puppies.

Although the breed is named after the Mexican state where they were discovered in the 1890's, there are very few in Mexico. Also there is a strong school of opinion that the modern Chihuahua may not be of Aztec origin, but rather a fairly recent import from the Orient where "dwarfing" of both plants and animals has long been a widely practiced art.

Practically all the Chihuahuas in Mexico are of United States origin, and the buyer who is offered a Chihuahua with the claim that it is a "pedigreed dog from Mexico," should view the purchase with skepticism.

Standard of the Breed

Smooth Coat

Head: A well-rounded apple-dome skull, with or without molera.* Cheeks

---

* Molera is defined as incomplete, imperfect or abnormal ossification of the skull.

and jaws lean. Nose moderately short, slightly pointed (self-colored in blond types or black). In moles, blues and chocolate, they are self-colored. In blond types, pink nose is permissible.

Ears: Large, erect when alert, but flaring at the sides at about an angle of 45 degrees when in repose. This gives breadth between the ears.

Eyes: Full but not protruding, balanced, well set apart—dark ruby or luminous. Light eyes in blond types permissible.

Teeth: Level.

Neck and Shoulders: Slightly arched, gracefully sloping into lean shoulders, may be smooth in very short types, or with ruff about the neck preferred. Shoulders lean, sloping into a slightly broadening support above straight forelegs that are set well under, giving a free play at the elbows. Shoulders should be well up, giving balance and soundness, sloping into a level back. (Never down or low.) This gives a chestiness and strength of forequarters, yet not of the "bulldog" chest; plenty of brisket.

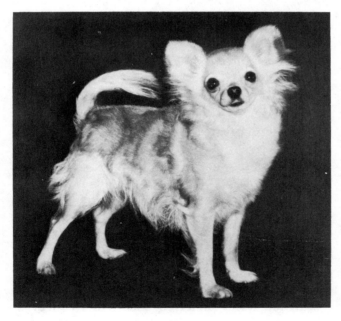

Long Coat Chihuahua
Ch. Ross Bonita Bambino
Owner: Albert H. Ross, Mobile, Alabama

Back and Body: Level back, slightly longer than height. Shorter backs desired in males. Ribs rounded (but not too barrel-shaped).

Hindquarters: Muscular, with hocks well apart, neither out nor in, well let down, with firm sturdy action.

Tail: Moderately long, carried cycle either up or out, or in a loop over the back, with tip just touching back. (Never tucked under.) Hair on tail in harmony with rest of body, preferred furry. A natural bobtail or tailless permissible if so born.

Feet: Small, with toes well split up but not spread, pads cushioned with fine pasterns. (Neither hare- nor catfoot.) A dainty, small foot with nails moderately long.

Coat: In the smooth, the coat should be soft texture, close and glossy. (Heavier coats with undercoat permissible.) Coat placed well over body with ruff on neck, and scantier on head and ears.

Color: Any color, solid, marked or splashed.

Weight: One to 6 pounds, with 2 to 4 pounds perferred. If two dogs are equally good in type, the more diminutive is preferred.

General Appearance: A graceful, alert, swift-moving little dog with saucy expression. Compact and with terrier-like qualities.

SCALE OF POINTS

Head, including ears	20
Body	20
Coat	10
Tail	5
Color	5
Legs	15
Weight	10
General appearance and action	15
Total	100

Long Coat

The long-coated variety of Chihuahua is judged by the same standards as the smooth-coated, except for the following:

Coat: In the long coats, the coat should be of a soft texture, either flat or slightly curly, with undercoat preferred. Ears fringed (heavily fringed ears may be tipped slightly, never down), feathering on feet and legs, and pants on hind legs. Large ruff on neck desired and preferred. Tail full and long (as a plume).

SCALE OF POINTS

Head, including ears	*20*
Body	*20*
Coat	*20*
Tail	*5*
Color	*5*
Legs	*10*
Weight	*5*
General appearance and action	*15*
Total	*100*

Disqualification: Too thin coat, that resembles bareness.

PEKINGESE

The sacred "lion dog" of the Chinese emperors was first brought to the western world when Queen Victoria received one in 1860 after the siege of Peking. Average weight 9 pounds; height 6 inches. Long, silky coat, white with markings; red or black.

There is no question of the royal ancestry of the "Peke." For over 2,000 years, the breed was confined rigidly to the imperial household of the Chinese emperors, and none existed outside the palace walls. According to old Chinese texts, these dogs were bred by court officials and each new puppy was brought personally to the emperor for his approval.

The few specimens brought to England in the 1860's proved prolific breeders and by 1898 the English shows featured large classes of the "lion dogs." While some few Pekingese were presented to Americans by the Chinese rulers in the late 1800's, the American imports were not bred extensively and most of the American Pekes are bred from British-imported stock.

Despite the many centuries of selective breeding, there are several different types and strains of Pekingese. To follow the classical terminology of the breed, the "lion dogs" have a rather massive front, a heavy mane and tapering hindquarters. The "sun dogs " are Pekes distinguished by their striking golden-red coats. The name "sleeve dog" is applied to the smallest Pekingese in accord with the belief that they were carried by Chinese noblewomen in the voluminous sleeves of their garments.

As with many other toy breeds, there is rather wide variance in weight and size. Present-day standards accept anything under 14 pounds, but some fanciers are more interested in a smaller Peke, and some are working for under-six-pound specimens without loss of quality.

Pekingese
Ch. Bu-Ku of Kaytocli and Miralac
Owner: Mrs. Everett M. Clark. Pound Ridge, New York

As a pet, the Peke is regal in his attitude, generally aloof to strangers, but intensely loyal to his master or mistress, and a good watchdog. Not made for outdoor romping, his coat requires care, but he is a hardy dog. Unfortunately too many pet Pekes receive too little exercise and too much food and are over-pampered and underexercised.

Standard of the Breed

Expression: Must suggest the Chinese origin of the Pekingese in its quaint-ness and individuality, resemblance to the lion in directness and independence and should imply courage, self-esteem and combativeness rather than pretti-ness, daintiness or delicacy.

Skull: Massive, broad, wide and flat between the ears (not dome-shaped), wide between the eyes.

Nose: Broad, black, very short and flat.

Eyes: Large, dark, prominent, round, lustrous.

Stop: Deep.

Ears: Heart-shaped, not set too high, leather never long enough to come below the muzzle, nor carried erect, but rather drooping, long feather.

Muzzle: Wrinkled, very short and broad not overshot or pointed. Strong, broad underjaw, teeth not to show.

Shape of Body: Heavy in front, well sprung ribs, broad chest, falling away lighter behind, lionlike. Back level. Not too long in body; allowance made for longer body in bitch.

Legs: Short forelegs, bones of forearm bowed, firm at shoulder; hind legs lighter but firm and well shaped.

Feet: Flat, toes turned out, not round, should stand up well on feet, not on ankles.

Action: Fearless, free and strong, with slight roll.

Coat, Feather and Condition: Long, with thick undercoat, straight and flat, not curly or wavy, rather coarse, but soft; long and profuse feather on thighs, legs, tail and toes.

Mane: Profuse, extending beyond the shoulder blades, forming ruff or frill around the neck.

Color: All colors are allowable. Red, fawn, black, black-and-tan, sable, brindle, white and parti-color well defined; black masks and "spectacles" around the eyes are desirable.

Definition of Parti-Color Pekingese: The coloring of a parti-colored dog must be broken on body. No large portion of any one color should exist. White should be shown on the saddle. A dog of any solid color with white feet and chest is not a parti-color.

Tail: Set high; lying well over back to either side; long, profuse, straight feather.

Size: Being a toy dog, medium sized preferred, providing type and points are not sacrificed; extreme limit 14 pounds.

Penalizations: Protruding tongue; badly blemished eye; overshot, wry mouth.

Disqualifications: Weight over 14 pounds; Dudley nose.

SCALE OF POINTS

Expression	*5*
Skull	*10*
Nose	*5*
Eyes	*5*
Stop	*5*
Ears	*5*
Muzzle	*5*
Shape of body	*15*
Legs and feet	*15*
Coat, feather and condition	*15*

Tail	*5*
Action	*10*
	———
Total	*100*

MINIATURE PINSCHER

The miniature pinscher is a Doberman pinscher in miniature, with the same structure and traits as his larger cousin. Average weight 8 pounds; height 11 inches. Short, glossy coat, black with tan markings or reddish brown.

The miniature pinscher is another of the German-bred dogs. Soon after the larger Doberman pinscher was developed as a true breed in Germany, fanciers began working for a toy breed with the characteristics and conformation of the Doberman. By 1895, they had succeeded in developing these toy dogs which bred true to type.

Unlike some of the other "toys," the miniature pinscher is a true dwarf specimen, with a sturdy, wedge-shaped body that is a scaled-down version of the larger pinscher. In addition, he has retained the traits of the Doberman. He is a highly intelligent dog who responds quickly to both housebreaking and training and makes an excellent watchdog.

Although they were introduced into the United States as late as the middle 1920's, the miniature pinschers, being natural showmen, made an immediate impression on the cognoscenti of the dog world and a number of them took best-of-group honors among the toys at leading shows.

Many former owners of larger breeds have found the miniature pinscher satisfies their need for true doglike qualities despite its small size. It is not at all toylike in behavior, and from the budget point of view, the food requirements of the "minpin," as he is called, are about one-seventh of a larger dog's needs.

In appearance, when at rest or in action, this breed much resembles a tiny deer. In fact, the breed was known in Germany as the *Reh Pinscher* or roe terrier, and the current practice of docking the tail and cropping the ears contributes to the desired deerlike look.

Standard of the Breed

General Description: The miniature pinscher originated in Germany and named the *Reh Pinscher* because it resembled in structure and animation a very small species of deer found in the forests. This breed is structurally a well-balanced, sturdy, compact, short-coupled, smooth-coated toy dog. He is naturally well groomed, proud, vigorous and alert. The traits which identify him

Miniature Pinscher
Ch. Rebel Roc's Casanova
Owner: Mrs. E. W. Tipton, Jr. Kingsport, Tennessee

from other toy dogs are his precise hackney gait, his fearless animation, complete self-possession and his spirited presence. *Faults:* Structurally lacking in balance, too long- or short-coupled, too coarse or too refined (lacking in bone development causing poor feet and legs), too large or too small, lethargic, timid or dull, shy or vicious, low in tail placement and action (action not typical of the breed requirements). Knotty overdeveloped muscles.

Head: In correct proportion with the body. From top; tapering, narrow with well-fitted but not too prominent foreface which should balance with the skull. No indication of coarseness. From front; skull appears flat, tapering forward toward the muzzle. Muzzle itself strong rather than fine and delicate, and in proportion to the head as a whole. Cheeks and lips small, taut and closely adherent to each other. Teeth in perfect alignment and apposition. From side view, well balanced with only a slight drop to the muzzle, which should be parallel to the top of the skull.

Eyes: Full, slightly oval, almost round, clear, bright and dark even to a true black, set wide apart and fitted well into the sockets.

Ears: Well set and firmly placed, upstanding (when cropped, pointed and carried erect in balance with the head).

Nose: Black only (with the exception of chocolates, which may have a self-colored nose).

Faults: Head too large or too small for the body, too coarse or too refined, pinched and weak in foreface, domed in skull, too flat and lacking in chiseling, giving a vapid expression. Jaws and teeth overshot or undershot. Eyes too round and full, too large, bulging, too deep-set or set too far apart, or too small, set too close (pig eyes). Light-colored eyes are not desirable. Ears poorly placed, low-set hanging ears (lacking in cartilage) which detract from head conformation. (Poorly cropped ears if set on the head properly and having sufficient cartilage should not detract from head points, as this would be a man-made fault and automatically would detract from general appearance.) Nose any color other than black (except for chocolates).

Neck: Proportioned to head and body. Slightly arched, gracefully curved, clean and firm, blending into shoulders, length well balanced, muscular and free from any suggestion of dewlap or throatiness. *Faults:* Too straight or too curved; too thick or too thin; too long or short; knotty muscles; loose, flabby or wrinkled skin.

Body: From top; compact, slightly wedge-shaped, muscular with well sprung ribs. From side; depth of brisket, the base line of which is level with the points of the elbows, short and strong in loin, with belly moderately tucked up to denote grace in structural form. Back level or slightly sloping toward the rear. Length of male equals height at withers; females may be slightly longer. From rear; high-set tail; strong, sturdy upper shanks, with croup slope at about 30 degrees, vent opening not barreled.

Forequarters: Forechest well-developed and full, moderately broad, shoulders clean, sloping with moderate angulation, coordinated to permit the true action of the hackney pony.

Hindquarters: Well-knit muscular quarters set wide enough apart to fit into a properly balanced body.

Faults: From top—too long, too short, too barreled, lacking in body development. From side—too long, too short, too thin or too fat, hips higher or considerably lower than the withers, lacking depth of chest, too full in loin, sway-back, roach-back or wry-back. From rear—quarters too wide or too close to each other, overdeveloped, barreled vent, underdeveloped vent, too sloping croup, tail set too low. Forequarters—forechest and spring of rib too narrow (or too shallow and underdeveloped), shoulders too straight, too loose, under-muscled or overmuscled, too steep in croup.

Legs and Feet: Strong bone development and small, clean joints; feet catlike, toes strong, well-arched and closely knit with deep pads and thick, blunt nails. Forelegs and feet—as viewed from the front—straight and upstanding, elbows close to the body, well knit, flexible, yet strong, with perpendicular pasterns.

Hind legs—all adjacent bones should appear well angulated with well-muscled thighs or upper shanks, with clearly well-defined stifles, hocks short, set well apart and turning neither in nor out, while at rest should stand perpendicular to the ground and upper shanks, lower shanks and hocks parallel to each other.

Faults: Too thick or thin bone development, large joints, spreading flat feet. Forelegs and feet—bowed or crooked, weak pasterns, feet turning in or out, loose elbows. Hind legs—thin underdeveloped stifles, large or crooked hocks, loose stifle joints.

Tail: Set high, held erect, docked to ½ to 1 inch. *Faults:* Set too low, too thin, drooping, hanging or poorly docked.

Coat: Smooth, hard and short, straight and lustrous, closely adhering to and uniformly covering the body. *Faults:* Thin, too long, dull, upstanding, curly, dry, area of varying thickness or bald spots.

Color: (1) Solid red or stag red. (2) Lustrous black with sharply defined tan, rust-red markings on cheeks, lips, lower jaw, throat, twin spots above eyes and chest, lower half of forelegs, inside of hind legs and vent region, lower portion of hocks and feet. Black pencil stripes on toes. (3) Solid brown or chocolate with rust or yellow markings. *Faults:* Any color other than listed; very dark or sooty spots. *Disqualifications:* Thumb marks or any area of white on feet or forechest exceeding ½ inch in its longest dimension.

Size and Weight: Size to range from 10 inches to 12½ inches at the withers, with a preference of 11 to 11½ inches, weight to be governed by size and condition, ranging from 6 to 9 pounds for males and 6½ to 10 pounds for females. A squarely built specimen within the size limit, in condition, will conform to weight range. *Faults:* Oversize, undersize, too fat, too lean.

SCALE OF POINTS

General appearance and movement (very important)	*30*
Skull	*5*
Muzzle	*5*
Mouth	*5*
Eyes	*5*
Ears	*5*
Neck	*5*
Body	*15*
Feet	*5*
Legs	*5*
Color	*5*

Coat	*5*
Tail	*5*
Total	*100*

POMERANIAN

A miniature of a Baltic sled dog, this breed's boldness belies its size. Average weight 6 pounds; height 7 inches. Profuse coat with curled, bushy tail, orange to black, white, parti-colored, brown and cream colored.

Few things are more frustrating to the owner of a German shepherd or poodle than to have a tiny Pomeranian walk off with honors in an obedience trial, leaving the larger contenders far behind.

And this has happened time and time again. The Pomeranian is one of the most trainable toy dogs. His ancestry shows in his appearance. His look is that of a spitz, his deep fur is that of the Icelandic and Lapland sled dogs.

Once the size of other sheepdogs, the breed was reduced in size by the breeders in German Pomerania to the point where a litter of newborn Poms can be held in one hand.

As do several other breeds, the Pomeranian owes much of his popularity to Queen Victoria, who established a kennel of Poms and exhibited the breed in British shows. With royal approval, they caught on in England and breeders began producing smaller and smaller specimens until the present standards were achieved, without loss of character, conformation or coat.

On leash or in the show ring, the tiny dog with his highly held tail and mincing gait makes a delightful appearance. In disposition, he is generally bold but not vicious and will sit placidly in the show ring minding his own business although surrounded by larger dogs.

The Pomeranian's double coat protects him against cold and sudden temperature changes and he is fairly hardy.

Standard of the Breed

Appearance: The Pomeranian should be compact, short-coupled, well knit in frame. He should exhibit intelligence in his expression, docility in his disposition, activity and buoyancy in his deportment, and should be sound in action.

Head: The head should be wedge-shaped, somewhat foxy in outline, the skull being slightly flat, large in proportion to the muzzle. In profile, it has a little stop which must not be too pronounced, and the hair on the head and

Pomeranian
Ch. Aristie Little Pepper Pod
Owners: Mr. and Mrs. D. C. Cloninger. Fort Worth, Texas

face must be smooth or short-coated. The muzzle should finish rather fine. The teeth should meet in a scissor grip, in which part of the inner surface of the upper teeth meets and engages part of the outer surface of the lower teeth. This type of bite gives a firmer grip than one in which the edges of the teeth meet directly and subjects them to less wear. The mouth is considered overshot when the lower teeth fail to engage the inner surfaces of the upper teeth. The mouth is undershot when the lower teeth protrude beyond the upper teeth. One tooth out of line does not mean an overshot mouth.

Eyes: The eyes should be medium in size, rather oblique in shape, not set too wide apart, nor too close together, bright and dark in color. The eye rims of the blues and browns are self-colored. In all other colors the eye rims must be black.

Ears: The ears should be small, not set too far apart nor too low down, and carried perfectly erect, and should be covered with soft, short hair. Trimming unruly hairs on edge of ears is permissible.

Nose: Should be self-colored in browns and blues. In all other colors should be black.

Neck and Shoulders: The neck rather short, well set in, and lionlike, covered with a profuse mane and frill of long, straight hair sweeping from the under-jaw and covering the whole of the front part of the shoulders and chest as well as the top part of the shoulders. The shoulders must be clean and laid well back.

Body: The body must be short and level, compact, well ribbed up and rounded. The chest must be fairly deep.

Legs: The forelegs must be well feathered and perfectly straight, of medium length and strength in due proportion to a well-balanced frame. The feet small, compact, standing well up on toes. The hind legs and thighs must be well feathered down to the hocks, and must be fine in bone and free in action. Trimming around the edges of the toes and up the back of the legs to the first joint is permissible.

Tail: The tail is characteristic of the breed, and should be turned over the back and carried flat, set high. It is profusely covered with long, spreading hair.

Coat: There should be two coats, an under- and an outer coat; the under-coat, is soft and fluffy, the outer coat long, perfectly straight and glistening covering the whole body, being very abundant around the neck and forepart of the shoulders and chest, where it should form a frill of profuse off-standing straight hair extending over the shoulders. The hindquarters should be clad with long hair or feathering from the top of the rump to the hocks. The texture of the guard hairs must be harsh to the touch.

Color: The following colors are permissible and recognized: black, brown, chocolate, red, orange, cream, orange-sable, wolf-sable, beaver, blue, white, and parti-color. The parti-color dogs are white with orange or black distributed on the body in even patches, and a white blaze is preferable. In mixed classes where whole-colored and parti-colored Pomeranians compete, the prefer-ence—if in other points they are equal—should be given to the whole-colored specimens. Sables must be shaded throughout with three or more colors, as uniformly as possible with no patches of self-color, the undercoat being a light tan color, with deeper orange guard hairs ending in black tipping. Shaded muzzle on sable permissible. Oranges must be self-colored throughout, with light shadings on breeching.

Size: The weight of the Pomeranian for exhibition is 3 to 7 pounds. The ideal size for show specimens is 4 to 5 pounds.

Color Faults

Major: Whole-colored dogs with a white chest or white foot or leg; black mask on an orange.

Objectionable: Black, brown, blue or sable should be free from white hairs; black-and-tan, and whites should be free from lemon or any other color.

Minor: Black mask on sable, shaded muzzle permissible, white shading or orange.

Other Faults

Major: Round, domy skull, undershot, pink eye rims, light or Dudley nose. Out at elbows or shoulders; down in pasterns; cow hocks; soft, flat, open coat.

Objectionable: Overshot, large round or light eyes, high or low legs, long toes, too wide in hind legs, trimming too close to show date, tail set too low on rump, underweight or overweight.

Minor: Lippiness, wide chest, tail curling back.

PUG

Originally a Chinese dog, the pug came to England via the East Indies in the middle 1600's and was for a long time the leading toy breed. Average weight 16 pounds; height 10 inches. Short, smooth coat, fawn with dark face or solid black.

The small pug bears the mark of the Chinese toy dogs, a large head, short nose, and tail curled over the back. During the "gay nineties," the pug was the mark of fashion, but then the Pomeranian, the "Peke" and the Japanese spaniel came along and obscured him.

In disposition, the pug is a spunky little creature, with many bulldog-like traits, but is more amenable to training. He needs far less care than many of the other toys and is essentially a house dog, preferring the warmth of a human residence to the call of the wild.

During the early 1930's this breed enjoyed a renaissance of popularity which is continuing. There is something most appealing about the mastiff-like look in such small size and the determined swagger of his small, cobby body and his coiled tail.

Now the pug is back among the twenty most popular breeds and his sponsors in the dog world are hopeful that he will move up in coming years to replace the rivals who displaced him decades ago.

Standard of the Breed

Symmetry: Symmetry and general appearance, decidedly square and cobby. A lean, leggy dog and one with short legs and a long body are equally objectionable.

Size and Condition: The pug should be *multum in parvo,* but this condensa-

Pug
Burleigh's Quincy Victoria
Owners: Mr. and Mrs. W. C. McCullough. Highland Park, Illinois

tion (if the word may be used) should be shown by compactness of form, well-knit proportions and hardness of developed muscle. Weight 14 to 18 pounds (male or bitch) desirable.

Body: Short and cobby, wide in chest and well ribbed up.

Legs: Very strong, straight, of moderate length and well under.

Feet: Neither so long as the foot of the hare, nor so round as that of the cat; well split-up toes; nails black.

Muzzle: Short, blunt, square, but not up-faced.

Head: Massive, large, round—not apple-headed, with no indentation of the skull.

Eyes: Dark in color, very large, bold and prominent, globular in shape, soft and solicitous in expression, very lustrous, and, when excited, full of fire.

Ears: Thin, small, soft like black velvet. There are two kinds—the rose and "button." Preference is given to the latter.

Markings: Clearly defined. The muzzle or mask, ears, moles on cheeks, thumb mark or diamond on forehead, back trace should be as black as possible.

Mask: The mask should be black. The more intense and well defined it is, the better.

Wrinkles: Large and deep.

Trace: A black line extending from the occiput to the tail.

Tail: Curled as tightly as possible over the hip. The double curl is perfection.

Coat: Fine, smooth, soft, short and glossy, neither hard nor woolly.

Color: Silver or apricot-fawn. Each should be decided to make the contrast complete between the color and the mask. Black.

SCALE OF POINTS

	Fawn	Black
Symmetry	10	10
Size	5	10
Condition	5	5
Body	10	10
Legs and feet	5	5
Head	5	5
Muzzle	10	10
Ears	5	5
Eyes	10	10
Mask	5	—
Wrinkles	5	5
Tail	10	10
Trace	5	—
Coat	5	5
Color	5	10
Total	100	100

TOY MANCHESTER TERRIER

This breed is a smaller edition of the black and tan rat terrier of England which has sired many of the terrier breeds. Naturally erect ears. Average weight about 8 pounds; height 8 inches. Short, glossy coat, black with rich tan markings.

The history of the toy Manchester terrier—named after the city in England where he was bred in Victorian times—illustrates the ups and downs of a breed. Originally a standard-sized terrier, the breed was reduced by countless generations of selective breeding to toy size. By the 1840's, the craze for smallness led to the breeding of specimens of these dogs that weighed as little as 2½ pounds,

Toy Manchester Terrier
Ch. Golden Scoops Tiffany
Owner: Mrs. Elsie Puleo. Dover, New Jersey

and a resultant loss of stamina almost wiped out the breed.

However, a reaction set in among the fanciers and the breed was gradually upgraded to the stage where the modern show classes for toy Manchesters are divided into two groups, with the larger for dogs weighing up to 12 pounds.

The short coat of the toy Manchester requires little care and he has the instincts of the terrier in a small package—aggressive, a one-person dog, always alert, with a keen, intelligent expression and a disposition that belies his small size.

Despite the efforts of modern breeders to build a more sturdy strain, many of these dogs are somewhat delicate and difficult to raise, and the novice owner who acquires a toy Manchester might do well to locate a veterinarian who is experienced in treating the toy breeds. Some owners have reported unfortunate reactions after their puppies have received their "shots," but the ones that get past puppyhood are generally long-lived and give many years of peppy companionship.

Standard of the Breed

Head: Long, narrow, tight-skinned, almost flat, with a slight indentation up the forehead; slightly wedge-shaped, tapering to the nose, with no visible cheek muscles, and well filled up under the eyes; level in mouth, with tight-lipped jaws.

Eyes: Small, bright, sparkling and as near black as possible; set moderately close together; oblong in shape, slanting upward on the outside; they should neither protrude nor sink in the skull.

Nose: Black.

Ears: Of moderate size; well set up on skull and rather close together; thin, moderately narrow at base; with pointed tips; naturally erect carriage.

Faults: Wide, flaring, blunt-tipped or "bell" ears. Cropped or cut ears disqualify.

Neck and Shoulders: The neck should be of moderate length, slim and graceful; gradually becoming larger as it approaches, and blending smoothly with the sloping shoulders; free from throatiness; slightly arched from the occiput.

Chest: Narrow between the legs; deep in the brisket.

Body: Moderately short with robust loins; ribs well sprung out behind the shoulders; back slightly arched at the loin, and falling again to the juncture of the tail.

Legs: Forelegs straight, and well under the body. Hind legs should not turn in or out as viewed from the rear; carried back; hocks well let down.

Feet: Compact, well arched, with jet black nails; the two middle toes of the forefeet rather longer than the others; the hind feet shaped like those of a cat.

Tail: Moderately short, and set on where the arch of the back ends; thick where it joins the body, tapering to a point; not carried higher than the back.

Coat: Smooth, short, thick, dense, close and glossy; not soft.

Color: Jet black and rich mahogany tan, which should not run or blend into each other but meet abruptly, forming clear, well-defined lines of color division. A small tan spot over each eye; a very small tan spot on each cheek; the lips of the upper and lower jaws should be tan, extending under the throat, ending in the shape of the letter v; the inside of the ears partly tan. Tan spots, called rosettes, on each side of the chest above the front legs, more pronounced in puppies than in adults. There should be a black "thumb mark" patch in the front of each foreleg between the pastern and the knee. There should be a distinct black "pencil mark" line running lengthwise on the top of each toe on all four feet. The remainder of the forelegs to be tan to the knee. Tan on the hind legs should continue from the penciling on the feet up the inside of the legs to a little below the stifle joint; the outside of the hind legs to be black. There should be tan under tail and on the vent, but only of such size as to be covered by the tail. *Fault:* White in any part of the coat is a serious fault, and shall disqualify whenever the white shall form a patch or stripe measuring as much as one-half inch in its largest dimension.

Weight: Not exceeding 12 pounds. In shows, classes are divided into two groups: under 7 pounds; and 7 to 12 pounds.

SCALE OF POINTS

Head (including eyes, nose and ears)	30
Neck and shoulders	10
Body (including chest and tail)	15
Legs and feet	15
Coat	10
Color	20
Total	*100*

YORKSHIRE TERRIER

A fairly new breed, developed in England within the last 100 years. A toy dog, average weight 7 pounds, height 8 inches. Coat is outstanding characteristic, long, silky, parted down back; steel blue with tan head and legs.

The Yorkshire terrier is naturally an alert and active dog. However, the stress on the dog's coat in the show ring forces owners who plan to show the dog to restrict its activity to keep the coat—which should reach the ground—in show condition.

Although the modern Yorkie has been bred down from larger dogs which weighed about 14 pounds, it is one of the sturdier and healthier of the toy breeds, and a number of members of the Yorkshire Terrier Club of America have reported dogs which have remained active to ages of eighteen and 20 years.

The novice planning to buy a Yorkie for show purposes should be prepared to spend many hours each week grooming the dog's coat and to keep the strands of the dog's coat in paper and cloth wrappers before a show. In addition, if planning to breed a bitch, a larger specimen (preferably over 8 pounds) should be chosen, as caesarian births are very often necessary and almost always so with a tiny bitch. To keep the breed down to size, the smallest males are generally matched to the largest bitches.

On the other hand, if the Yorkie owner is not interested in breed shows, the coat may be cut shorter and then the dog requires little grooming.

Yorkshire Terrier
Ch. Abon Hassen's Lady Iris
Owners: Mr. and Mrs. Theron C. Trudgian. Denver, Colorado

One unexpected characteristic of the Yorkshire is its response to obedience training. Many Yorkies have done exceedingly well in obedience trials in recent years and a number of the Yorkshire fanciers' clubs have set up obedience classes with outstanding success.

As a rule, the Yorkshire is not a finicky eater. However, some strains show a tendency to vomiting, but this is often controlled by withholding food for a day or so and feeding small quantities of baking soda solution or a few drops of pure witch hazel in water.

Standard of the Breed

General Appearance: A long-coated toy terrier, the coat hanging quite straight and evenly down each side, a parting extending from the nose to the end of the tail. The animal should be very compact and neat, the carriage being very upright, and having an important air. The general outline should convey the existence of a vigorous and well-proportioned body.

Head: Rather small and flat, not too prominent or round in the skull, nor too long in the muzzle, with a perfectly black nose. The fall on the head to be long, of a rich golden tan, deeper in color at the sides of the head about the ear roots, and on the muzzle where it should be very long. The hair on chest a rich bright tan. On no account must the tan on the head extend on to the neck, nor must there be any sooty or dark hair intermingled with any of the tan.

Eyes: Medium dark and sparkling, having a sharp, intelligent expression and placed so as to look directly forward. They should not be prominent, and the edge of the eyelids should be of a dark color.

Ears: Small, V-shaped, carried semi-erect and not far apart, covered with short hair, the color a very deep rich tan.

Mouth: Perfectly even, with teeth as sound as possible; an animal having lost any teeth through accident not a fault, provided the jaws are even.

Body: Very compact, and a good loin. Level on the top of the back.

Coat: The hair on the body moderately long and perfectly straight (not wavy), glossy like silk, and of a fine silky texture. Color, a dark steel blue (not silver blue) extending from the occiput (or back of skull) to the root of tail, and on no account mingled with fawn, bronze or dark hairs.

Legs: Quite straight, well covered with hair of a rich golden tan a few shades lighter at the ends than at the roots, not extending higher on the forelegs than the elbow, nor higher on the hind legs than the stifle.

Feet: As round as possible, and the toenails black.

Tail: Cut to medium length; with plenty of hair, darker blue in color than the rest of the body, especially at the end of tail, and carried a little higher than the level of the back.

Tan: All tan hair should be darker at the roots than in the middle, shading to a still lighter tan at the tips.

SCALE OF POINTS

Formation and terrier appearance	*15*
Color of hair on body	*15*
Richness of tan on head and legs	*15*
Quality and texture of coat	*10*
Quantity and length of coat	*10*
Head	*10*

Mouth	5
Legs and feet	5
Ears	5
Eyes	5
Carriage of tail	5
Total	*100*

3

FEEDING YOUR DOG

of years, dogs have lived with people, eaten what the people ate, and apparently have thrived on it. However, in recent years, the manufacture and sale of dog food has become one of America's thriving industries. Currently, sales of prepared dog food in cans, packages and bags have totaled about $350 million a year. This growth of the dog-food industry has been accompanied by an intensive newspaper, magazine and television barrage to convince the dog owner that he is failing in his duty to his pet if he feeds him brand "X" instead of the sponsor's product.

Most of the commercial dog foods are adequate. However, like everything else in the market place, you get what you pay for. The lower-priced dog foods will necessitate additional feeding of meat to keep your dog in good shape; many of the higher-priced foods provide almost everything the dog needs.

From the point of view of nutrition, there is little difference whether you use a good grade of canned dog food, biscuits, meal or kibbled food. All contain about the same proportions of proteins, minerals, fat, carbohydrates, crude fiber, and so on. Some manufacturers add a small amount of charcoal to aid the animal's digestion and to help prevent the formation of intestinal gases. The lower-priced foods are padded out with cereal and other low-cost food products to add bulk to the package or can.

Most dog owners today find it more convenient to buy prepared dog food than feed table leftovers or prepare special menus for their dogs.

READ THE LABEL

Read the label before buying any dog food. Most reliable food packers today provide a label which describes the ingredients of the product—whether it is beef, horse meat, lamb or meat by-product, liver or whatever else it contains.

In addition, the label usually provides an analysis of the contents. For example, one of the foods often recommended by veterinarians contains:

Crude protein	*not less than*	*13.5%*
Crude fat	*not less than*	*7%*
Crude fiber	*not more than*	*1.5%*
Ash	*maximum*	*0.5%*
Charcoal		*.01%*
Sodium Nitrite		*.001%*

Generally, a food which runs fairly close to this analysis should provide a suitable diet.

FEEDING YOUR PUPPY

A normally healthy puppy should be fully weaned at the age of seven or eight weeks and should be ready to enjoy a soft diet for several weeks and then gradually become accustomed to normal "doggy" meals. In the wild state, the mother would chew and regurgitate the food for the puppy for several weeks until it is ready for more solid foods. In raising a more civilized puppy, its food should be mushy at first, with the addition of more solid foods each week.

FEEDING PRINCIPLES FOR THE PUPPY

For the past hundred years there has been almost as much research in canine nutrition as in human. While many of dog-feeding research projects have been conducted by dog-food companies and the end results have something of the atmosphere of the "independent research laboratory" findings that are so frequently reported in television commercials, much has been learned about the dog's need for specific food elements.

It has been pretty definitely established that the first months in a dog's life are the most important for body building and that his health and longevity depend to a considerable extent on his early diet (and on the diet of his mother during her pregnancy).

GENERAL DIET REQUIREMENTS

Proteins. These provide the amino acids, the "building blocks" required for growth and tissue repair. The puppy's protein requirements are high, since puppyhood is the period of fastest growth. Milk, cheese and meats are rich in protein. However, there is considerable difference in composition between dog's milk and the cow's. Some puppies cannot digest cow's milk; some will throw it up. If you should encounter that problem, try adding a bit of lime water to the milk and beat a raw egg into it. If that doesn't work, substitute a light beef or chicken broth for the milk in the puppy's diet.

Fat. Puppies usually require about 8 per cent fat in their diet to provide energy and a healthy skin and coat.

Carbohydrates. These are a source of ready energy for the active puppy. Properly cooked carbohydrates can be digested by a puppy, but avoid over-feeding of starchy foods.

Vitamins. Several research projects with "controlled" subjects have shown that the normal puppy diet may not provide sufficient vitamins. Symptoms of vitamin deficiency are dull coat, skin ailments, poor appetite, lack of vitality and lowered resistance to disease.

A powdered or liquid vitamin supplement is on the "must" list for puppy feeding and should be mixed with his food once daily.

Minerals. Calcium and phosphorus are necessary in proper proportion for building tooth and bone structure. Iron, cobalt and copper for blood formation, and other trace elements for nerve, muscle and other body structure. It is often helpful to sprinkle bone meal on one of the puppy's meals daily, but avoid overdosing him with bone meal.

THE PUPPY'S DIET

If you should acquire a puppy under seven or eight weeks of age, try to find out what his diet has been and keep him on that for another week or two. If you have no idea of his previous diet, feed him much as you would a very young human infant—mainly milk and a baby cereal (pablum or the like) and pre-pared infants' foods.

Once the puppy is fully weaned, diet should consist mainly of milk (whole or evaporated, or the mixture suggested above); raw or slightly boiled ground beef, lamb, mutton or horse meat; liver or viscera; dry cereals (Shredded Wheat is recommended, Wheaties, Rice Crispies or other not-too-sweet cereal); puppy meal or biscuit; egg yolk; cottage cheese; buttermilk; strained vegetables; good quality canned dog food.

As to amount, a good rule of thumb is to feed a dog about one-half ounce of food per pound of body weight per day; growing puppies about twice this amount. However, this may vary somewhat, depending on breed, amount of exercise, climate, and especially on the individual dog. Some dogs just seem to have more active appetites than others.

PUPPY AND DOG FEEDING CHART

It is not necessary to become a slave to your dog. The following chart shows the number of daily feedings for puppies of different ages and for adult dogs. Space the feedings to meet your own schedule. Don't overfeed your dog or puppy with between-meal tidbits, but if you enjoy his obvious appreciation of snacks, you needn't be overstrict always.

Age	Weaning to 3 months	3 months to 6 months	6 months to 1 year	Over 1 year
Number of daily feedings	4	3	2	1 or 2

A suggested diet

Food groups

Group A
Milk
Eggs
Buttered toast
Cereals

Group B
Raw or boiled beef
Horse meat
Lamb or mutton
Liver, heart or kidney
Canned dog food
Cottage cheese
Buttermilk
Milk
Biscuit
Kibble
Puppy meal

Try for a common-sense balance in the diet of your puppy or dog. Remember that the dog's taste sensations are not like yours. What seems a monotonous diet to you may appeal to him. Avoid feeding anything that is spicy or hot; however, he does need a certain amount of salt in his diet.

For puppies needing four feedings daily, pick the morning meal from Group A; the noon and evening meals from Group B, and the bedtime feeding from Group C. For puppies on the three-meals-a-day schedule, the morning feeding from Group A, and the other two meals from Group B. For dogs requiring one or two meals daily,

Whole wheat bread
Whole wheat cereal
Strained vegetables
Meat broth or soup
Powder or liquid vitamin
    supplement
Bone meal
Cod liver oil
  Group C
Warm milk
Cereal

selections may be made from either Group A or B and may be fed at any time during the day.

When you begin housebreaking the puppy, cut down on the amount of liquid in the evening meal. Try to set up and keep to a fairly regular feeding schedule. However, a puppy can miss a feeding with no ill effects; a grown dog can get along with no food for twenty-four hours or longer.

NOT FOR YOUR DOG!

Do not give your puppy raw pork products, poultry bones, chewing gum, candy, peanuts, popcorn, soft drinks or chocolate; they may upset his digestive system. However, don't panic if your puppy does gobble up something on this "verboten" list or something else that you think should not be in a young canine's diet. The dog's digestive system—even that of a puppy—is pretty much the same as a wolf's. Usually if he swallows something too offensive, it will promptly come out again, and don't worry if your puppy upchucks occasionally. This is a very common puppy trait, although persistent vomiting may require a visit to the veterinarian.

One of the most frequent types of phone calls to a veterinarian begins, "My puppy has just eaten. . . ." The end of the sentence may be anything from gummed paper, part of a louvered door, a green apple, a nylon sock, a rubber band, or almost anything a puppy can get into its mouth. Unless the substance is an actual poison, there is little cause for worry. It will either come up soon through the mouth or you may have the somewhat unpleasant task of helping it out through the other end of the puppy a bit later.

THE PROPER FEEDING DISH

The type of feeding dish you use for a puppy doesn't matter much. If it is low enough for the puppy to get at the food, it is low enough for him to climb into it, and you can expect your puppy to walk right into and through his meal. Just use a damp sponge or paper toweling to clean him up afterward.

Most dogs are sloppy eaters. Many of the fancy feeding dishes in the pet shops were designed by people who obviously never had to clean up after a dog's dinner.

Match the size of the dog's dish to the amount of food you will be giving him. The dish should be as heavy as possible, as the kind that slides around the floor makes it harder for the dog to eat and leaves a wider trail of dog food for you to clean up, if your dog is to do most of his eating indoors. Some metal dog-food dishes are made to fit into frames that are fixed to the floor with rubber suction cups, and there are also wide rubber dishes that cling to the floor.

Also, match the dish with your dog's head. A dog with long floppy ears will get his ears into the food unless he has a high dish with a rather narrow-top opening. A dog with a wide, bulldog type head needs a dish with plenty of room to move around in.

ABOUT DRINKING WATER

There are two schools of thought regarding drinking water for the dog. A young puppy probably gets enough moisture in his semiliquid diet and will use a drinking dish as a bathtub. For an older dog, you can give him water three times a day, or leave a dish of water available to him at all times. Some dogs will overdrink if they have too much water available and may suffer stomach upset. But, by trial and error, you and your dog will soon arrive at a satisfactory drinking-water arrangement. Incidentally, many apartment or house dogs soon learn that there is a supply of water in the toilet bowl and will drink from it if they can reach it.

FOOD FROM STRANGERS

Frequently the newspapers report epidemics of dog poisoning, and if you can, it might be a good idea to train your dog not to take food from anyone except a member of the immediate family. Although this training runs against a domestic dog's natural disposition, it can be accomplished. With some dogs, it can be achieved merely by severe verbal correction if the dog attempts to pick up food from the street or accepts it from a stranger, and by being consistent with this correction until it takes hold.

Another technique that may work is this: Have some person whom the dog does not know (to provide an unfamiliar scent associated with the food) prepare a piece of meat by slicing it and inserting some strong condiment; and let him put the morsel down where the dog can get it. A few instances in which the dog finds that alien food has a disagreeable taste may teach the dog to restrict his eating to his home territory.

PROBLEMS IN DOG FEEDING

One of the most common problems in feeding a house-raised dog is that of the finicky eater. Dachshunds, Boston terriers and many of the toy breeds tend to be problem eaters. Often this is due to the owner's attitude. Letting the dog go hungry until he eats what he is offered will usually solve the problem. However, the average dog owner is not hard-hearted enough to do that.

In rare cases, the dog's refusal to eat may reach the stage where it becomes necessary to have a veterinarian keep him alive by intravenous injections, although there may be no evidence of any organic condition which would prevent the dog from eating. But most often the dog will eat when he is hungry. The average dog is smart enough to ignore his own food if he is constantly fed from the table, and most house pets seem to prefer food from the dinner table to food from their own dish.

Most dogs are suspicious of any change in their diet. If your dog refuses to eat when you offer him a new kind of food, or when you add a vitamin to his food, try hand-feeding the first few mouthfuls. Hold a few pieces of the unfamiliar food in your hand; let the dog sniff it first, and then you will usually find that he will swallow the tidbit from your hand and presently finish the food in his dish. But be careful not to carry this to the point where the dog expects to be hand-fed. Many dogs will become pampered parasites with a little encouragement.

Another method is to add a bit of soup broth, gravy or whatever you have on the stove or the table to his new food, to give it a richer flavor and induce him to try it. Holding the dog's head down into the food dish and shouting at him to eat will only fray your temper and excite the dog.

There is no excuse for the pet dog that growls or snaps at a person who approaches him while he is eating. In the wild state, a dog may have to fight to protect his food, and a puppy raised in a kennel where he had to compete with other puppies for food may have developed the habit of standing protectively over his food. When the dog is young, this habit can be broken. Occasionally play with the puppy while he is eating and pick a morsel out of the food dish and hand it to him. As part of the game, pick him up and carry him a foot or two from his food, then put him down and let him go back to it. If he snarls or shows any resentment, correct him rather severely.

It is not difficult to teach a dog the meaning of "Drop it!" And with proper training, your dog should drop anything he has in his mouth, even a tasty piece of garbage, when he hears that command. Begin when the dog is young. First make a game of letting the dog hold his end of a stick or piece of thick cloth. Tell him to "Drop it!" and blow in his nostrils, or tap his snout to make him let go. Then praise him for cooperating, or reward him with a tidbit or piece of dog candy. Later, correct him if he does not obey the command. When he gets a bit older, discipline him if he fails to drop an object on command.

COMMON SENSE APPROACH TO DOG FEEDING

If you read a technical treatise on canine feeding, you will find yourself enmeshed in vitamins, lipotropins, bioflavonoids, niacin, minerals and other dietetic technicalities. Don't let all that frighten you.

The dog's appearance and actions are your guides as to whether he is getting the proper amount of the correct food. After a satisfactory meal, a puppy's abdomen should be nicely rounded and "bouncy" to the touch. The fur of the puppy and older dog is another proper-food indicator. If the coat is not shiny and healthy-looking, it may indicate a lack of fat in his diet.

The older dog should be lean, with a good layer of flesh over his ribs and flanks. Any tendency toward obesity should call for a reduction in food or a change in diet, with a cutting down of carbohydrates and biscuit-type foods.

The dog's elimination is another important key to his diet sufficiency. Normally, his stools should be solid. If you feed a meal-type food, his stools will be bulkier than from a kibble or meat diet. Frequently, a dog's stools will be loose for a day or so after a change in his diet from one type of food to another. However, persistent diarrhea may indicate some illness; and alternate loose and good bowel movements may, especially in puppies, indicate the presence of worms.

4

YOUR DOG'S HEALTH

START OFF WITH A HEALTHY PUPPY

TRYING TO BUILD a sickly puppy to healthy maturity is almost always a losing battle. Ethical dog breeders invariably remove the sickly specimens from a litter before offering the puppies for sale, but still many unfit puppies are sold each year. And once the purchaser becomes attached to his pet the constant trek to the veterinarian can become a costly and disheartening routine. As a matter of self-protection, any puppy that is bought should be subject to approval by a veterinarian. The usual procedure is to allow the buyer a 24-hour period in which to have the puppy examined by a veterinarian. If the puppy is rejected, the seller should be shown a note from the veterinarian giving the reason for rejection, and the purchase price should be refunded. Many humane associations and dog shelters allow a try-out period during which a puppy or dog may be returned and exchanged for another pet.

Buying a puppy even from a reputable, ethical breeder always entails a certain risk. Some heredity defects do not show up for a considerable time, and many dog diseases have a rather long incubation period during which the puppy or dog may appear healthy. So far as health is concerned, there is little evidence to support the common belief that a mongrel or mixed-breed dog is usually healthier than a purebred dog.

A frequent point of discussion among dog fanciers is the rather rapid deterioration of a breed soon after the particular breed becomes popular. That is a point to watch if you are buying a dog of a popular breed. It often happens that a type of dog catches the public fancy and the breeders overproduce in order to cash in on the demand. Many experts blame the popularity of the movie dog Rin Tin Tin for a long decline in the quality of German shepherds

—although the breed has improved in recent years; and television's Lassie is being blamed for a profusion of inferior collies.

SIGNS OF HEALTH

Always look a gift dog—or one you are considering buying—in the mouth. The healthy dog should have clean teeth and healthy-looking gums. And smell his breath. While occasional halitosis may result from something he has eaten, the dog's breath should normally not be offensive.

A puppy should be lively, should have a neatly rounded but not too prominent belly, and a smooth coat free from patches or blemishes. His eyes should be clear, without discharges. However, a reddish appearance at the corner of the eye may be the inner eyelid (the haw), which is prominent in some breeds.

When you take the puppy to the veterinarian, he should take the puppy's temperature, examine the eyes, ears and anal region, "sound" his lungs, and check his bone structure for soundness. Keep in mind, however, that even the most skilled veterinarian can report only on the puppy's state of health. It is impossible for him to tell whether a puppy has "championship" potential.

PUPPY AND DOG CARE

Assuming that you start off with a healthy puppy or dog, you should have fun with him (or her) as with a member of your family, and keeping a dog healthy is no big problem. Dogs, except for some of the toy breeds which require special care, are naturally sturdy animals. Over many millennia dogs have become accustomed to man's way of life and they can live happily in a hut on the desert or in an air-conditioned city apartment.

The dog's instincts are geared to enable him to survive, and all he needs is a little common-sense cooperation from his owner. The dog's problem is that civilization has been imposed on him. In his normal existence, a dog would not be given a bath in a heated apartment and then rushed out into the cold winter air, or ride in a car at fifty miles an hour with the breeze blowing in his ears. In his wild state, the dog eats when he can, then rests to digest his food. Let your dog enjoy a dog's life. Follow a sensible feeding plan (discussed in the previous chapter), give him exercise, a clean place in which to sleep, and human companionship. Many of the best obedience and field dogs lead a double life—affectionate as pets, and hard-working at their jobs.

THE NECESSARY "SHOTS"

Many dogs who have never seen the inside of a veterinarian's office have lived to a healthy old age. But dogs in a city or suburban environment need protection against diseases which spread among the dog population.

Usually when you acquire a puppy you will be told that he has already received his puppy shots for immunity against distemper. But before he is allowed to run loose, or even walk in the streets on lead, he should be given his "permanent" shots. The vaccination given dogs by most veterinarians protects them against distemper, hepatitis and leptospirosis, which are the three most prevalent canine virus diseases. Usually they are given in a series of three shots, and some veterinarians recommend booster shots during a dog's adult life to strengthen the degree of protection. Until a dog has received this protection it is unwise to allow him to have much contact with other dogs or even to let him sniff people's shoes which can carry an infection in from the street.

Many areas require rabies inoculations to protect dogs from that highly contagious virus disease. However, there is criticism of promiscuous rabies inoculations in regions where no cases of rabies have been reported for some years. Your best bet is to be guided by the regulations, if any, in your area, and the advice of your veterinarian. Incidentally, a dog that is foaming at the mouth is not necessarily a "mad" rabid dog. Some dogs foam at the mouth if they eat or drink anything which has an unpleasant taste.

EXTERNAL PARASITES

Fleas, lice, ticks and mites may infest your dog, but control is fairly simple and the fear of having him bring pests into the house is no valid reason against owning a dog.

Fleas can be kept from your dog by dusting him with flea powder once a week and also by sprinkling the powder occasionally around his sleeping quarters. The species of flea which is found on dogs prefer dogs to humans and will seldom attach themselves to a human when a dog is around. However, if the dog is away from home for a while, the fleas may shift to human hosts.

Lice attach themselves to the dog and breed on him, laying their eggs in his hair where they are visible as tiny silverish or black specks; these will hatch into new generations of lice if left undisturbed. The cure is a liberal application of insecticide, repeated until the insects have been destroyed.

From the writer's observation, ticks have increased in number and annoyance in the northeastern part of the United States. Reports from the Public Health Service indicate that cases of humans contracting fever from the Rocky Mountain tick are prevalent in wider areas.

On a short-haired dog the ticks can generally be seen. The female tick is a fat, bean-shaped insect, grayish in color; the male is much smaller and reddish brown. The parasite attaches itself to the dog by burying its head in the dog's skin. From a short-haired dog the tick can be removed with tweezers or with a piece of absorbent cotton or tissue. But first make the tick withdraw his head. This is done by touching him with the glowing end of a lighted cigarette (it can be done easily without burning the dog) or by touching it with iodine. Destroy the pest by burning or dropping it in kerosene.

On longer-haired dogs the problem calls for a very thorough application of powder which is described as a tick killer, or by using one of the liquids for this purpose. A serious infestation may require a dipping in an insecticide solution.

Most ticks are acquired when the dog goes through brush or tall grasses where the ticks lie in wait for a host and drop down and attach themselves. After cleaning the dog, spray or powder his sleeping areas to catch any ticks that may be there. Ticks are not merely bloodsuckers; their danger is in the infections they may carry.

Mites are tiny insect-like creatures which cause a reddish spot to form on the skin of dogs they infect. Like ticks, they cling to tall grasses and brush and attach themselves to passing dogs, and are the cause of different forms of mange. But mites yield to treatment with the proper insecticides. However, the different kinds require different treatment, so it's best to check with a veterinarian if the dog persists in scratching. A reddish skin spot may be a sign of mange.

INTERNAL PARASITES

Most puppies require one or more wormings to get rid of worms they were born with or have managed to acquire while living with their mother and littermates. Contrary to common belief, worms do not come from a dog's eating candy or sweets; and garlic will not kill or drive out the worms.

If a dog is well wormed in puppyhood, prevented from eating garbage and other filth, and kept free of fleas, he should remain worm-free.

The types of internal parasites common to dogs are: whipworm, tapeworm, roundworm, hookworm, heartworm, and *Coccidiodes* (a microorganism which affects mainly puppies).

Coccidiosis is caused by *Coccidiodes,* a small, one-celled parasite which is supposedly spread by flies. It is highly contagious and causes intestinal irritation and often bloody diarrhea. Generally the condition will work off in about three weeks in an adult dog, but it may be highly dangerous to puppies, often attacking entire litters.

Whipworms attach themselves to the intestines. They are filament-like worms, about one-half inch long, but with a fine "whip" at the front of their body which may be several times the body length.

The most common tapeworm is the flea-host type which lives in the body of the flea and enters the dog when he eats a flea. The tapeworm head is liberated during the dog's digestive process and reaches the intestinal tract, where it attaches itself and grows additional segments until the worm may be well over a foot long. Pieces break off and may be seen in the dog's stool, or in what looks like brown seeds under the dog's tail. Occasionally a piece may be seen moving in the dog's stool. Controlling fleas prevents infection. Other forms of tapeworm may be acquired from pork which is not properly cooked, from raw fish, or from rabbit meat.

Roundworms are fairly common. The dog eats the eggs of the worm, or a puppy can be born with the eggs in his body. The worms follow a rather involved life pattern in which they spend part of the life cycle in the dog's blood, then finally fasten themselves in the intestine where they grow to a length of up to five inches. They are not seriously dangerous to older dogs, but may weaken a puppy considerably.

The hookworm is a tiny parasite, only about five-eighths of an inch long, but with a voracious appetite for blood. It receives its name from the hooks around its mouth by which it fastens itself to the intestinal wall. In one stage the hookworm is able to bore through the dog's skin, and finally arrives in the intestine where it fastens itself and sends its eggs out in the dog's stool.

Heartworms are rather rare. They are spread by the bite of a mosquito which introduces the worm's larvae into the blood stream. The larvae finally work their way into the dog's heart. Some have been found 8 inches long and $\frac{1}{16}$ of an inch thick. However, they can be removed by various medicines and veterinary treatment. Coughing when the dog tugs at the leash may sometimes be an indication of heartworm.

Treatment

Reading about worms may make the internal parasite situation seem worse than it really is. Adult dogs can usually develop a resistance to worms and often the worms die in the dog's body and pass out with his stool without any treatment. There are a number of home worm remedies available in pet stores which may be effective against specific worm parasites if used according to directions.

Continued scratching or licking of the rectum, or intermittent loose bowels may indicate worms. If you take your dog to the vet for treatment, take along a sample of his stool, as microscopic examination will help the veterinarian identify the type of worm that has infested your dog.

SOME SYMPTOMS—AND EXPLANATIONS

Many new dog owners spend time and money on unnecessary visits to the veterinarian. Some apparently horrible things may seem to be happening to your dog when actually there is little reason to become alarmed.

Often an owner is horrified to see his dog running around in a frantic state, shaking his head violently, flapping its ears, and perhaps stopping from time to time to rub an ear against the floor or the furniture. Most often this is merely because a flea has gotten into the ear and the dog is trying to dislodge it, or a bit of wax may be annoying him. The head shaking usually stops after the flea has departed or the wax has worked loose. However, if it persists for a considerable time, it may indicate ear canker (if your dog has long, floppy ears), or some middle-ear trouble.

Throwing up soon after eating is common among many of the breeds with bulldog-type heads and bodies, and also among some other dogs. Most often, the dog will promptly re-eat his regurgitated meal if you let him, with no harm. However, too frequent "up-chucking" of food by an adult dog may indicate that something is wrong and calls for a medical check-up. If the dog throws up a white foamy substance in large volume, that may indicate illness, especially if it is preceded by gagging or coughing. Also, if the vomit is yellowish or greenish and persists, it may be serious.

Another alarming sight is to see your dog dragging his rear along the ground, and constantly licking his anal region. This is most often because the anal glands have accumulated a secretion which the dog is trying to squeeze out. You can help by holding the dog firmly and squeezing the glands around his anus with absorbent cotton until a rather smelly liquid comes out. If neglected, these glands may form abscesses which burst, or require lancing by the veterinarian. Some dogs are prone to the condition and may require squeezing-out several times a year.

After a bowel movement, your dog may begin to run around excitedly in a tight circle, rubbing his rear on the ground and trying to bite at his anus. If you hold him, you will probably find that he has been trying to eject a swallowed piece of string or cloth or fiber which has become stuck in his anus and won't come through. This requires your help in pulling it free.

Dog are subject to many respiratory ailments which are very similar to human colds and pneumonia. The symptoms are much the same. A dog with a cold may have a running nose, weepy or caked eyes, accompanied by a cough and sniffles. Treat him as you would a child with the same condition. Keep the dog warm and comfortable; give him aspirin, and cut down on his exercise. However, if he doesn't get over it in a few days, it should call for a vet's opinion. Often coughing simply means that the dog has swallowed some grass or dirt and is trying to clear his throat.

Some dogs even show symptoms of hay fever—running eyes, sneezing, etc. and the like. But this usually disappears rather quickly.

Dogs also may suffer from asthma, sore tonsils (dogs have tonsillectomies, too), but a persistent dry cough may sometimes indicate the beginning of distemper.

Loose bowels may be the result of a change in diet, or, if very frequent, may indicate that the dog needs a worming; in a puppy, continuous watery bowel movements may be a sign of some illness.

THE DOG'S TEMPERATURE

The dog's temperature is a good indicator of his state of health. Any serious condition will cause his temperature to rise from the normal 100.6 to 101.5 F.; although excitement may cause a temporary rise of a degree or so. If your dog is accustomed to being handled, taking his temperature is no problem. Use a human-type rectal thermometer, sterilize it in alcohol, rub vaseline over the tip and insert it in the rectum. Hold the dog while the thermometer is in him, as he will instinctively try to sit down to remove the object from his rectum. Take the reading after a few minutes. Remember that the dog's normal body temperature is higher than that of the human, so disregard the "normal" marker on the side of the thermometer.

THE SICK DOG

If your dog is really sick he will show it by his appearance and actions.

Refusal of meals for more than a day; a long period of lassitude; and considerable change in the dog's disposition, are signs of illness. Generally, the dog's coat gives an indication of his state of health, and a change from his usual sleekness may show that something is wrong.

POISONING

If you know that your dog has swallowed a specific poison, call the local SPCA or a veterinarian to learn the proper antidote and how to administer it.

A fairly safe emergency treatment is to pour a solution of half water and half regular-strength hydrogen peroxide down the dog's throat, which should make him vomit. Then when he has stopped gasping, give him some epsom salts in water to clean out his intestines. Save some specimens of the vomit and stool to help the veterinarian identify the type of posion. Don't give him any food or water until you have consulted the veterinarian.

Milder forms of food poisoning may identify themselves by hivelike bumps over the dog's body and face, which may become so large that the eyes are almost closed by the swellings. Withhold food and water, and get the dog to the veterinarian as soon as possible. If you cannot obtain veterinary service for some time, put the dog on a strict diet of barley or oatmeal water until you can have him examined.

5

GROOMING YOUR DOG

of grooming your dog requires should be an important consideration in your choice of a pet. A breed such as the Yorkshire terrier, that has been bred for generations for his long, silky coat, requires constant grooming. The poodle and many of the terriers require frequent coat care for a good appearance. If you are a city dweller and used to having things done for you, the trips to the canine beauty parlor can put quite a dent in your budget.

Generally, the longer-haired dogs require more frequent grooming to keep their coats in condition and to prevent the hair from matting. The short-haired breeds can get along with occasional brushing.

And while we are on the subject of coats, it might be well to consider the problem of shedding. Contrary to the belief of many, the short-haired dogs often shed much more than do the long-haired and the shed hair will cling tenaciously to clothing and furniture. Before buying a dog it would be well to discuss the matter of dog hairs with the women of the family. Some breeds shed almost not at all and these would appeal to the fastidious housekeeper. (This trait is noted in the description of the various breeds in this book).

THE GROOMING TOOLS

The new dog's "layette" should include a comb, a brush, a hound glove and a stripping knife. The preferred comb is one of steel with rather dull—not pointed—teeth. If your dog has a profuse coat or long feathering you should buy a comb with heavy teeth set wide apart. A finer-toothed comb is better for use on a dog with a short coat.

There are scores of different types of dog brushes on the market, and an informed sales person can help you choose the proper one for your dog. The length of the bristle should be chosen according to the length and density of the dog's coat; long-haired dogs require a deeper bristle. For dogs with a heavy or wire-haired coat, the bristles should be very stiff, while a brush only slightly stiffer than the ordinary human hairbrush works well on a short-haired or sparsely coated dog.

The hound glove gives a glossy finish to dogs whose hair lies close to the body. It is especially recommended for use on all terriers, setters, spaniels, and smooth-coated dogs. Incidentally, one of the best ways to give your dog's coat a glossy look is to rub it thoroughly with the palm of your hand. The oil in the human hand imparts a fine luster to a dog's coat. In fact, if you observe the grooming section of a dog show, you will often see the handlers giving their dogs a good hand-rub before taking them into the show ring.

The stripping knife, or dog dresser, is used for the removal of dead hairs and to keep the dog trimmed according to the style of its breed. To use this dog tool, hold the knife in the palm of your hand, the end resting against the heel of the hand and the first finger wrapped around the shank. The hair that is to be removed should be pressed against the knife with the thumb. A slight upward twist of the wrist brings the stripping edge in contact with the hair. Remove only a few hairs at a time.

Chalk is used in grooming white-coated dogs, especially terriers. Rub it in well before the dog is stripped, to prevent the hairs from slipping through your fingers during the stripping process. In addition to cleaning and whitening the coat, the use of chalk improves its texture, especially for breeds having a naturally hard coat.

Use the dull-pointed scissors to trim and straighten the line of the ears, legs and belly, also to trim the feet and between the toes.

IMPORTANT NAIL CARE

City dogs have one advantage over country dogs. A dog who gets his exercise on pavements usually keeps his nails worn down so that he will not need frequent nail trimming. The country dog, exercising on soft ground, should have his nails cut or filed about once a month. If the nails are allowed to grow too long, they force the dog to walk flatfooted. Also the pounding of overlong nails on roads can become painful and is a frequent cause of lameness. If the dog's nails are allowed to grow beyond the point where they are nourished by the quick, they are likely to become dead and brittle and may fracture and be torn off. Also, the dog with longer nails has less of a "grip" on smooth floors and may easily suffer a bad fall indoors.

Dogs' nails may be trimmed by clipping or filing—using either the special nail clippers or a fairly rough wood file. Many dogs who object violently to having their nails clipped will endure filing without complaint.

When trimming a dog's nails, avoid cutting into the quick, which is the live, pink flesh within the nail. If your dog has white nails it is easy to see the quick from any angle. If the dog has darker nails you may find it easier to locate the quick from the underneath portion of the nail. It has a soft, spongy appearance and stands out against the hard, brittle nail texture. If you should happen to cut or file into the quick, you can stop the bleeding with a few drops of antiseptic or some alum powder.

FILING AND CLIPPING A DOG'S NAILS

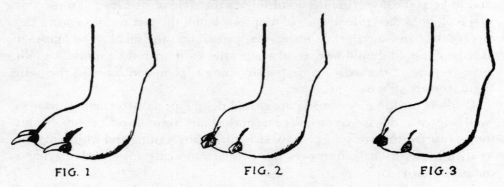

FIG. 1   FIG. 2   FIG. 3

Figure 1 shows the average nail before cutting, with the tip of the nail extending beyond the quick.

Figure 2 shows the nail cut close to the quick. If the nail is left like this, is should wear down evenly in a few days.

Figure 3 shows the nail after filing, with a thin layer of protective shell left over the quick.

When using a file, draw it in one direction only, from the top of the nail downward in a round stroke to the end of the nail or underneath. You will need considerable pressure during the first few strokes in order to break through the hard surface of the nail. After the first few strokes use an easier pressure.

BATHING YOUR DOG

Some of the most socially acceptable dogs have never had a bath! In fact, bathing of dogs is overdone by the great majority of dog owners. Too frequent bathing robs the dog's fur of the natural oil his skin produces and which in itself is a protection against dirt. A dog can roll in dirt or mud, shake a few times, lick a few dirty spots, and be perfectly clean in a short time.

Even the lightest-colored dogs can be kept clean with widely spaced baths. A number of companies put out dog cleaners in powder form or in pressure cans that do an effective job and eliminate the need for frequent baths. These "dry" baths are particularly good for wire haired dogs such as the fox terrier. These cleaners remove the doggy odor along with the dirt.

Unless your dog rolls in something smelly, he need not be bathed more often than once a month. The water should be temperate, and you can add a small quantity of disinfectant to inhibit fleas.

One reason why so many dogs fight against a bath is that they have had the unpleasant experience of soapy water in their eyes or ears. Professional dog bathers often stuff the dog's ears with cotton at the beginning of the bath and put a few drops of castor oil into each eye to protect against soap and water. If you observe a swimming dog, you'll see that he always keeps his ears and eyes out of the water.

In bathing your dog, use a good quality of dog soap. Keep a thick towel handy to dry the dog immediately after the bath. Part of the bathing program should include cleaning the inner part of the ears with a damp cloth to remove any accumulation of dirt and wax.

Rinse the soap out thoroughly to prevent the hair from tangling, if yours is a long-haired dog, and to avoid leaving soap deposits on the skin which can cause a scaly condition. If your dog's hair is inclined to snarl, a rinse with a little vinegar added to the water may help.

Dry the dog thoroughly before letting him out, and be careful not to let him run out of a heated house while damp into the cold outer air. In bathing a young puppy, it is advisable to give him a bath the last thing at night and to leave him in a warm, draft-proof place until morning.

You'll probably feel like grooming the dog after his bath, but never comb a long-coated dog while the hair is wet, as the comb will tear out live hair.

6

CLIPPING YOUR OWN DOG

to be clipped every few weeks can prove expensive. But by buying a hand clipper or an electric clipper, with practice you can cut down the expense of owning one of the breeds that must be clipped often. It will be easier for you if you begin clipping the dog's coat when he is about eight or ten weeks old to accustom him to the sound of the clippers and to being handled. With a little persistent training, almost any dog will learn to stand on a table or high bench and allow you to work on him.

As you read the "standards" of the different breeds you will see how the clipping is designed to bring out the best points of each. Although you do not have to clip any dog, certain breeds will be more comfortable if they are trimmed and will lose their characteristic appearance if their coats are allowed to grow long. The hair of poodles, for example, tends to "cord" if not trimmed, and an untrimmed poodle is an ungainly looking specimen of dogdom.

A characteristic of the spaniel is a dense coat, but sometimes the hair grows too thick. If this is true of your dog, it is necessary to strip out the excess hair over the entire body. When you are finished, the coat should lie smoothly over the body outline, and should not appear bushy or bunched up anywhere. Next, proceed as follows:

1. Trim the "feelers"—long coarse hairs—from the muzzle and above the eyes.

2. Smooth the skull and cheeks. Remove the hair where the ears join the skull. Your objective: to make the ears appear to be set as far back and as low on the skull as possible.

3. Trim the outside of the ears slightly at the top where they join the skull, leaving more hair at the base of the ears. Trim closely the inside of the ear and

SPANIELS
(Cocker, Springer, Clumber)

the part of the neck which the ear covers, so that the ear will hang flat and close. Use your scissors to trim the edge of the ear evenly.

4. Trim the hair from the underpart of the jaw and evenly down the neck.

5. Trim the brisket lightly to avoid a bushy effect.

6. Straighten the feathering on the front legs, using scissors.

7. Clean the shoulders where the coat may be bumpy or too thick.

8. Clean feathering from the hocks.

9. Clean feathering from the tail, but not closely.

10. Trim the hair to the shape of the foot, but leave enough hairs to cover the nails. Do not trim between the toes, but work from underneath, clipping between the pads. The final effect should give the foot the appearance of a sound, hard, round, compact paw.

If your spaniel is being used for field work or runs around in brush, you should make the dog more comfortable by clipping closely on the brisket, ears, legs and underparts of the body to avoid tangling by burrs, reduce ticks, and prevent being ripped by underbrush.

The spaniel's coat should receive a daily brushing with a long bristle (not wire) brush. Brush in the direction the hair grows to achieve a fairly flat, slightly wavy coat. A hand rub will then produce a desirable sheen on the coat.

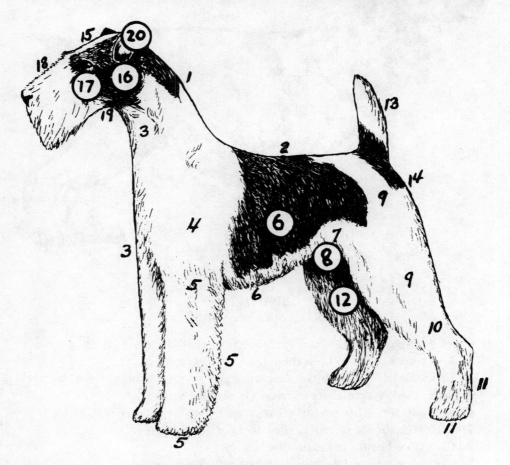

WIRE-HAIRED FOX TERRIER

1. Trim the neck closely and evenly and continue in the same way down the back.

2. Trim the back level and fine, but not as closely as the neck.

3. Trim the front part of the neck and brisket very closely, leaving just a bit more hair as you work down to where the forelegs join the body.

4. Trim the front shoulders closely and evenly.

5. Trim the front legs to straightness. Trim mainly on back line of legs. It may be necessary to take out a few hairs on the front and outside of the forelegs where they join the shoulders, to obtain the effect of a straight line from the top of the shoulders down to the feet—from the brisket to the top of the toes. Remove superfluous hair from edges of the feet and around toes; then shape feet to roundness.

6. Shape the ribs to follow the body conformation. Work the hair evenly from a closely trimmed back to a fairly heavy coat on the lower part of the chest and ribs. Clean the under part of the chest to prevent shagginess. Trim the under line of the chest to follow the body line.

7. Take the loin out closer than chest, but not too fine; trim the under line closely to emphasize the tuck-up.

8. Remove snarled or heavy hairs from the belly.

9. Trim here from a fine back to heavily coated thigh.

10. From the middle of the thigh to hock, trim only shaggy hairs.

11. Trim the back line of hock in a straight line. Remove any excess hairs from between toes and feet; shape to roundness.

12. Trim the insides of hind legs clean down to hock joint.

13. Trim the tail evenly, but not too closely, to a tip toward head. Trim fine in rear where it joins the stern.

14. Trim the stern very closely where it is joined by the tail; leave hair heavier toward the hind legs.

15. Trim the skull very closely. Leave eyebrows fairly heavy over the inside corner of the eyes. Leave very little hair over outside corner. Trim eyebrows evenly and closely over the outside corner of the eye; leave plenty of length over inside corner.

16. Trim cheeks closely from the outside corner of the eye to the corner of the mouth to give the desired expression.

17. Trim slightly from the inside corner of the eyes downward to the corner of the mouth.

18. Trim the top of the muzzle from the space between the eyebrows to the nose to give a straight-line front on top of the skull.

19. Leave the chin whiskers and brush them forward, then clean under the jaws from the corners of the mouth back to the neck.

20. Clean the ears closely inside and out and straighten the ear edges.

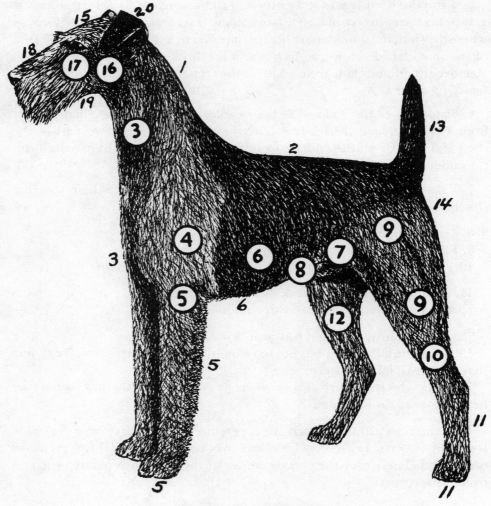

AIREDALE TERRIER

1. Trim the neck closely and evenly down into the back.
2. Trim the back level, but not as closely as the neck.
3. Trim the front part of neck and brisket very closely, leaving a bit more hair as you work down to where the front legs join the body.
4. Trim the shoulders evenly and closely.
5. Trim the front legs to straightness, working from the rear line. Remove

a few hairs from the front and outside of the front legs where they join the shoulder to give a straight line from the top of the shoulder to the feet and from the brisket to the tips of the toes. Use scissors to trim excess hair from the edges of the feet and between the toes. Shape the feet to roundness.

6. Shape the ribs to follow the body conformation. Work the hair evenly from a closely trimmed back to a fairly heavy coat on the underpart of the ribs and chest. On the underpart of the chest remove any shaggy hairs. Follow body line in trimming chest.

7. Trim out the loin closer than the chest, but not too fine. Emphasize the tuck-up.

8. Trim shaggy or snarled hairs from the belly.

9. Trim here from a fine back to a fairly heavy-coated thigh.

10. From the middle of the thigh to hock leave natural hair; trim only shaggy hairs.

11. Trim back of hock straight. Trim excess hairs from the edges of the hind feet and between the toes. Shape the feet to roundness.

12. Trim the insides of hind legs clean. Try to give a clean, even line to the hind legs from the rear view.

13. Trim the tail closely to a tip toward the head; trim very fine where it joins the stern.

14. Trim the stern very closely where it is joined by the tail, working it heavier toward the hind legs.

15. Trim skull very closely. Leave eyebrows rather heavy over the inside corners of the eyes; leave very little over the outside corners. Trim eyebrows evenly and closely at the outside corners of the eyes, leaving plenty of length over inside corners.

16. Trim cheeks closely from the outside corners of eyes to the corners of the mouth.

17. Trim very slightly from inside corners of eyes downward to the corners of the mouth to give desired Airedale expression.

18. Trim hairs on top of the muzzle from slightly between the eyebrows to the nose to give straight line from the top of the skull.

19. Do not trim the chin whiskers, but brush forward and trim clean under jaw from the corner of the mouth back to the neck.

20. Clean off ears closely inside and out; straighten the edges with scissors.

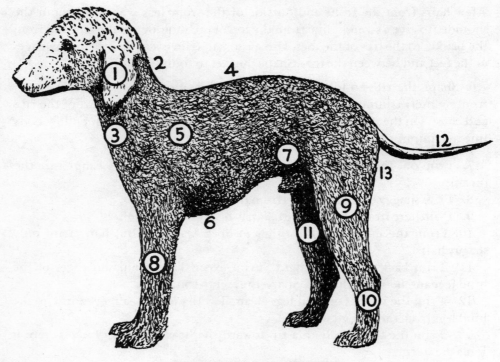

BEDLINGTON TERRIER

    The Bedlington is one of the "double-coated" dogs. In the natural state he grows a hard, wiry outer coat which is generally sparse. This outer coat should be removed by plucking before starting to trim the softer inner coat.

    The sheeplike appearance of the Bedlington's head is improved by correct trimming of the topknot, or pompadour. This pompadour should start at the tip of the nose and be slightly and increasingly raised as it travels up the muzzle. It should be extravagantly domed at the top of the head; then evenly decreased until it blends smoothly into the neck, just below the point where the skull and neck join.

    To emphasize the "sheep" look, the flews of the lips, the underpart of the jaw and the cheeks should be trimmed very closely.

    It may take a bit of practice to get the desired look. The pompadour should blend evenly into the closely trimmed muzzle and cheeks. Try to visualize an actual dividing line between the built-up area and the closely trimmed area as running directly from the sides of the nostrils to very slightly below the outside corner of the eye, then to just below the point where the ear joins the head and from that point very closely back into the neck.

1. Clean the hair from the inside and outside of the ear, leaving a long and ragged-edged but smooth tassel on the tips of the ears.

2. Trim the back and sides of the neck evenly into the back.

3. Trim the underpart of the neck very closely, leaving slightly more hair as you work down toward the brisket.

4. Trim the back not quite as closely as the neck, trying to emphasize the roached (rounded) appearance of the back over the loin.

5. Trim the sides of the chest and shoulders very closely and flat.

6. Leave as much hair as possible on the underpart of the chest to emphasize its depth. Trim the shaggy hairs.

7. Trim the loin very closely and fine.

8. Remove shaggy hairs from the front legs. Trim any hairs from the top outside of the front legs, trying for a straight and narrow appearance when viewed from the front. Trim around the feet, following the natural "hare foot" contour.

9. Trim the hind legs evenly, leaving slightly more hair as you work toward the hocks.

10. Remove any shaggy hair from the hocks.

11. Trim the insides of hind legs down to the hocks.

12. Trim the tail extremely close on underpart and sides. Leave some hair on top of the tail for half its length; trim the rest of tail closely.

13. Trim the stern, under the tail, closely.

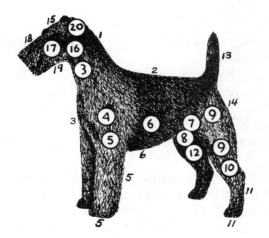

WELSH TERRIER

1. Trim the neck evenly into the back.

2. Trim the back level, but not as closely as the neck.

3. Trim the front part of neck and brisket closely, leaving just a bit more hair as you work down toward to where the front legs join the body.

4. Trim the front shoulders evenly and closely.

5. Trim the forelegs to straightness, trimming mostly on the back line. If necessary, take out a few hairs from the front and outsides of the forelegs where they join the body to get the effect of a straight line from the top of the shoulder to the feet and from the brisket to the tips of the toes. Trim any excess hair from edges of feet and between toes. Shape feet to roundness.

6. Trim the ribs to follow the body conformation. Work the hair evenly from a closely trimmed back to a rather heavy coat on the underparts of the ribs and chest. On the underparts of the ribs and chest leave the natural growth of hair, removing only enough to prevent shagginess.

7. Trim the loin cleaner than the chest, but not too fine. Trim the under line with scissors to emphasize the tuck-up.

8. Trim shaggy or snarled hairs from the belly.

9. Trim this area from a finely trimmed back line to a fairly heavily coated thigh.

10. Trim only shaggy hairs from the middle of the hock to the thigh.

11. Trim the back line of the hock straight. Remove superfluous hairs from the edges of the feet and between the toes and shape to roundness.

12. Trim insides of hind legs clean down to the hock joint. Work for a clean, even line of the hind legs from a rear view.

13. Trim tail evenly, but not very closely and "tip" the head. Take out fine hair in rear where the tail joins the stern.

14. Trim the stern very closely where it is joined by tail. Work the coat heavier toward the hind legs.

15. Trim the skull very closely. Leave eyebrows rather heavy over the inside corners of the eyes; leave very little over the outside corners. Trim the eyebrows evenly and closely over the outside corners. Leave plenty of length over the inside corners.

16. Trim the cheeks closely from the outside corners of the eyes to corners of the mouth.

17. Trim slightly from in front of the eyes to the corners of the mouth.

18. Trim the top of the muzzle from slightly between the eyebrows to the nose. Work for a straight line from the top of the skull.

19. Leave the chin whiskers. Clean under the jaw from the corners of mouth to the neck.

20. Clean ears closely inside and out. Straighten the edges.

SETTERS (English, Gordon, Irish)

1. Trim the muzzle of feelers (long, thick hairs) and work it to perfect smoothness.

2. Smooth the skull and cheeks closely and take out hair where the ear joins the skull. The objective is to make the ears appear to be set as far back on the skull and as low as possible.

3. Trim the outside of the ears slightly where they join the skull, leaving more hair toward the bottom. Trim the insides of the ears and the part of the neck covered by the ears, to enable the ears to lie closely against the head. Use scissors to trim the edges of the ears, rounding them slightly on the bottom.

4. Clean the hair from the under part of jaw down the neck evenly.

5. Remove enough hair from the brisket to avoid bushy appearance. When the hair is brushed down straight, it should fall evenly to make a graceful line from the neck into the front legs.

6. Straighten feathering on the front legs slightly and even the hairs growing out over the toes.

7. If necessary, clean the hair on shoulders.

8. Trim a very few hairs from the loin to show some tuck-up, but do not emphasize this feature.

9. Trim the fringe on the hocks evenly.

10. Trim the feathering on the tail to a graceful, even curve tapering to a point toward the tip. The tail must never appear bushy. If the hair on the tail is too thick, it should be thinned out with a stripping knife. If the setter is to be used for field work, some owners prefer to trim closely the long hair on the brisket, ears, legs and underparts of the body.

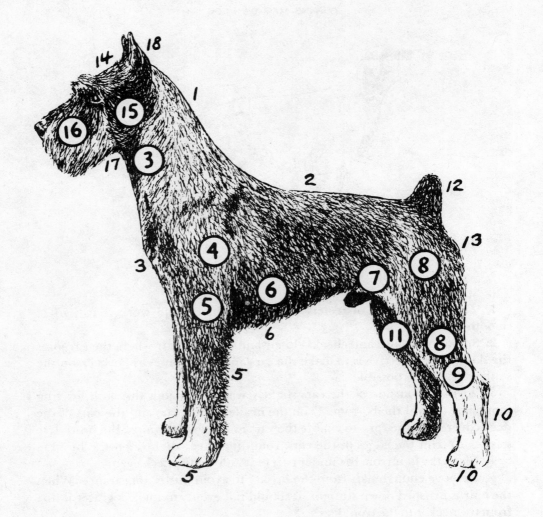

SCHNAUZER

Miniature, standard and giant schnauzers are trimmed in the same way.

1. Trim the neck evenly into the back.

2. The schnauzer's hair may grow against the grain and be unruly on the back, so trimming must be done carefully to obtain the desired results. Trim hairs to even length, but not too closely. Work for an even back line and to avoid a shaggy appearance.

3. Trim neck and brisket rather closely, leaving a bit more hair as you work down toward the point where the front legs join the body.

4. Trim the shoulders closely down into the front legs.

5. Now trim the forelegs to straightness. Work mostly on the back line. It may be necessary to remove a few hairs from the front and sides of the forelegs, where they join the body, to give a clean line from the shoulder to the sides of the feet and from the brisket to the tips of the toes. Trim excess hairs from the sides of the feet and between the toes.

6. Trim from the back down the ribs, leaving the hair slightly heavier on the underpart of the ribs and chest. Trim the under line of the chest to follow the body line.

7. Trim the loin closer than the chest and trim the under line to emphasize the tuck-up.

8. Trim the back legs from the back to the middle of the thigh fairly closely.

9. From the middle of thigh to the hock, trim out shaggy hairs, but do not clip closely.

10. Trim the rear line of the hock to straightness with scissors. Trim any excess hairs from the sides of the feet and between the toes.

11. Trim the insides of the rear legs clean.

12. Trim the tail of shaggy hairs, but do not clip closely.

13. Trim the stern fairly closely and evenly.

14. Trim the skull closely, leaving fairly heavy eyebrows. Leave more eyebrow over the inside corner of the eye than over the outside corner.

15. Trim the cheeks closely from slightly behind the eye and slightly behind the corner of the mouth.

16. Do not trim the whiskers on muzzle or chin, except to shorten hairs where necessary to blend them slightly with cleanly trimmed cheek.

17. Clean under jaw from slightly behind the corner of the mouth back into the neck.

18. Trim the ears clean, inside and out, and straighten the edges with scissors.

KERRY BLUE TERRIER

1. Trim evenly along the neck and down into the back.

2. Trim the back evenly and level the top line.

3. Trim the underpart of the neck and brisket closely, leaving a bit more hair as you approach the lower part of the brisket, where the forelegs join the body.

4. Trim the shoulders evenly down into the forelegs.

5. Leave the hair on the forelegs except for a slight trimming to straighten. Trim along the back line of the legs to get the proper effect. You may have to remove a few hairs from the front and sides of the forelegs, where they join the body, to obtain the desired straight line from the shoulder to the ground and from the brisket to the tips of the toes. Clean the hairs from between the pads and shape the foot to roundness.

6. Trim the sides from a rather closely trimmed back to an almost full coat on the underpart of the ribs and chest. Trim the under line of chest to follow the natural body line.

7. Trim the loin just enough to show the tuck-up.

8. Trim from the back to middle of thigh evenly, leaving the hair a bit heavier on the leg.

9. From middle of the thigh to the hock joint, remove only those hairs which give a shaggy look.

10. Using scissors, trim the back line of the hock evenly. Trim hair from between toes and shape the feet to roundness.

11. Trim the tail evenly but not too closely. Remove any hairs that appear to make tail longer than it is.

12. Trim shaggy hairs from the stern. Strip most closely where the tail joins the body, leaving heavier hair toward the bottom of stern and rear of legs.

13. Trim the top of the skull very closely, leaving plenty of eyebrow. *Note:* Do not trim between the eyebrows as with most other terriers.

14. Trim the cheeks leaving hair slightly longer than on the skull. Work evenly but quickly into a heavy beard on the foreface.

15. Trim slightly under the eyes to slightly behind the corner of the mouth.

16. Trim the ears closely inside and out. Straighten edges with scissors.

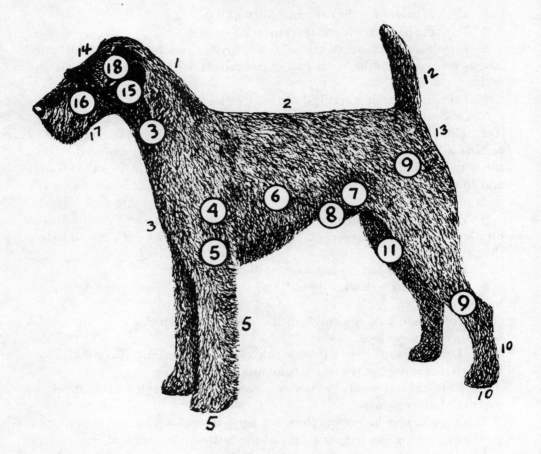

IRISH TERRIER

1. Trim the neck very closely and evenly into the back.

2. Trim the back evenly, but not as closely as the neck.

3. Trim the front part of the neck and brisket closely, leaving just a bit more hair as you work down to where the forelegs join the body.

4. Trim the front shoulders evenly and closely.

5. Trim forelegs slightly to emphasize straight lines. Work mainly on the back line. Remove excess hair from the edges of the feet and between the toes; shape the foot to roundness.

6. Shape the ribs to follow the natural body conformation. Work from a finely trimmed back to a fuller coat on the underpart of the ribs and chest. Remove any shaggy hairs from the sides and under the chest.

7. Trim the loin, but do not emphasize tuck-up; work rather for a smooth line.

8. Trim snarled or shaggy hairs from the belly.

9. Trim the thighs from the back line to the hock, removing enough hair to show a definite outline of leg.

10. Straighten the line of the hock and trim excess hairs from the edges of feet and between toes; shape rear feet to roundness.

11. Trim inside of hind legs down to the hock joint.

12. Trim the tail evenly, but not too closely, with a rounded tip toward the end.

13. Trim the stern closely and evenly.

14. Trim the skull very closely. Leave eyebrows, but not too heavy. Leave a bit more over the inside corner of the eye than at the outside corner.

15. Trim the cheeks clean back from the corner of the mouth.

16. Trim under the eyes to emphasize typical Irish terrier expression.

17. Clean under the jaw from the corner of the mouth to the neck. Leave the chin whiskers uncut and brush them forward.

18. Clean ears inside and out; straighten the edges with scissors.

Special Care of the Feet

A great many Irish terriers suffer from horny or cracked pads. Strangely, foot troubles are common to both Irish dogs and horses. One theory for this is that the animals or their ancestors, in their native climate, were used to run on a soil which was more boggy and damp than ours. The drier soil and climate dries out their feet, causing this condition.

When you groom your Irish terrier, examine his feet carefully. Remove any loosened horns or edges, being very careful not to cut into the live flesh. Many owners of these dogs massage their pads each day with olive oil or borate of glycerine to cure this condition. While the soreness lasts, the dog should be exercised only on grass.

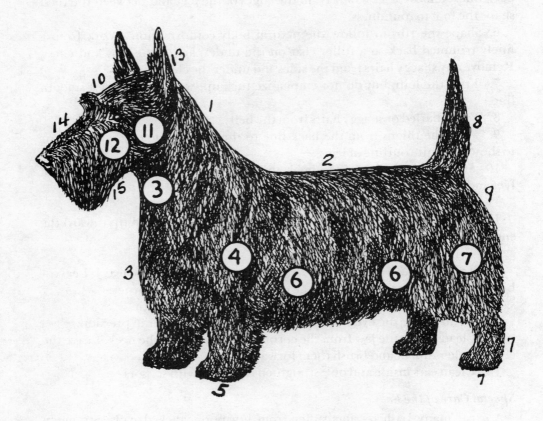

SCOTTISH TERRIER

1. Trim the neck and back evenly. The back should show a straight, level line.

2. Trim the back level, but not too fine.

3. Trim the front of the neck closely, but as you work down to the brisket, leave hairs long but not shaggy. Never trim any hairs that would detract from the desired appearance of a dog built close to the ground.

4. Trim the shoulders enough to blend the body of the dog to the forelegs with a clean, even line.

5. Do not trim the forelegs. Although the Scottie's legs are naturally somewhat bent, the hair should be combed to camouflage that shape and make them appear straight from either front or side view. Trim any excess hairs from the feet and between the toes. Shape the feet to roundness.

6. Trim the hair evenly from the finely trimmed back to an absolutely full coat on the underpart of the ribs and chest. Viewed from the front, the dog should not appear shaggy or bulgy, but should carry a look of breadth and substance.

7. Remove only shaggy hair from the thighs. Trim the back line of the hock straight. Remove excess hair from the edges of the feet and between the toes. Shape the rear feet to roundness with scissors.

8. Trim the tail to a point, leaving it fairly heavy at the base.

9. Trim the stern fairly close where the tail joins, but work it quickly into the long hair below, which helps give the rear-view impression of a dog heavy and low to the ground.

10. Trim the skull very closely, leaving considerable eyebrows.

11. Trim the cheeks from the outside corners of the eyes to the corners of the mouth.

12. Trim very lightly from the inside corners of the eyes to the corners of the mouth to give desired Scottie expression.

13. Trim the back and edges of the ears rather fine. Leave hair on insides of ears to blend into the skull.

14. Trim between the eyebrows and part the hair over the muzzle and comb downward and forward.

15. Leave the chin whiskers, but clean the hair off the underpart of the jaw from the corners of the mouth back into the neck.

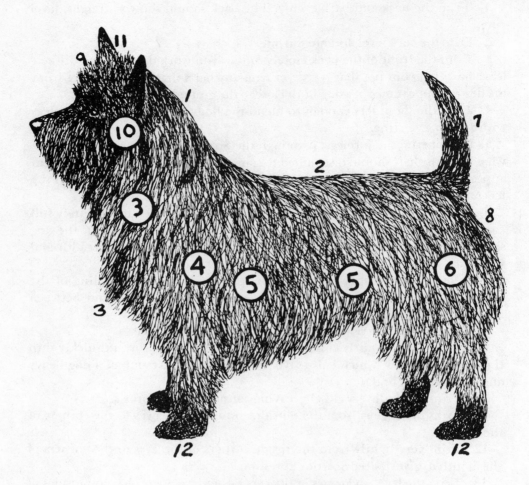

CAIRN TERRIER

Stripping is necessary for the long-haired cairn terrier to keep his coat healthy and to emphasize the desired alert, game appearance characteristic of the breed. His shaggy look should be preserved, but his trim should bring out his good points.

1. Pluck the dead hairs from the neck and trim slightly. If your particular cairn is inclined to be heavy in the neck or coarse-haired, take out more hair.

2. Pluck the dead hairs and trim the new coat, just enough to give a level back line.

3. Trim the neck and brisket slightly.

4. Remove any bumpy or patchy places from the shoulders. Leave the hair somewhat shaggy, but not profuse.

5. Trim the sides of the body to follow the body conformation.

6. Trim the upper parts of the thigh slightly. Leave the hair longer and shaggier on the lower part, just above the hock joint.

7. Trim the tail so that it remains bushy, but not too shaggy. Work for a thick base, to a finer forward tip. Remove any hairs that seem to make the tail longer than it is.

8. Trim any hairs from the stern that give it a bunchy appearance, but do not remove fringe. Trim most closely where the tail joins the stern.

9. Trim enough hair from the skull so that about half of the ear stands clear.

10. Trim the hair around the cheek to follow the conformation of the head.

11. Remove all long hair from backs and sides of the ears. With scissors, straighten the edges of the ears.

12. Shape the feet to roundness with scissors.

POODLES

(Standard, miniature, and toy)

Clipping is essential to the poodle. Other long-haired breeds which should be trimmed may not look right if they are left untrimmed. But leave a poodle untrimmed and the dog is in for trouble. If the poodle's coat is allowed to grow haphazardly without care, his coat will form into thin, round mats, which become cordlike as they grow longer. These tightly twisted cords often reach the ground and interfere with dog's activities, and are almost impossible to keep well groomed. In the official classification of poodles there is a "corded poodle" category, but these are almost never seen. The poodle with a clipped coat is referred to as the "curly poodle."

While the present-day poodle clips may seem affected to the non-poodle owner, they really have a practical and a historical background. In the Middle Ages, the poodle was a sporting water dog, used as a retriever from water. The long ruff covering the chest gave protection against cold water, and the shaved hindquarters made the dog better streamlined for swimming. From this practical clip developed the show clips now seen in the show ring and outdoors.

The Poodle Clips

If you are planning to enter your poodle in breed shows, three different types of clips are permitted: The *puppy clip,* the *English saddle,* and the *continental.* However, many poodle owners prefer the simpler *kennel clip* or the more elaborate *Royal Dutch.*

Monthly clippings add considerably to the expense of maintaining a poodle, and many owners find that the investment in a set of tools and a bit of practice in a do-it-yourself clipping program is satisfactory.

To keep your poodle well groomed calls for the following equipment: Small-animal electric clippers with detachable heads; barber shears (blunt-pointed); a carder (an oblong implement with a short handle, similar to a fur brush); a rake for pulling through mats of tangled hair; a comb with teeth two or three inches long; a brush with stiff extra-long bristles; and tweezers to remove hair from the outer ear.

A grooming table of convenient working height that stands securely and is covered with rubber matting will make the grooming project easier.

Poodle (Puppy Clip)

Some Clipping Techniques

The following suggestions make the clipping somewhat less formidable. Clip the face, feet and forelegs with the dog in a sitting position. For body clipping and work with scissors, keep the dog standing.

Shortening the hair on the chest and under the tail will give your poodle a more compact appearance. However, if your poodle appears short-legged, shorten the hair underneath the body and chest to make him look taller.

Remove the hair underneath and in front of the ears so that they lie close to the head. But if the dog happens to have a broad skull or high-set ears, leave some hair to disguise these faults.

It is recommended that you first clip your poodle at about eight or ten weeks to get him accustomed to the treatment. If you are going in for the Royal Dutch or English saddle clips, wait till the poodle is about six months old or older. The change from the puppy coat to the richer adult coat takes place at about fourteen to eighteen months, but the poodle does not generally reach his prime coat until he is about three years old.

Poodle (English Saddle Clip)

Poodle (Continental Clip)

Poodle (Kennel Clip)

Poodle (Royal Dutch Clip)

7

PRINCIPLES OF DOG TRAINING

THE SECRET
of enjoying a dog can be expressed in one word: training! An untrained dog
is just an animal who happens to domesticate himself in your home. Training
a dog not only enables you to enjoy him thoroughly and makes him an accepted canine citizen of your neighborhood, but it gives the dog an opportunity to develop his capabilities. It is unfair to take a dog who has the ability to
learn and not give him the chance to develop himself.

Training a dog will not break his spirit or turn him into a robot. Unlike
other animals, which must be trained by punishment, the dog is the one domestic animal with an instinctive desire to please his master. The problem of
dog training is not with the dog so much as the master. If you can get across
the communications barrier and show the dog what you want him to do, he will
do it.

There are no tricks or mysteries to dog training. It is a relatively simple
process, based on these four principles:

1. A practical knowledge of how a dog's mind works
2. Constant repetition of training exercises
3. Suitable recognition of a dog's progress, with praise for a satisfactory
performance; correction for misbehavior or failure
4. Patience

It is best if one member of the family establishes himself as the master of the
dog. For some reason, most dogs seem to respond more quickly to a masculine
trainer, perhaps because the male voice carries more authority than the female.

In training a dog you must be aware of the limitations of the dog's brain. In

266

the beginning, a dog will be uncertain of what is expected of him. Normally, a dog may not fully understand a command until he has been made to carry it out a number of times. And in dog training a "number of times" may be anywhere from twenty to fifty.

SOME SPECIFIC TECHNIQUES

Vocal commands should be given firmly and clearly. The tone and sound of the voice—not the actual words used—are the qualities that will influence the dog. And, in using vocal commands, keep the words simple and always use the same words for the same command. For instance, in calling the dog in for meals always use the same call, whether "dinner," "food," "eats," or "come and get it." In the beginning, always precede any training command with the dog's name to get his attention. Then pause for an instant before giving the command.

Next to the voice, gestures are the chief means of influencing dogs. Often a gesture and a voice command are combined. In the early stages of training, exaggerate both the voice commands and the gestures. As training proceeds, the exaggeration is reduced.

It is essential that the dog be made to carry out the same command over and over until he can make the desired response without delay. Repetition is even more important in dog training than in human learning. Use the leash as a training aid to show the dog what is expected of him. However, both you and your dog can go stale and lose efficiency by overpracticing any one command during a session of training. It is better to go on to something else or let some time elapse before returning to practice the command that is not getting the desired response.

And perhaps most important of all, the trainer must never lose patience or show irritation. If he does, the dog will become harder to handle because he takes his cue from the trainer. Patience is one of the prime requisites of a dog trainer, but it must be coupled with firmness. The moment the dog understands, obedience must be demanded if the dog is to be a prompt and accurate worker. Dog training takes time and understanding.

From the beginning of training, the dog should never be permitted to ignore a command or fail to carry it out completely. He must learn to associate the trainer's command with his execution of it. He should never be allowed to expect that there is anything else for him to do but obey. He must learn that he will have to do what the trainer commands, that he will have to carry out the command completely, no matter how long it takes. Laxity on the part of the trainer on even one occasion may result in an attitude or mood of disobedience that may lead to difficulty in further training. When the trainer is sure that the dog knows what is expected of him but is being willfully stubborn, the trainer may handle the leash firmly, and if necessary punish the dog with harsh vocal criticism.

The aim of "correction" is improvement, not reprisal. A dog does not understand the abstract principles of right and wrong according to human standards and praise and correction are the means of teaching him what he is expected to learn.

It is seldom necessary to resort to physical punishment to teach a lesson to a sensitive dog. Withholding praise, a rebuking tone, even "No" said reprovingly, are usually sufficient punishment. If the dog is stubborn or insensitive, correction in his case must be more severe. The correction must be made to fit the dog as well as the misdeed. Timing in correction is very important. The correction, whatever form it takes, must always be administered immediately after the dog misbehaves. A dog cannot relate punishment with a misdeed committed at some time previous to the punishment.

Real punishment should be inflicted as a last resort, and only for deliberate disobedience, stubborness or defiance when the dog has learned better. He must never be punished for clumsiness, slowness in learning, or inability to understand what is expected of him. Punishment for such reasons, intead of speeding training, will have the opposite effect. The word "No" is used to indicate to the dog that he is doing wrong. "No" is the only word used as a negative command. It should be spoken in a stern and reproving tone. If this form of reproof is not successful, the dog should be chained or kenneled. A dog is never slapped with the hand or struck with the leash. The hand is an instrument of praise and pleasure to the dog and he must never be allowed to fear it. Beating with the leash will make him shy of it and lessen the effect of its legitimate use. The dog's name is never used in connection with a correction.

Whenever a dog successfully executes a command, even though his performance is slow, he should be rewarded with a pat on the head and obvious praise. Praise and reward may take the following forms: kind words, patting, allowing a few minutes romping, allowing the dog to perform his favorite exercise, including free run and play.

In serious dog training it is generally inadvisable to reward the dog by feeding him tidbits. However, in teaching him tricks, use the tidbits if you wish to give him more incentive to perform.

Every training session must conclude with petting, praise and encouragement for the dog, in order to keep up his enthusiasm for the work. If the dog's performance does not warrant praise, then allow him to perform some exercise he knows so that he will earn the reward legitimately.

PSYCHOLOGY OF THE DOG

In order to train a dog effectively, it is necessary to go a bit beyond the principles of dog training and have some knowledge of the dog's psychology and physical traits.

The dog's world differs from the human in some very specific ways. His world is predominately one of odors. His nose tells him countless things about his environment that completely escape humans. He is also more sensitive to sounds. His vision is considerably inferior to human vision, and for this reason he depends less upon it. He prefers to approach closely to objects that must be examined. However, his sensitivity to the movement of objects compares favorably with human sensitivity of this kind.

In training a dog as a house pet and companion you must concern yourself primarily with his senses of vision and hearing.

A most striking difference between the retina of the dog's eye and human retina is that the former lacks a fovea (a small pit or depression). When a man focuses his eyes upon any object, the light reflected from that object is thrown upon the fovea of the retina. He can see many objects besides that, but they are seen indistinctly. This can be tested readily enough by focusing the eye upon any word on this printed page and then trying to see how many other words can be read without moving the eye. The words reflected on the non-foveal portions of the retina are blurred and poorly defined. Since the dog lacks a fovea, one may expect that even an object upon which he focuses is seen less clearly than it would be by humans. It seems certain that a dog can most conveniently and comfortably see objects which are at a distance of 20 feet or more.

However, the dog compensates for lack of visual acuity by his keen perception of movement. This is a type of visual stimulation to which dogs seem very sensitive. If any object is moved ever so slightly, most dogs will detect and respond to the movement. This acuteness has been noticed in many psychological laboratories. Pavlov observed that the slight movement of an object in the vertical plane could be distinguished by dogs from movement in the horizontal plane, and also that discrimination between clockwise and counter-clockwise motion was possible.

In training, this means that your dogs can easily learn to respond to a number of different hand signals. But do not make the mistake of expecting him to learn by watching another dog obey commands or go through an exercise.

Tests made in Russia and Germany have shown that dogs hear sounds too faint to affect human ear. In one test, a German shepherd at a distance of 24 meters (a meter is 39.37 inches) responded to a sound which a man could not hear at a distance of more than 6 meters. It seems apparent, too, that dogs hear sounds of higher pitch than affect human ears; the "dog whistle" which calls the dog by a blast that a person cannot hear operates on this principle.

From practical experience, it seems that in dog training, inflection, actual words and gestures all play a part. It may be necessary to give commands to a dog at night or when the master cannot be seen, so it is important that the dog be trained to respond properly without benefit of gesture. Most dogs can readily be instructed to respond to a number of oral commands. Some of them appear to understand most accurately the feeling of the master as it is conveyed by his voice. A word spoken in an encouraging tone will elate the dog; a cross word will depress him. Some dogs, however, cannot be reached effectively through the ear, and these must be trained by gesture and use of the leash to guide them through the desired exercises.

THE DOG'S SENSE OF SMELL

In advanced training, tracking, and in training of "scent" hounds, the dog's uncanny sense of smell comes to the fore. Dogs so far surpass humans in the keenness of smell that it is difficult to imagine the nature of the sensations they receive. Just as it is impossible for the color-blind dog to know what colors are, so it is impossible for the human to conceive of the vast range and chemical shadings of odors to which dogs are so sensitive.

The dog's nose is ideally adapted for the detection of minute particles of odorous substances. The snout is kept moist by a glandular secretion and is extremely sensitive to slight currents of air. Upon feeling such a current, the head is turned into the wind, the animal clears its nostrils and sniffs. A generous sample of the air passes into the nasal cavity and over the mucous membrane, which is richly innervated with the finely subdivided endings of the olfactory nerves. This mucous membrane is supported on an intricate convoluted bony structure which provides a maximum surface with a minimum obstruction to the circulation of air. By comparison, the human nose is a crude apparatus for smelling, yet even the human nose can detect chemicals borne by the air in such extreme dilution that they cannot be identified by the most sensitive chemical tests. In general, studies have shown that dogs can respond to odor traces of all known sorts and in dilutions far more extreme than can be detected by man. Furthermore, they can distinguish between odors which seem identical to human beings; for example, the difference between natural and artificial musk.

BASIC HOME TRAINING FOR YOUR DOG

Housebreaking a dog is no serious problem if you keep in mind that a dog is a naturally clean animal. He does not want to soil the place where he sleeps and plays. The most important factor in housebreaking is *confinement*. If you give a puppy free rein and allow him to run all over the house, you are in for trouble. As soon as you bring the puppy into your home, barricade a quiet, draft-free corner and keep him there for several weeks. First thing in the morning, after every meal, or after any active play, and last thing at night, take him outdoors, or stand him on pile of newspapers if you are trying to paper-train him.

When he does his "business" in the desired place, praise him. When he makes a mistake, let him know that you are displeased with him.

Many young puppies manage all right during the day, but get into trouble at night. You can help by cutting down on the liquid content of the day's last meal. Also, try tying the puppy on a short leash near his bed, long enough so that he can move around, but not long enough so that he can get out of his bed. When he wants "out," he'll whine or bark and ask to be taken out. This may be a little hard on the human members of the family, but if a few of them take turns it isn't too bad, and it is good training for the puppy. After a few weeks, the puppy should be able to control himself during the night.

Use some one short word that the young dog learns to associate with relieving himself. Use this word when you are urging him to "go." This will help him learn which areas are permissible and which are forbidden. Also, train the dog to use different types of places. A dog that has learned to go on the grass can be uncomfortable and his training may be set back when you have him on a city street. If you have a city dwelling dog, teach him that the gutter is the proper place.

Be firm with your puppy when it comes to house cleanliness, but don't try to rush him. Until he is about four or five months old, he just hasn't the muscular control, and even a well-meaning dog may occasionally make mistakes. Many of the smaller, more excitable breeds may "dribble" from excitement when some person they recognize comes into the room.

LEASH TRAINING

First accustom the young dog to wearing a collar. When he has become acclimated to his new home and has had his preventive inoculations, you can begin training him to walk on the streets. The preferred leash (although "doggy" people always call it a "lead") is the six-foot-long webbed cloth type with a loop on one end and a snap on the other, to catch on to the dog's collar.

No matter what size or breed your dog is, he should be taught to walk on your left side. Hold the leash firmly in your right hand, using the left hand to correct the dog if he tries to act up. Expect to run into some trouble. A dog does

The chain link training collar is an important tool in training a dog to obedience. When put on properly, as shown here, it is slack when the leash is loose, tightens when the leash is pulled.

not like to walk on lead, but after a while he accepts it philosophically. Some breeds accept it sooner than others, and many owners of terriers face a long struggle to determine at which end of the lead the control lies.

One trick in teaching leash-walking is this: Most dogs prefer coming to going, so carry the dog or let him walk in his own way some distance from home. Then use the leash on the return trip.

You will find leash-training much easier if you use a "choke" collar, even, with a small dog. The collar is not as horrible as the name implies. It is a chain-link collar with a ring at each end. When the dog pulls, the collar tightens, but it wouldn't hurt him. When he eases up, the collar eases, and he soon learns that walking along politely is more comfortable than fighting the collar. With one of the larger, stronger breeds, the choke collar is a "must." Very few experienced dog people advocate the use of a shoulder harness, as it makes control of the dog difficult and may actually harm the dog by pulling his shoulders out of position if he constantly fights it.

TEACHING THE "HEEL"

"Heel" is a universal dog command. It is an order to the dog to walk along at your left knee, and to come to a sit when you stop. And it is surprisingly easy to get any dog to do this.

Don't try to get your dog to begin heeling until he is about six to eight months old. Snap the leash to the free end of the choke collar. Hold the leash in your right hand with some slack, and keep the slack of the leash running through your left hand. (This is simpler than it reads.) Start off walking briskly, constantly repeating the dog's name and the word "heel!" The faster you walk, the easier it is for the dog to get the idea. If he lags behind, try to encourage him to catch up by patting your thigh or calling him to "heel." If necessary, jerk him forward with the leash. When he is staying at heel, encourage him with words of praise; use the scornful "No" when he forges ahead or lags behind. Remember these three points: (1) constantly repeat the dog's name and the word "heel"; (2) walk briskly; and (3) praise him for staying at your left knee.

The average dog begins to get the idea of heeling in one training session of about a half hour, broken into ten-minute exercises with rests between. If you are training a young dog and get absolutely no response, it may be because the dog is not yet ready for this lesson; or that you are walking too slowly and not being severe enough in your corrections.

Dog is taught to walk at owner's side as close to left knee as possible (heeling).
Hold leash in right hand, use left to urge dog along, pat or correct him.

How to turn right is taught by suddenly turning sharp and jerking leash.

Left turn is taught by lifting right knee or foot against dog's chest and neck.

When practicing "heeling," keep the dog's attention by talking to him, and use your left hand as a lure to keep him at your side.

Teach dog to sit by jerking up on leash, pushing down on dog's rump.

"STOP" AND "SIT"

Part of the "heeling" exercise calls for the dog to come to a sit without any command when you stop. As you stop, jerk the dog back, pull up on the leash, and push down on his hindquarters. That will put him in a sitting position. Then relax the leash and praise him, but keep alert to push him back to a sit if he begins to get up when he hears a word of praise. He may at first think it is an invitation to play. As soon as you get pull-head-up, push-rear-end-down routine working, begin to use the verbal command "sit" every time you stop. After a while, you will find that you can eliminate the command and the dog will automatically come to a sit when you stop. Then when you start off again, the dog will rise and walk along with you. As a guide to the dog, always start off with the left foot, the one nearest the dog, because he learns to use it as a signal.

After some practice—ten or fifteen minutes an evening or afternoon—for about nine or ten weeks, the dog and you should reach the point where you can dispense with the leash and your dog will walk along at your side. However, when you first try "free" heeling keep up a running conversation with the dog to keep his attention; repeat the word "heel." Praise him constantly, and at the first sign of lagging or forging ahead, sap back the leash and be firm in your correcions. But the dog should be letter-perfect in heeling on leash before you work him free of the leash.

"SIT" ON COMMAND

With the leash, your voice and your left hand, you should have no trouble teaching your dog to sit on command. While saying "Sit," pull up on the leash and push his rear end down with your left hand. If he tries to lie down, use your critical "No!" and pull him back to a sitting position. Keep the dog in a sitting position for a moment, and back away slowly to the end of your leash. Then try walking around him, keeping him sitting. With a little repetition, your dog will soon respond to the verbal command to sit. If you use a finger-pointed-downward gesture each time you give the "sit" command, the dog will soon respond to that signal also and drop to a sitting position. After a while keep the dog sitting while you walk away a short distance. Use the command "Stay" to keep him in place. Don't use the dog's name with the command to "stay" as he may have the idea that any command that begins with his name means that he must do something and he'll start up.

"DOWN" ON COMMAND

When your dog has learned to sit on command, you can proceed to the next

From a "sit" facing you, teach the dog to "come" on command; later he will come when called even if running free.

"Lie down" is taught by pulling the dog's head down. Draw leash under your foot. Always praise the dog when he obeys your command.

Later the dog should drop down to position whenever the hand signal is given.

step in training—to lie down on command. The basic idea at first is to get the dog down while repeating the command "Down." When he is down, praise him and hold him down for a moment so that he'll know what's expected of him.

First problem: getting the dog down. With a small, quiet dog, you may be able to do this by making him sit, and then pulling his front feet forward while pressing his shoulders down. With a larger dog, you may have to kneel alongside him and wrestle him to the ground while repeating "Down!" Another technique is to stand with one foot over the leash and pull the leash up under your shoe so that you force the dog's head and shoulders down.

This usually takes some time and doing, so don't lose your patience. It will usually take numerous repetitions until the dog gets the idea. When the dog begins to get the idea, start using a hand gesture. Raise your left hand, palm down, somewhat like a threatening gesture while giving the vocal command.

When the dog does go down, try to keep him down. If you praise him too lavishly, he will jump up, so just stroke him gently to let him know he's doing the right thing. And don't try at first to correct the dog if he rolls over on his back while he's down, or stretches out on his side. The important thing is to get and keep him down. Later on he will lie in a proper doglike position.

One of the steps in "advanced" obedience work is exercises with a wooden dumbbell. First get across the idea that he is expected to pick up the dumbbell.

As soon as he responds regularly to the "Down" command and the hand signal, try walking a short distance away; then take longer walks away, keeping him down with a sharp command if he begins to rise. After some practice you should be able to leave him for as long as five minutes, even while you are out of sight, and find him lying in the same spot when you return. And he should drop when he hears the command even when you are a distance away from him. In obedience trials the handler may use either a verbal command or a hand signal to drop his dog.

In retrieving, dog must pick up dumbbell when ordered, never drop it. Hold dog's jaws against dumbbell gently but firmly insisting that he hold it.

At the "finish" of a dumbbell exercise, the dog should come to a "sit" in front of the handler, give up dumbbell on command.

The goal of obedience training: a dog that will get along with other dogs and with people. This scene at a convention of the National Industrial Recreation Association shows a varied group of trained dogs, each patiently holding his dumbbell and watching the trainer for the next command.

SOME DISCIPLINE PROBLEMS

Barking: A dog's barking can be controlled. However, some breeds are more inclined to be noisy than others. Poodles, for instance, can seldom be restrained from their characteristic yelping. Many of the toy dogs are noiser than the larger breeds. You can usually raise your dog to be a barker or a nonbarker. If you are raising your dog to be a watchdog, then when he first barks at footsteps outside the door, tell him that he is a good dog and encourage him. But if you are living in an apartment or in a closely developed suburb, your barking dog can create a serious problem with landlord or neighbors.

Dogs dislike sharp, loud noises. If you want a nonbarker, you must start training him almost from puppyhood. At the first bark, slam a book or rolled-up newspaper sharply against a table or wall, and shout "No!" Continue this program, and as soon as the dog associates the fact that his barking brings an unpleasant effect, he'll stop barking. However, when you are playing he may bark with excitement, and let him. A dog needs some freedom of action.

As for the dog that barks when he's left alone—that calls for a bit of shock treatment. One method that oftens work is this: Walk out of the room slamming the door behind you and than wait outside. If you hear whining or barking, slam the door with the flat of your hand as hard as you can and shout "No!" If the noise inside continues, walk back inside and reprove the dog severely, but only with your voice. Repeating that a few times should cure even a confirmed complainer.

Even a dog that has been trained not to bark will usually bark in an emergency, and some dogs that never raise their voices in city apartments become good watchdogs when they move out to summer homes.

Automobiles: Although some dogs seem to develop road sense and manage to cross heavily trafficked streets, the automobile is listed as the number one killer of dogs. If your dog is given the freedom of an unfenced yard, he must be trained not to go into the street. The first time you catch him at this offense, drag him back to the same side of the curb and let him know in no uncertain terms that he has committed a serious crime. This is one occasion when a bit of physical punishment may be used to enforce the lesson. Some breeds are born "roamers" and a dog on the track of a rabbit or a male following the scent of a female in heat will certainly forget training, so the answer may be a fenced-in run or a long chain or leash.

Car chasing is another dangerous habit some dogs acquire. Try to nip it in the bud. One method is to tie a long rope on the dog's collar. When he tries to take off after a car, snap him back as hard as you can, and then punish him.

If that doesn't work, you might get someone to ride by in a car, and when the dog goes after it, have the driver stop the car and come out with a leash or length of rope and let him have the end of it. Or you might have the person lean from the car and squirt him with a water pistol containing a little ammonia diluted in the water. A habitual car chaser must be confined, as he is a menace to the neighborhood and to himself.

Jumping on People: Most puppies and many dogs express their joy at meeting people by jumping up and putting their front paws on them. When a puppy does this it may be cute, but a 60-pound dog's paws on a summer dress can be rather annoying.

This habit can be broken quickly. Just grab the dogs forepaws when he jumps up and step on his rear toes with a little pressure. Or, every time he does it, slap his nose and ask everyone else to do it. That should effect a cure in a short time.

8

OBEDIENCE TRIALS

AFTER YOU
have trained your dog, you have an opportunity to test your ability as a trainer, and your dog's performance, in competition with other dogs and their trainers. Obedience trials have been added to many dog shows within the last twenty-five years. Most of the competitors in these shows are amateur handlers who have trained their own pets. Basically, the obedience trials are a test of the dog's skill in responding to the commands which make him a good companion, not in performing "tricks."

The obedience trials which are held in connection with regular breed shows, and the separate obedience trials run by obedience training clubs are open only to purebred dogs which have been registered with the A.K.C. or are eligible for registration. However, in many localities the S.P.C.A. or the humane societies conduct obedience classes and shows which are open to all dogs.

Dogs which qualify under the American Kennel Club regulations receive "degrees" for obedience work, and these degrees are listed in their registry in the stud books. The first obedience degree is Companion Dog, for which the dog earns the right to have the letters "C.D." appear after his name. Next comes the Companion Dog Excellent (C.D.X.); and highest is the Utility Dog (U.D.) In addition the dog can also qualify for a Tracking Dog Certificate, which adds the coveted "T.D." to his name.

HOW OBEDIENCE TRIALS OPERATE

The obedience Trials are divided in three classes: Novice, Open, and

Utility. The Novice and Open classes are subdivided into Class A for amateur handlers only, and Class B for both amateur and professional. Utility classes are not divided.

The dog starts his competition in the Novice class, which leads to the Companion Dog degree. To qualify and win what is known as a "leg" on the degree, the dog must score at least 170 points, and at least 50 per cent of the points for each test. After qualifying in three shows before three different judges, he becomes a Companion Dog.

THE NOVICE CLASS

Test	Maximum Score
1. Heel on leash	35
2. Stand for examination by judge	30
3. Heel free (off leash)	45
4. Recall (come on command)	30
5. Long sit (1 minute)	30
6. Long down (3 minutes)	30
Maximum total score	200

THE OPEN CLASS

In the Open class, which leads to the Companion Dog Excellent degree after qualifying in three trials, the dog must show a good ability at heeling "free"; retrieve a wooden dumbbell from the floor or ground, and then over a hurdle; must take a broad jump on command and perform the "long sit" and "long down" with the handler out of sight. In the "recall," he must start toward his handler on command, then drop on command and come on another signal.

Test	Maximum Score
1. Heel off leash	40
2. Drop on recall	30
3. Retrieve on flat	25
4. Retrieve over obstacle	35
5. Broad jump	20
6. Long sit (3 minutse)	25
7. Long down (5 minutes)	25
Maximum total score	200

THE UTILITY CLASS

The first parts of the Utility class tests stress the dog's training in scenting an object handled by his trainer. The handler comes into the ring with fifteen small objects, each about a good mouth-holding size for his dog. Five must be of leather, five of wood, and five of metal. The judge selects one object of each type and these in turn are handled by the handler and then put out on the floor or ground individually by the judge, who uses tongs so as not to interfere with the "scent" imparted by the handler. The dog must then, on command, go out to the thirteen objects, pick up the one which has been handled, and retrieve it, bringing it back to the handler.

In the "seek back" the handler is ordered by the judge to heel the dog within the show ring, following orders to turn at different points. On the judge's signal a small object, generally a glove or key case, is dropped by the handler without the dog's seeing it. Dog and handler return to the starting point and then the dog is ordered to find and bring back the object.

In the "signal" exercise, the handler must use only hand signals—no voice—in going through an elaborate heeling routine, and the dog must sit and then drop on recall, all on hand signal.

In the "directed jumping," the dog must jump over a hurdle and a high-jump bar, in turn, at the handler's direction, returning to the handler after each jump.

In the "group examination," the handlers stand their dogs and leave the ring. The judge then examines each dog and, when he has completed this, calls the handlers back into the ring. The dogs must remain standing without moving during all this time.

Test	Maximum Score
1. Scent discrimination—Article 1	20
2. Scent discrimination—Article 2	20
3. Scent discrimination—Article 3	20
4. Seek back	30
5. Signal exercise	35
6. Directed jumping	40
7. Group examination	35
Maximum total score	200

THE "TRACKING" DEGREE

The tracking test is always conducted outdoors and separately from the obedience trial or dog show. To earn this degree, your dog must first be approved by an approved tracking judge, then must successfully complete a tracking test judged by two judges and in which three or more dogs are competing.

In this test, the dog is required to follow a stranger's trail and locate a missing object at least 440 yards from the starting point. The dog works in a shoulder harness on a leash or rope 30 feet long, and must not be guided. The trail is laid about thirty minutes before the test and includes at least two turns.

A starting flag is set up and then another marker thirty paces from the start to indicate the trail. From then on, the dog must follow the trail by scent.

PREPARING FOR OBEDIENCE TRIALS

The dog's response to commands despite the presence of other dogs and people is an important part of his obedience performance. Although you can train your dog yourself, he will probably be better prepared for an obedience trial after some schooling in a dog obedience class. Obedience training clubs throughout the country give you a chance to train your dogs—and learn your part in obedience work—with other dog owners. In many communities, obedience classes for dogs are given in schools as part of the adult education program. In some cities the S.P.C.A. runs obedience classes. By inquiring at pet shops or asking your veterinarian, you can probably locate an obedience class near you, or you can get a list of dog-training facilities by writing to the Gaines Dog Research Center, 250 North Street, White Plains, N. Y. 10625.

Generally the classes run for ten weeks, one evening a week, and it is advised that you spend about a half hour each day in "homework" with your dog. Some obedience clubs have a year-round program in which you start your dog training at any time and continue as long as you wish.

Complete information about obedience trials and instructions for making a set of standard hurdles and broad jump (which are adapted to the size of your dog) may be had by writing to the American Kennel Club, 51 Madison Avenue, New York, N. Y. 10010. Ask for the free booklet "Regulations and Standards for Obedience Trials."

9

THE DOG SHOW

WHEN YOU
walk into a dog show, it is colorful, exciting and confusing. Different kinds of
dogs are parading around the rings; some are standing while judges examine
them. From time to time, groups of dogs leave the rings and others come in.
Then there are frequent bursts of applause as the judges line up a group of
dogs and hand out ribbons, trophies and envelopes containing cash prizes.

When you go to a dog show—assuming that you are new to the dog world—
two things will help you understand what is going on. Above each ring is a
sign which identifies the breed being judged in that ring. A catalog (usually
priced at a dollar) lists each dog entered by an identifying number that also
appears on the handler's arm band.

In addition to competing for the ribbons, trophies, and cash prizes—which
are usually nominal, the dogs also compete for "championship" points. When
a dog has won 15 points at a number of shows he is known as a champion and
the designation "Ch." appears before his name in the official kennel club
records. The show regulations set up by the American Kennel Club are quite
complicated. In some of the larger shows as many as 4,000 dogs appear, and all
or most of the 116 breeds recognized by the A.K.C. There are also "specialty"
shows in which dogs of one breed compete for points and prizes.

As the judges select the winners in the different classes, they match the dogs
before them against the accepted "standard" of the breed. Reading the standards of the different breeds in this book will give you an idea of just what
qualities the judges are seeking and what characteristics are considered faults.

THE DOG SHOW CLASSES (AMERICAN)

There are five official classes for each breed entered in a show:

Puppy Class: Open to dogs six months but not more than twelve months of age, up to and including the first day of the show. Only dogs born in the United States or Canada are eligible.

Novice Class: Open to dogs six months of age or older that have never won a first prize at a show (except wins in puppy classes). Only dogs born in the United States or Canada are eligible.

Bred by Exhibitor Class: Open to all dogs except champions six months of age or older, owned and exhibited by the same person or kennel who are the recognized breeders on the American Kennel Club records.

American-Bred Class: Open to dogs that are not champions, six months of age or older, born in the United States after a mating which took place in the United States.

Open Class: Open to dogs six months of age or older, with no other exceptions made.

In addition, many shows set up special classes such as for locally bred dogs or with other limited requirements.

The male dogs and bitches in each class are judged separately, and four prizes are awarded in each class. The dogs that win first place in their class are then eligible for the "winners" class, which is also divided according to sex— winners dog and winners bitch.

Then the two winners of the breed compete for "best of winners."

Now, the situation gets a bit complicated, because a dog of your breed with his championship already won may have been entered in the "specials" class and your dog must go up against any "special" entries, assuming that he has been selected each time by the judge.

In the breeds which are divided into different varieties, winners are chosen for each variety in a similar manner. Then comes the "group" competition. All the different breeds are divided into six groups. Although the grouping is presumably based on the use made of each breed, the division is rather arbitrary. The groups are: sporting dogs; hounds; working dogs; terriers; toy dogs; nonsporting dogs—the miscellaneous group. The best of each group is selected and then these six winners—in an all-breed show—come into the ring for the final honor, selection as "best in show."

In addition to the "winners," "reserve" winners are named by the judges so that in case the winner canceled for any reason, the reserve winner is advanced to the winning role.

BENCHED AND UNBENCHED SHOWS

The announcement of a dog show states whether it is a "benched" show or an "unbenched" show. If the show is benched it means that stalls are set up on the grounds or in the building and the dogs must be kept in these stalls during the show, except when they being judged or exercised. In an unbenched show, the dogs must remain on the show grounds or in the building during the show. Also, an "exercise" area is provided at shows—one section for males, one for bitches, where the dogs may be taken to relieve themselves during the show.

HOW TO ENTER YOUR DOG IN A SHOW

Announcement of coming dog shows are listed in the different breed publications and in the general dog magazines, and in the monthly *Pure-Bred Dogs,* the official magazine of the American Kennel Club. Also, most daily newspapers give some publicity to dog-show announcements. If you would like to receive notices of coming dog shows, write to the nearest licensed "superintendent," who will place you on his mailing list to receive the announcements, called "Premium lists." These announcements give all details of the show, the prizes, names of judges, classes, and so forth.

The leading dog-show superintendents are:

Berhrendt, Mrs. Bernice, 470 38th Ave., San Francisco, Calif. 94121. Mrs. Helen M. Busby, Mrs. Norah F. Randolph.

Bradshaw, Jack, III, 727 Venice Blvd., Los Angeles, Calif. 90015. Mrs. Jack Bradshaw, Barbara Bradshaw.

Brown, Norman E., Route 2, Box 256, Spokane, Wash. 99207. Mrs. Anita W. Brown.

Crowe, Thomas J., P. O. Box 20205, Greensboro, N. C. 27420. T. N. Bloomberg, Ralph W. Cox, Miss Dorie Crowe, Mrs. Nina R. Crowe, Herbert H. Evans, Richard C. Heasley, Walter A. James, Mrs. Barbara Moss Mulvey, James E. Mulvey, Stuart S. Sliney, Durwood H. Van Zandt.

Jones, Roy J., P. O. Box 307, Garrett, Ind., 46738. Mrs. Elizabeth F. Jones, Dale D. Neukom.

Keller, Lewis C., P. O. Box 11, Mohnton, Pa., 19540. Mrs. Lewis C. Keller, Harold Weaver.

Mathews, Ace H., 11423 S.E. Alder Street, Portland, Oregon 97216. Mrs. Nancy J. Mathews.

Onofrio, Jack, P. O. Box 25764, Oklahoma City, Ok., 73125. Leon F. Krouch, Raymond W. Loupee, Dorothy M. Onofrio.

Thomsen, Jack, P. O. Box 726, Santa Fe, New Mexico 87501. Mrs. Doris A. Lewis, Mrs. Ann Thomsen, Mrs. Nancy L. Walden.

Webb, Marion O., 500 North Street, P. O. Box 546, Auburn, Indiana 46706. Mrs. Betty Dennis, Robert G. Foster, Mrs. Lillie Pion, Stephen Bryant Walter, Mrs. Dorothy Webb.

Winks, Alan P., 2009 Ranstead Street, Philadelphia, Pa., 19103. Mario Fernandez, Randolph V. Fite, Thomas J. Gillen, Robert P. Rio, Charles W. Ruppert, Mrs. Joseph H. Spring.

When you receive the premium list, fill in the entry form carefully, making sure that you have properly described your entry and the class you wish to enter and send it with the required fee to the superintendent or the club secretary. Note that entries close about two weeks before the show.

SHOWING YOUR DOG

About a week before the date of the show you receive in the mail your admissions card to the show with your dog's catalog number and (if a benched show) his bench number. It is perhaps unwise to enter a show unless you have attended a few to see just what is required of the entrants and their dogs. Shortly before you are called into the ring you will receive from a steward a numbered arm band which you wear while showing your dog. The important thing is to follow the judge's instructions as to walking, gaiting or standing your dog.

However, you should face the fact that the amateur handler showing his own dog is going against big odds in the show ring. The professionals, breeders, kennel owners and professional handlers make their living from dogs, and the show ring is the place where they exhibit and build up their merchandise. The ribbons and championships they win add to the value of the dogs and enhance the price of their puppies and the stud fees they receive for their male dogs.

If you have a really good dog, you would probably do better if you engaged a professional handler to show him in the ring, as the "pros" know how to bring out a dog's better points and to overshadow his faults. Also, if your dog is one of the breeds in which grooming is important, a professional trim is almost a "must" before going into the ring.

MATCH SHOWS

One way to get some experience in showing your dog, and also to have his quality appraised by judges before going to the expense of a "point" show, is to enter "match" shows. These are local, informal shows run by dog clubs under sanction of the Kennel Club. No points are awarded at these shows toward championships, but ribbons and trophies are awarded to winners. Many of the same judges who handle the point shows also officiate at match shows. The match shows are run very informally and the judges and other dog owners will help you get an idea whether your dog's conformation and coat make him a possible champion. The secretary of your breed club or local dog club can inform you of match shows in your vicinity and they are also listed in the dog publications. No advance registration is required to enter a match show. You pay your entry fee, usually fifty cents or a dollar when you arrive. Also, most match shows have puppy classes for three- to six-month-olds, and some include a match obedience contest.

THE RULES AND REGULATIONS

The American Kennel Club, 51 Madison Avenue, New York, N. Y. 10010, will send a free copy of "Rules Applying to Registration and Dog Shows" to any person requesting it. This 60-page booklet makes interesting reading for those interested in showing dogs or in learning about the technical aspects of registering and showing a purebred dog.

10

FIELD TRIALS

IF YOUR favorite breed is a sporting dog, hound or spaniel, you can spend an interesting day at a field trial, as a spectator or participant. Held outdoors, these field trials give dogs and their owners a chance to compete under simulated hunting conditions, working on live game. In the field trial the dog is not judged on his conformation and appearance as in the show ring, but on his ability to work at his specialty.

Announcements of field trials are carried in the *American Field Magazine* and in the *A.K.C.* magazine. In addition, placards are usually posted in sport shops, and, on the day of the trial, road signs with arrows leading to the scene of the trial are placed for some miles around.

HOW FIELD TRIALS OPERATE

Field trials are divided into different classifications, according to the breeds of dogs competing and their type of field work.

THE SPORTING DOGS

The pointing breeds run on pheasant, quail and other game birds. Where wild birds are not plentiful, pheasants or quail are released for the trial. The pointers include: English setter, Irish setter, Gordon setter, pointer, German short-haired pointer, pointing griffon, Brittany spaniel, and Weimaraner.

The retrievers, in their trials, retrieve ducks or other waterfowl. The retrievers include: Labrador retriever, Chesapeake Bay retriever, Irish water spaniel, American water spaniel, golden retriever, flat-coated retriever, and curly-coated retriever.

The spaniels flush and retrieve game of all types. The hunting spaniels include: cocker spaniel, springer spaniel, clumber spaniel, Sussex spaniel, field spaniel, English cocker spaniel, and Welsh springer spaniel.

THE HOUNDS

Field trials are limited to five of the hound group. The beagle, basset and greyhound run on rabbits; the foxhound and coonhound on their favorite game.

In addition there are night hunts and field trials conducted by the United Kennel Club members for a number of hound types which are not recognized by the A.K.C. These include: American black-and-tan coonhound, bluetick coonhound, plott hound, redbone coonhound, and walker (treeing) coonhound.

Most popular in this country are the beagle trials and the trials for pointing dogs.

THE BEAGLE TRIALS

The beagle trials are run almost exactly like an actual hunting trip, except that guns are not used. And it is fascinating to see the change that takes place in the beagle when he sets out on the trail of a rabbit.

The beagles run in braces of two, and the order in which they run and the braces are decided by a drawing. After the entire field has had one run, the judges select the best workers and run them again in braces. As many as five series may be run before the judges select the four winners and the "reserve" winner. An elaborate point system depending on the number of entries, requiring a total of 120 points and three "firsts," leads to the field championship known as "field champion of record."

In addition to the formal field trials, many clubs hold informal sanctioned matches at which no points are awarded.

BIRD DOG TRIALS

Trials for the pointers and retrievers are generally run in the spring and fall in the northern part of the country and in the winter in the South. Training the dog for field-trial work and hunting has been dealt with extensively in many books which are available in most libraries and bookstores for the dog owner who wants to read up on the subject before starting to train his dog.

Generally there are different stakes (classes) for dogs of different ages and separate stakes for amateur and professional handlers.

The owner of a hunting-type dog will find that his pet seems to have an almost uncanny instinct for his own type of field work, and many puppies seem to "know" what is expected of them almost the first time they are given a chance to work out in the field.

11

DESIGN FOR A DOGHOUSE

NOT ALL
dogs are privileged to live in the house, and many dogs actually prefer the out
of doors. If your dog is to have outdoor living quarters, this dog house, described here, and designed by the American Humane Association, will be
adequate for the average-sized dog.

A flap of several folds made of either burlap, canvas or an old carpet nailed
over the doorway will keep out drafts and give added warmth.

A dog living out of doors should have a fenced-in yard or run. If not, he
should be on a light chain fastened to an overhead clothesline or on a swivel
stake. The swivel stake can be purchased at most pet-supply houses, and is also
advertised in most dog magazines, and is simple to install A chained dog should
have easy access to his house, food and water.

GUIDE TO CONSTRUCTION

Walls: The structural details for each of the four walls is found on the construction plans. A more detailed corner view shows how the corner joints
are made. When assembled, the four walls make a box.

Floor: The floor is constructed of tongue-and-groove boards and is 4 feet
square. For adequate ventilation and to keep free from dampness, the floor is
nailed at right angles to three 2 × 4-inch cross members, as shown in the two
views of the floor diagram.

Partition: This panel is the windbreak. It is constructed of the tongue-and-
groove boards and these are held in place by four 1 × 2-inch stringers.

Roof: The roof section consists of the top surface constructed of tongue-and-

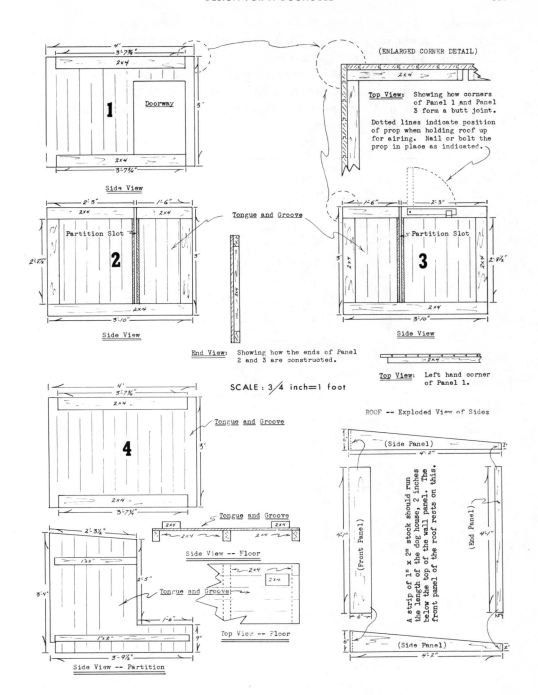

(ENLARGED CORNER DETAIL)

Top View: Showing how corners of Panel 1 and Panel 3 form a butt joint.

Dotted lines indicate position of prop when holding roof up for airing. Nail or bolt the prop in place as indicated.

Side View

Doorway

1

2x4

Partition Slot

2

Side View

Tongue and Groove

Partition Slot

3

Side View

End View: Showing how the ends of Panel 2 and 3 are constructed.

Top View: Left hand corner of Panel 1.

SCALE: 3/4 inch = 1 foot

4

Tongue and Groove

Tongue and Groove

Side View -- Floor

Tongue and Groove

Top View -- Floor

Side View -- Partition

ROOF -- Exploded View of Sides

(Side Panel)

(Front Panel)

(End Panel)

A strip of 1" x 2" stock should run the length of the dog house, 2 inches below the top of the wall panel. The front panel of the roof rests on this.

(Side Panel)

groove stock. The side panels are constructed of 1 × 6-inch stock as shown in the plans. The two stops that position the roof when opened for airing are made of 2 × 4-inch stock and are 8 inches long.

Note that the two side walls are slotted vertically for the partition. Slide the partition down the slots parallel with the front wall with partition opening away from the door. To simplify moving or cleaning, this doghouse may easily be separated into its four components.

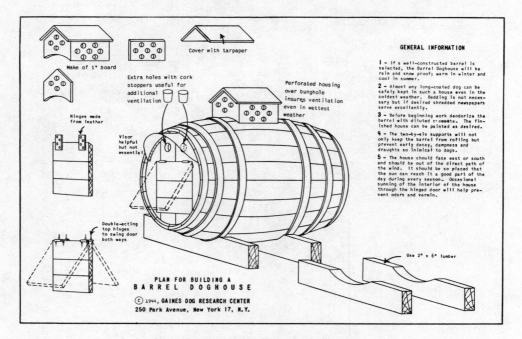

Plan for Building a Barrel Dog House

12

A GLOSSARY OF "DOG" LANGUAGE

ONE OF
the problems of dog owning is the encounters with experts who use the technical language of the dog world and expect anyone at the end of a leash to understand them. The following list covers most of the terminology of dogdom, and particularly the terms which appear in the "standards" of the different breeds and which may not have meaning to the novice dog owner.

ALMOND EYE—an almond-shaped eye with the outer corners slanting upward towards the ears; typically found in the bull terrier.

ANGULATION—the angle at which the bones fit together at a joint; particularly the angle of the hindquarters at stifle and hock (which *see*).

APPLE HEAD—rounded or domed skull.

ARTICULATION—the joint between bones.

ASCOB—any solid color other than black.

BAT EAR—an erect, batlike ear, rounded at the tip, as found in the French bulldog.

BEARD—the long hairs or tuft under the dog's chin.

BELTON—a mixture of blue- or orange-and-white hairs in the dog's coat.

BOBTAIL—a docked or short-cut tail.

BREECHING—hair on the inside of the hind legs of the dog; on some breeds, hair on the rear of the rump and on the outer side of the hind leg.

BRINDLE—a coat streaked or spotted with a darker color.

BRISKET—the part of the dog's chest between and just behind the forelegs.

BROKEN-UP FACE—the typical face of the bulldog, Pekingese, and others, with receding nose, projecting jaw, deep stop and wrinkles.

BRUSH—a bushy tail.

BUTTERFLY NOSE—parti-colored nose.

BUTTON EAR—ear folding forward close to the head and pointing towards the eye, typical of the fox terrier.

CANINE TEETH—four sharp-pointed teeth between the incisors and the bicuspids. The upper pair sometimes called eyeteeth.

CANKER—an ulcer-like, spreading sore; most often of the inner ear.

CHOPS—the lower cheeks.

CLODDY—thickset and low to the ground.

CLOSE-COUPLED—short in the loins and back.

COBBY—short-bodied.

CONFORMATION—the structure or form of the dog's body.

COW-HOCKED—with hocks turned inward.

CREST—ridge of the neck of the dog.

CULOTTE—hair growing on the thighs of some breeds, such as the Pomeranian.

DAM—the female parent of the dog.

DEWCLAW—the extra, useless claw or toe found on the inner side of the leg just above the foot.

DEWLAP—the loose fold of skin hanging from the throat in the bulldog, bloodhound and similar breeds.

DISH-FACED—with a concave outline between the eyes and the tip of the nose.

DOCK—cutting or shortening the tail.

DOWN-FACED—with a muzzle tilted downward.

DOWN IN PASTERN—a pronounced angle between the ankle and the paw, or a weak sloping pastern.

DUDLEY NOSE—flesh-colored nose.

EWE-NECKED—with a concave outline along the top of the neck.

FAWN—pale, yellowish brown color of coat.

FEATHER (FEATHERING)—fringe of hair along the tail and back of the legs.

FIDDLE FRONT—with bowed forelegs.

FLAG—the tail; used most often in speaking of setters.

FLEWS—loose, hanging parts of the lips, as in the boxer and bulldog.

FRILL—fringe of hair around the neck.

FRONT—forepart of the chest and forelegs.

FURROW—indentation from the middle of the forehead to the top of the skull as in bulldog and other breeds.

GAIT—manner of walking or running.

GAY TAIL—a tail that is carried erect.

GRIZZLE—gray, or streaked with gray.

HAREFOOT—long narrow, rabbit-like foot.

HAW—a red membrane inside the lower eyelid.

HOCK—the joint corresponding to the human ankle.

INCISORS—front teeth between the canines.

KNEE—joint in the foreleg between elbow and foot.

LEATHER—the external part of the ear.

LIVER—reddish- or purplish-brown color.

LOADED SHOULDER—a heavy shoulder, overmuscled below the withers.

LOIN—part of the back on either side of the backbone between hipbones and ribs.

LOOSE SHOULDER—a shoulder that juts out at an angle from the body and is loose in movement.

LOP-EARS—ears that hang down loosely and swing away from the cheek.

MANE—long hair growing from the top or sides of the neck as in the collie.

MANTLE DOG—one whose chief body color is other than white.

MASK—a dark shading on the muzzle. Seen in the great Dane, boxer, and others.

MERLE—gray ground color with splotches of black, or bluish gray, as in the blue merle collie.

MUZZLE—projecting part of the dog's head; the mouth, nose, and jaws; the foreface.

ORANGE BELTON—white coat, flecked with orange.

OTTER TAIL—a tail thick at the base and tapered at the tip.

OVERSHOT—the upper part of the jaw extending over the lower.

PAD—the under part of the foot.

PADDLE—a gait in which the forefeet are thrown out to the side when trotting.

PARTI-COLORED—of two or more different colors with neither color predominant.

PASTERN—part of the foreleg between knee joint and foot.

PENCILING—black markings against tan background on the toes.

PIPE-STOPPER TAIL—a short, stubby tail.

PLUME—a feathery tail.

POMPOM—the ornamental tuft left on the tail or body when the dog is clipped.

PRICK EAR—an ear carried stiffly erect.

RACY—long in body and legs and slight in build.

RINGTAIL—tail that curls in a circle.

ROACH-BACK—a curvature of the back, rising behind the withers and over the loins and down the hindquarters; typical of the greyhound.

ROSE EAR—the ear folding backward, showing part of the inner ear when viewed from the front.

RUFF—collar of bushy hair.

SABLE—black or very dark-brown color.

SCREWTAIL—short, kinky, twisted tail.

SHELLY—with a flat, narrow body.

SICKLE TAIL—tail curled upward, in the form of a sickle.

SIRE—the male parent.

SLOPING SHOULDER—shoulder slanting back and upward to the withers.

SNIPY—rather sharply pointed, weak muzzle.

SPAY—to remove the ovaries of a female dog.

SPLAYFOOT—a foot with the toes spread wide apart.

STAND-OFF COAT—profuse coat with the hairs standing straight out from the body.

STERN—another term for the tail.

STIFLE—joint of the hind leg, corresponding to the human knee.

STOP—the space between the top of the skull and the muzzle.

SWAY-BACK—with an abnormal downward curve of the spine.

THROATY—excessive loose skin under the throat.

TOY DOG—any one of the various small breeds.

TUCK-UP—having the belly drawn up under the loin; notably among the greyhounds.

TRUMPET—the slight depression or hollow on the skull, appearing on either side behind the orbit or eye socket, corresponding to the temple in man.

TULIP EARS—ears carried erect with some forward curve.

TWIST—a curled tail.

UNDERSHOT—with the lower part of the jaw extending beyond the upper.

WALLEYE—a bluish eye, resembling a glass eye; seen often in the blue merle collie.

WEEDY—lean, lacking substance in build.

WHEATEN—pale, yellowish brown color.

WHIP TAIL—stiff, straight tail.

WHISKERS—long hairs on the chin and muzzle.

WITHERS—highest part of the back, between the shoulder blades. (Point at which height is measured.)

DOG SHOW TERMS

BENCH—the stalls in which dogs are kept on exhibition at a show.

BENCHED SHOW—a show in which the dogs are required to be kept in the stalls except when in the ring or being exercised.

BEST OF WINNERS—the dog chosen by the judge as the best of all entries in the regular official classes of a breed.

CHAMPION—a title awarded by the British or American Kennel Club to a dog which has won at least 15 points in officially recognized shows; at least 6 points must have been won at major shows and under different judges.

GROUP—the six divisions into which the A.K.C. has divided the recognized breeds; sporting; hound; working; terrier; toy, and nonsporting groups.

HANDLER—the person showing the dog; professional handlers work under A.K.C. licenses.

LICENSED SHOW—a show given by a club not an A.K.C. member club, but under A.K.C. rules and at which championship points may be awarded.

LISTED DOG—a dog which is eligible for A.K.C. registration, but which is not registered; may be shown up to three times by payment of an additional 25¢ listing fee.

MEMBER SHOW—a show given by a club which is a member of the A.K.C. (*Note:* Clubs, not individuals, make up the membership of the American Kennel Club.)

MISCELLANEOUS CLASS—classes at shows which are outside the regular official classes; generally for the rarer breeds which have not won A.K.C. recognition, but which are considered purebred dogs.

IRREGULAR CLASSES—classes for special entries outside the regular official classes, such as locally bred dogs.

PREMIUM LIST—the official announcement of a show, listing the prizes, judges, details of the show, etc.

RESERVE WINNER—the entry chosen by the judge as second to the winner's dog or winner's bitch; to be moved up in the event the winning dog or bitch is disqualified.

SANCTIONED MATCH—an informal show at which no official points may be won.

SPECIALTY SHOW—a show for an individual breed, offering championship points; may be held separately or as part of a larger show.

STEWARD—the ring assistant to the judge.

SUPERINTENDENT—the professional arranger of a show.

WINNER'S DOG—the dog which is chosen best of the winners' class, among the first-prize winners from the other five official classes.

WINNERS' BITCH—the bitch which is chosen best of the winners' class among the first-prize winners from the other five regular official classes.

OBEDIENCE TRIAL TERMS

COMPANION DOG (C.D.)—a title awarded by the A.K.C. to a dog which has qualified in three Novice trials under different judges.

COMPANION DOG EXCELLENT (C.D.X.)—a title awarded by the A.K.C. to a dog which qualified in three Open trials under different judges.

DOWN—the exercise in which the dog drops to the ground on verbal command or hand signal.

DROP ON RECALL—an exercise in the Open class in which the handler calls the dog from across the ring, then drops him on signal from the judge, and finally calls him to a front-sit and then to heel.

DUMBBELL—a wooden dumbbell which the dog retrieves on command and brings to the handler; size varies according to size of the dog.

HEEL—the exercise in which the dog follows closely with his head at the handler's left knee; also the dog's sitting closely by the handler's left side on command or signal.

HIGH JUMP—an exercise in which the dog takes a high jump on command and returns to the handler.

HURDLE AND BAR JUMP—in the advanced Utility class an exercise in which the dog takes a bar jump and a hurdle jump on signal command from the handler.

NOVICE CLASS—the first class in obedience trials for dogs which have not won the C.D. title.

OPEN CLASS—The second class in obedience trials for dogs which have won the C.D. title.

RECALL—the exercise in which the handler calls the dog from across the ring. The dog must come briskly across the ring and sit in front of the handler, facing him.

FINISH—the judge's order at the end of each exercise at which the dog must come to the heel position on the handler's signal or verbal command.

LEG—a dog acquires a "leg" on receiving a qualifying score toward an obedience title.

SIGNAL EXERCISE—a part of the Utility class work in which the handler must control the dog by hand signals only, with no verbal commands.

SIT—an exercise in which the dog is required to remain in a sitting position without moving; for one minute in Novice class with handler across the ring; for three minutes in Open class with handler out of the ring and out of sight.

STAND FOR EXAMINATION—an exercise in which the dog must submit to manual examination by the judge without moving or showing resentment.

TRACKING—held separately from the obedience trial, a test in which the dog must qualify by following a stranger's scent over an outdoor trial and find a leather object at the end. On qualifying, the dog receives the title of Tracking Dog (T.D.)

UTILITY—the highest class in obedience trial competition, open to dogs with the C.D.X. title.

U.D.T.—Utility Dog Tracker, the degree awarded to dogs which have completed the U.D. requirements and the Tracking test.

FIELD TRIAL TERMS

ACTION—the manner in which the dog moves in the field.

BACK (OR BACKING)—the dog coming to a point when he sees another dog pointing; also called "honoring" the other dog's point.

BACK-CAST—searching to the rear.

BRACE—the dogs are tried in pairs; each pair is the "brace."

BYE—if the stake contains an uneven number dogs, the last drawn dog runs alone; or the judge may select a brace mate for him.

CAST—a search for game in one general direction without an abrupt turn.

CHASING—running after flushed birds.

DIVIDED FIND—when two dogs are found pointing and it cannot be determined which dog first made the point.

DRAW—the drawing of the names of dogs to determine the order in which they will run and their pairings.

DROPPING ON POINT—the dog's dropping to the ground when it scents a bird.

FLUSH—to cause a bird or birds to fly.

RANGE—the distance from his handler at which the dog hunts.

SECOND SERIES—after the first braces have been run, a second series may be run by dogs chosen and paired by the judges.

STANCH—to remain still on point until the birds are flushed.

STEADY—to remain in the pointing position after the shot is fired.

NEWLY POPULAR BREEDS

In the last few years, a number of breeds, mainly among smaller dogs, have gained in popularity among American dog fanciers. Shown here are some of the leading show dogs among these newly popular breeds.

Lhasa Apso
Ch. Keke's Ha-Le
Owner: Mrs. A. Ann Hoffman

Shih Tzu
Ch. Paisley Ping Pong
Owner: Miss Joan Cowie,
Nanjo Kennels

Silky Terrier
Ch. Lu-Jon's Lord Cagney of Tunney
Owner: Helen and Don Thompson,
Don-El Silkies

Vizla
Ch. Puerco Pete Barat
Owner: Joseph F. Cunningham, A.K.C. Judge

The relative popularity of the different purebred dogs is shown in the latest figures from the American Kennel Club, indicating the registrations among the different breeds. The Poodles, for example, showed registration of over 250,000.

BREED	*Placings*	*BREED*	*Placings*
Poodles	1	Keeshonden	43
German Shepherd Dogs	2	Basenjis	44
Beagles	3	Silky Terriers	45
Dachshunds	4	Welsh Corgis (Pembroke)	46
Miniature Schnauzers	5	Chow Chows	47
St. Bernards	6	Vizslas	48
Irish Setters	7	Chesapeake Bay Retrievers	49
Labrador Retrievers	8	Newfoundlands	50
Collies	9	English Setters	51
Pekingese	10	Welsh Terriers	52
Chihuahuas	11	Borzois	53
Cocker Spaniels	12	Schipperkes	54
Doberman Pinschers	13	Great Pyrenees	55
Basset Hounds	14	Australian Terriers	56
Shetland Sheepdogs	15	Miniature Pinschers	57
Pomeranians	16	Kerry Blue Terriers	58
Great Danes	17	Standard Schnauzers	59
Yorkshire Terriers	18	Bloodhounds	60
Brittany Spaniels	19	Irish Wolfhounds	61
German Shorthaired Pointers	20	Gordon Setters	62
Golden Retrievers	21	Whippets	63
Boston Terriers	22	Manchester Terriers	64
Boxers	23	Pulik	65
Scottish Terriers	24	Italian Greyhounds	66
Old English Sheepdogs	25	Bedlington Terriers	67
Siberian Huskies	26	English Cocker Spaniels	68
English Springer Spaniels	27	Rhodesian Ridgebacks	69
Fox Terriers	28	Bull Terriers	70
Pugs	29	German Wirehaired Pointers	71
Lhasa Apsos	30	Irish Terriers	71
Afghan Hounds	31	Bullmastiffs	73
Dalmatians	32	Rottweilers	74
Cairn Terriers	33	Pointers	75
Samoyeds	34	Belgian Sheepdogs	76
Weimaraners	35	Skye Terriers	77
Norwegian Elkhounds	36	Japanese Spaniels	78
Airedale Terriers	37	American Water Spaniels	79
West Highland White Terriers	38	Salukis	80
Bulldogs	39	Papillons	81
Alaskan Malamutes	40	Giant Schnauzers	82
Maltese	41	Bouviers Des Flandres	82
Shih Tzu	42	Norwich Terriers	84

BREED	Placings	BREED	Placings
Welsh Corgis (Cardigan)	85	Affenpinschers	101
American Staffordshire Terriers	86	Komondorok	102
Mastiffs	87	Foxhounds (American)	103
Belgian Tervuren	88	Flat-Coated Retrievers	104
Dandie Dinmont Terriers	89	Irish Water Spaniels	105
Sealyham Terriers	90	Border Terriers	106
Black & Tan Coonhounds	91	English Toy Spaniels	107
Lakeland Terriers	92	Otter Hounds	108
Greyhounds	92	Foxhounds (English)	109
Brussels Griffons	94	Welsh Springer Spaniels	110
Briards	95	Harriers	111
Bernese Mountain Dogs	96	Curly-Coated Retrievers	112
Wirehaired Pointing Griffons	97	Clumber Spaniels	113
French Bulldogs	98	Field Spaniels	114
Scottish Deerhounds	99	Belgian Malinois	115
Kuvaszok	100	Sussex Spaniels	116

ACKNOWLEDGMENTS

The author wishes to express sincere thanks to the many dog fanciers whose help has made this book possible. The secretaries of the different breed clubs have been most helpful. Mr. Harry Miller and staff of the Gaines Dog Research Center have always been most cooperative. Dr. E. G. Fuhrman, president of the United Kennel Club, and officials of the *Field Dog Stud Book* are thanked for providing copies of registration forms. Much of the information on dog nutrition and feeding has been made available by the U.S. Vitamin and Pharmaceutical Corporation. The Quartermaster Corps of the U.S. Army has aided in the sections on dog training and care, which are based on their long military experience with the dog-service personnel. The Durham-Enders Razor Corporation has been kind in allowing use of illustrations and techniques on clipping and grooming the different breeds.

Especial thanks are due to members of Suffolk Obedience Training Club of Long Island and the Dog Fanciers Luncheon Club of New York City, who have shared the benefits of their accumulated knowledge of so many different breeds; and to Dean White, editor of *Our Pet World* magazine.

The material on dog bites is adapted from "Epidemiology of Dog Bites," a paper prepared by Henry M. Parrish, M.D., assistant professor of preventive medicine, University of Vermont College of Medicine. The data on "Characteristics of Biting Dogs" was prepared under the direction of Frank B. Clack, V.M.D., M.P.H., chief public health veterinarian; Dr. James F. Mock, V.M.D., public health veterinarian of the Allegheny County Health Department, Pittsburgh, Pa.; and Duane Probst, D.V.M, research assistant in the department of veterinary science, University of Wisconsin, Madison.

INDEX